HOLDING UP THE SKY

A STORY OF OVERCOMING CHILDHOOD

HOLDING UP THE SKY

A STORY OF OVERCOMING CHILDHOOD

LESSIE AULETTI

atmosphere press

Prelude

I am old now, probably as old as Anne Marsh when I met her so many years ago. I see her face, its smile a permanent fixture amidst wrinkles and freckles. That smile has left crinkles at the edges of her eyes and upward creases beside her curved mouth, cheeks and lips touched only with her own inner blush of pink. I stand before the full-length mirror in my bedroom and see myself, short, a little chubby, with dirty blond hair returning to the platinum of my youth. It is uncanny, but to my eyes, I see so much of Annie in that reflection—age, height, stance, smile. And heart. I am sure I got my heart from that dear Quaker lady.

I am no relation to Anne; no common blood flows through our veins, yet some fluke of fate directed our souls to a common path. It would be hubris to believe she chose me. If it is true, as many believe, that we are born with our fates writ upon our foreheads, it was inevitable that we would meet.

Recently I discovered that we did have something in common. Most of my family came from Scotland, leaving behind everything to stake a claim in the mostly unexplored vastness that became the United States. Some left their homes because they were Quakers, and thus neither could, nor would, engage in war either for or against England. Anne's ancestors fled Scotland for similar reasons.

Do our souls pick their companions for eternity's journey? I choose to believe that they do.

CHAPTER I
In Which the Plot is Hatched

The first time I saw the old woman I was crouched on my hunkers, hidden deep in the tall, uncut late winter grass hay. My brother Danny and two of his little buddies stood at the creek's edge twenty feet from where I peered, unseen, from between the tall grass stalks. They had the flies of their pants unzipped and were concentrating on who could pee with the most accuracy, using a large maple leaf floating in an eddy pool against the far bank for target practice. They took turns, laughing and gesturing with glee, rating each other's attempts on a scale from one to ten. Eventually, the boys ran out of ammunition, zipped up their pants, and resorted to throwing rocks.

I was so intent on watching the contest without making a sound that I missed the rustle of approaching footsteps. When the hand touched my shoulder, I startled and fell plop on my behind, wounding my dignity (if I had had any) worse than my fanny. I let out a screech and scrambled to my feet. Danny's head shot round as if on a swivel. He spotted my blue shorts and striped tee shirt bright against the soft golds and tans of standing hay, his brows beetling together in an ominous scowl as he recognized me.

"Was you spyin' on us? You was, wasn't you, Leah! Oh boy—are you gonna get it!" Daniel shouted and shook his fist in my direction, his face glowing crimson as he realized what he and his buddies had been doing. The boys turned as a unit and splashed down the creek, muttering among themselves and plotting retribution.

"What was that all about?" queried a pleasant voice behind me. "I didn't mean to startle thee, girl. Are thee all right?"

"Well, I guess not—Danny's gonna get me for watchin'. Why'd you sneak up on me like that?" I grumbled as I rose to my feet and rotated to put a face to the voice—a wrinkled, tanned gnome face, backlit and featureless.

The oldest person I had ever seen crouched before me, offering a steadying hand. I flinched from her as if she held a firebrand and bolted a few feet straight backward. She stood up, brushing dust and grass stems from her long, black skirt. The gnome-face split apart with a wide grin. "What is thy name, little one?" she inquired pleasantly. With one wide-eyed sweep, I cataloged her decidedly peculiar appearance, ciphered in her odd way of talking, and concluded with absolute certainty that she was my enemy. Mama would not have approved such a split-second determination as she had taught me to always give a stranger the benefit of the doubt, and for a second, I wavered, until I heard Danny's wicked snicker from across the creek. He was out there with his friends conjuring up some nasty torture to get even with me for my prying eyes. No doubt, it was her fault. My resolve hardened and I turned my back to her and ran for the woods.

I thought nothing more of the old woman until a few

weeks later when school had let out for the summer and the long days before fall lay ahead.

We had spent the early part of an unseasonably warm June morning playing hide-and-seek by the creek that meandered diagonally through the cow pasture and slid into the cool shadows of twenty acres of mixed trees, swampland and grassy meadows. "We" included my older brother Daniel, our younger brother Robbie, and me.

In theory, Danny—the eldest—was in charge. In fact, he left the responsibility for Robbie to me, the only girl. Danny picked on Robbie and teased me without mercy. Robbie tattled to Mama, who gave him plenty of extra hugs and kisses. I tried not to complain. Danny eventually got even with me if Mama punished him, while I ended up with one of her heart-to-heart talks about learning to ignore my brother's torture. Sporadic attempts to even the score brought swift retribution from both brother and parents.

Danny and I envied Robbie. He was, after all, "the baby," Daddy's pride and joy and Mama's little man. His arrival had put Danny's nose out of joint on two accounts; he was no longer the only son, and he was now the eldest son, as well, and expected to assume responsibilities he did not want.

I became the middle child, forever doomed to keeping the peace. No longer the baby, but never the eldest, I wore my "middle childness" like a second skin. I loved Robbie, regretting only that he was not a sister, and usually tried to protect him.

Danny's growing resentment had resulted in a recent increase in teasing aimed principally at me. School was "out" for the summer, and Mama had assigned to Danny the responsibility for Robbie's well-being while we were outside.

"Golly, Mom! How'd ja expect me to have fun with my friends this summer if I always got a little kid taggin' along. It's bad enough that Leah's always spyin' on us—I can just hear what the guys are gonna say."

Mama sat in her rocker next to the oil stove reading the paper. She didn't blink. "If these boys are your friends, Danny, they'll understand. No doubt some of them have little brothers of their own." She directed her attention back to the headlines in *The Sun*.

"But Mom...!"

Mama put her paper in her lap and raised her left eyebrow, a sure indication that she was becoming annoyed. Danny backed up out of her reach but held his ground.

"I'm sure you don't want Daddy to hear how selfish you've become, do you? He works awfully hard for us—all day in the shipyard, then home to milking and chores."

Danny didn't move.

"This would just break his heart, Danny." Mama's attempt at making Danny feel guilty fell on deaf ears. Danny shifted his weight and cleared his throat.

"How about Leah? Why can't she watch out for Robbie. She's a girl, after all. She should babysit, not me!"

"You know your sister takes on her share of responsibilities around here, and I haven't heard her complain." Mama's voice sounded irritated, a tone that didn't escape my brother's attention. He shrugged his shoulders and smiled.

"A guy's gotta try, ya know."

Mama allowed that a guy could try all he wanted. The facts

remained that the mantle of responsibility had fallen to the eldest son. Unfortunately, the mantle rested on resentful shoulders. Danny glared at me as he slouched into the playroom; I knew I was in for a rough summer. The conditions required for "Hatchet Annie's birth" were now in place. They waited only for a game of hide-and-seek to set them in motion.

At that particular moment beside the creek, I was "it." I dutifully hid my eyes and counted while the boys scrambled for hiding places within our designated hiding area. We had established these boundaries after a prolonged game left Robbie misplaced in the twenty-acre woods—a nerve-wracking experience causing us many anxious minutes while I diverted our mother's attentions and Daniel searched for the distantly screaming Robbie. Fortunately, Mama had not found out.

After my count reached one hundred, I set out to find them.

Danny took great delight in ambushing me, so he usually hid along the wooded boundary area. This is where I concentrated my search. Today he dropped at me from an overhanging tree limb, narrowly missing knocking the stuffing out of me. He smiled widely, his Jack-o-lantern grin revealing the gaps in his front teeth. "Almost gotcha that time. Now, just try'n catch me before I touch base." He streaked off, cackling wildly, with me in hot pursuit.

I still remember our laughter sparkling through the clean-smelling air, how grass and flowers and dust feel beneath my feet, and the sting of tree shoots as they slap my bare legs. I nearly catch him once, then trip on a blackberry vine and sprawl ungracefully into a currant bush. Danny is safe at base before I finish brushing dried grass from my knees.

"Well," he gloated, "unless you catch the squirt, you're gonna be IT again. Have I got a great place to hide then! You'll NEVER find me! Want me to help ya get him?"

Of course, I refused. Danny always offered to help me; he also counted on my turning him down. I would have accepted gladly but for my pride. I retaliated by showing him my tongue, then turned on my heel, and set about searching for Robbie in all his favorite places. Behind me, I could hear Danny laughing wickedly. He was planning some new torment at my expense of that I was sure.

By the time I heard my little brother rustling in the tall grass, I was ready to retaliate. Unfortunately, Daniel was older and far too big for me. Poor Rob was just the right size—an available and impressionable victim—barely hidden in creek weeds. Now, what could I do that would not get back to Mama?

At that moment, a wrinkled, grey-haired woman steps across the creek ten feet in front of me and begins searching diligently along the creek bank. I instantly recognize my nemesis from earlier. Today she wears an ankle-length black skirt above sandals, a white high-collared blouse, and a fringed black shawl. A small hand axe protrudes from a basket slung over her shoulder. She still looks older than dirt, and she has not seen me. Danny has not yet exacted revenge for the spying incident—no doubt he has something special planned, but so far has not found the perfect time to inflict it. In the meantime, she fits my purposes perfectly!

I slipped quietly into the grass behind Robbie, putting my hand over his mouth so he couldn't make a noise, and hissed in his ear.

"Shhh! Don't make a sound. Do you see that old woman on the path?" My hand moved up and down as Robbie nodded his head. "Do you know who she is?" My hand followed Robbie back and forth. "Well," I murmured, "that's Hatchet Annie, and she'll get you if you make any noise—so don't!"

The scheme had sprung full-blown into my mind in a heartbeat. It was so perfect—so diabolical—so delicious! One recent Saturday afternoon, Mama had taken us to see a re-run of *The Wizard of Oz*. Danny and I had stared, open-mouthed, at the color film as Dorothy, the Cowardly Lion, et al adventured their way through Oz.

Robbie spent the majority of the matinee hiding beneath his seat, terrified out of his wits by the Green Witch. Not even the lure of buttered popcorn could coax him onto Mama's lap. When the house lights came up, she got down on her knees on the theater floor covered with sticky discarded soft drink cups and candy wrappers and pulled him, kicking and screaming, out of hiding. In the following weeks, he would awaken in the night from dreams of the Green Faced Lady, as he called her, and either Danny or I would creep out of bed and comfort him, sometimes taking his sobbing little body into our own beds. After he peed in Danny's sheets, however, he left the in-bed comforting to me! Now along came this old woman, suitably dressed. Unfortunately, her face was not green and she was not riding a broom, but otherwise, she was perfect for the part.

Robbie took one look at her and gasped. He leaped from his grassy hiding place and fled for home, emitting a shrill, high-pitched shriek of utter terror. Watching his little back disappear through the tall grass left me giddy with power. I laughed victoriously to myself. Oh, this was perfect! Absolutely perfect! Endless possibilities for torturing Robbie ticker-taped across my mind.

Abruptly, the old woman whips around, keen eyes taking in the situation. Those eyes, blue-grey as the winter sky, meet mine—her mouth screws up in disapproval—and she shakes her head sharply. Then, she crosses the creek and melts into the bushes on the other side. I stick out my tongue at her disappearing back, shrugging off that niggling part of my conscience that feels compassion for my little brother's terror. After all, Mama will give him extra hugs and kisses, and Daddy will call him his little man and take him up on his shoulders (as he used to do with me) and sing to him in Czech. Besides, it isn't my fault that Robbie is chicken!

With a light heart, I skipped for home base to tag Robbie IT. I actually whistled all the way! It did not occur to me that the Fates (or my big brother Daniel) might play a heavy hand in retribution.

CHAPTER 2
In Which the Plot Thickens and I Gain an Accomplice

By the time I came up the path from the creek, Robbie had disappeared into the garden where Mama kneeled, setting bedding plants in long, even rows. She gave me a quizzical look as I ambled by but didn't call me over. I could see Robbie mumbling through his tears and gesturing wildly. Mama hugged him close, gently wiping his face where eye leaks had left ribbons of clean skin tattooing his grubby cheeks. He pointed towards me, but she smiled and told him that his sister would always protect him from harm. His little eyes got huge as saucers and he shook his head hard at Mama. She patted the bottom of his denim overalls and turned back to her planting. Apparently, I was off the hook for the moment.

After lunch, Robbie refused to play by the creek, so Danny amused himself by locking me in one of the rabbit hutches—unfortunately, the home of our huge buck. Danny suspected I was somehow responsible for Robbie's sudden aversion to the creek in general, and hide-and-seek in particular, and threatened to leave me locked in until I confessed.

"I'll just go away for a while. Maybe you'll be in the mood

to talk when I get back." Danny sounded like a character in one of his favorite Red Ryder movies. "Better hope that buck likes you better'n he likes me, Leah. He's one mean sucker!" Danny whistled through his teeth as he disappeared around the corner.

The buck rabbit and I eyeballed each other, our noses separated by no more than two or three inches. A child larger than I would not have fit into the hutch. As it was, I crouched on all fours, the chicken wire floor cutting into my knees and palms, facing a full-grown male Dutch rabbit. He had long, yellow teeth and he'd worn the white hair off over his nose by pressing it for hours through the chicken wire walls while he lusted after the lady rabbits in adjacent hutches.

Danny was correct in his assessment of the buck. I had had a run-in with him before. Daddy had given me the duty of feeding and watering the rabbits after assigning hutch-cleaning duties to Danny. Consequently, the rabbits were usually well fed and watered, but could rely on clean hutches only on the weekends when Daddy inspected.

Every day, I saw the buck grow more desperate to reach the does housed next to him. Daddy said he would just have to suffer, or we'd be "ass deep in long ears," whatever that meant, but the present arrangement didn't seem fair to me. All the other rabbits were two to a hutch. He must be feeling lonely, I reasoned, especially since he was the only boy.

One morning, I took pity on him. After filling every pen's weighted bowls with pellets, I cleaned and refilled the hanging water bottles. As I worked, Thumper (I actually thought of him in Disney terms at the time) gazed pleadingly at his lady loves and ignored his food.

"Don't you worry, Thumper," I crooned. "As soon as I finish the water, I'll put you in a hutch with some of your friends." Thumper crouched on his belly and fixed his brooding eyes on the adjacent pair of Agouti-colored lovelies. I talked to the rabbits as I worked.

"Now, you should all get a turn being friends with Thumper." I paused from the water bottles and spoke directly to the hutches. "He can visit with you two, first!" I stepped up to the selected hutch and fastened the last remaining water bottle in place, then turned my attention to Thumper. "Come on, Thumper, Mama's gonna move you right now."

I turned the little wooden latch on the buck's hutch and opened the door just far enough to admit my head and shoulders. Arms outstretched, I leaned forward and gathered Thumper to my chest. With the swiftness of a professional assassin, the ungrateful beast ripped my forearms to shreds with his strong, claw-tipped hind legs. My shrieks of pain brought Daddy on the run. He snatched me from the hutch, leaving the rabbit spinning on his nose, and flipped the hutch door shut.

"What were you thinking," questioned Daddy as he applied Iodine and bandages to my bleeding wounds. "That rabbit could have taken off your nose or put out an eye. My God, Cookie—I never thought you'd actually try to move him!"

"Why did he hurt me, Daddy?" I sniffled through my tears. "I was only tryin' to help him!"

"It's a good thing you didn't, baby. If you had—Oh Lord! Those does would have been pregnant in a heartbeat. I shudder to think how we'd ever eat up that many rabbits if you had actually let him visit in every hutch!"

"You mean he's a husband?" I was shocked. Although I knew about the birds and the bees (and cows, pigs, chickens, etc.) like every farm kid, it hadn't crossed my mind that my sweet little Thumper had ulterior motives!

I should have known! I should have remembered the lesson Danny, Robbie and I learned oh, so well the previous Easter when some well-meaning relative presented us with three identical fluffy half-grown white bunnies with pink eyes. Danny quickly grew bored with chasing his bunny, so she joined the rabbits in the hutches. Robbie's bit him on several occasions, and soon joined her sister in captivity. Only my bunny, my sweet Daisy Dreamer, learned to snuggle close and eat from my hand. It became apparent to Daddy, however, that somewhere along their short journey to our part of the woods the three ladies had met up with some neighborhood's lothario. Daisy Dreamer quickly developed a bulging tummy that squirmed and writhed in a provocative manner.

"Better take her to join the others," Mama remarked to Daddy. "We don't need Leah adopting an entire litter."

I wasn't exactly sure what Mama meant, but no amount of pleading kept Daddy from whisking Daisy Dreamer off to join her sisters. I visited every day, of course, taking her bits of carrot and clover and grasses from the pasture. She remained friendly while her two sisters ignored me completely. I lifted her out of the hutch, being careful not to release the other two who made a hop for it the moment my hand touched the little turn knob that kept the wooden, chicken wire-covered door closed. Daisy's tummy grew daily.

She needs to run around, I tell myself. She is used to hopping about in the playroom while Mama cringes and cleans up little rabbit poops. I let her loose in the covered area between identical rows of hutches, encouraging her to get some exercise, then return her to the hutch she shares with her sisters.

A few days after school resumed post-Easter break, I came home and changed from my clothes into the jeans and flannel shirt I usually wore around the farm. With Mama's permission, I took some carrot and potato peels from the compost container near the kitchen sink and sped down to the barn to cosset my fat little bunny. I saw right away that Daddy had separated the sisters, one to a hutch, and had placed a nice, cozy hay-lined box in each new home.

How are you feeling today," I crooned as I opened Daisy Dreamer's hutch door. She seemed lethargic—droopy eared and grouchy, not the slightest bit interested in the proffered vegetable peels. A scuffling sound in the adjoining hutch attracted my attention. Danny's rabbit had dragged something out of her box and was busy trying to stuff it through the hutch's chicken wire flooring.

"Whatcha got there, dearie?" I leaned forward and realized to my horror that the 'something' had legs and ears! It was a fully formed baby rabbit—perfect in every way—except it was black. I reeled back in horror; Danny's rabbit was killing her own baby!

Now Daddy's remark about the 'litter' made sense. If Danny's rabbit had babies, maybe Daisy was also in the family way. My delight at the thought of many little Daisy babies erased the senseless action of infanticide I had just witnessed. Now my attention switched to the object of my affection who had retreated into her nesting box.

"You probably don't feel so good," I crooned to Daisy Dreamer. "I'll just put these vegetables into your bowl, and you can eat them later."

As I withdraw from the hutch, I hear a curious noise coming from Daisy's little house—an odd little crunching, slurping sound—that sends a shiver down my spine. I snatch up the box, only to discover, to my horror, the reason why my sweet little bunny is not hungry. She has already eaten and is now finishing up the last scraps of her own babies! I could still identify tiny black feet and other ragged, partly chewed body parts.

I jerked my head back so quickly that I smacked the back of it on the hutch frame, not pausing to close the door or secure it with the little spinning wooden latch. I howled all the way to the house, not sure if the pain I felt came more from the head or the heart.

Mama let me cry. She checked out the lump on my head, but nothing could ease the big divot in my insides. After a cup of warm cocoa, we walked back to the barn. Daisy had polished off the last of her offspring and was busy grooming herself, licking the remains from her paws. Mama secured the hutch.

"I don't know what to tell you, honey. Maybe Daddy will know why the rabbits did such a nasty thing. He'll be home soon."

We walked back to the house in silence.

Daddy did provide an explanation of sorts. He said that in nature if the mother perceives that an offspring is not perfect, she kills it and eats the body to pay back the energy it took to produce it.

"It's Mother Nature's way, Cookie. There's always a reason why these things happen. I think the does were shocked because the babies were black, not white like themselves. The babies must have had a black daddy rabbit."

"But why should it make any difference what color her babies are?" I sobbed in despair on my daddy's shoulder.

"It shouldn't, honey—really it shouldn't, but some things are just not for us to understand. Nature is neither cruel nor kind—just practical. A mother rabbit can't afford to raise babies that won't survive."

"But they were perfectly good little babies. Why didn't she know that Daddy?"

"Ah, Cookie—she's just a rabbit, after all. It's only us humans that see things more than one way—and we don't always do a very good job at it."

Daddy took the three Easter bunnies to a friend up the road. Danny was disappointed that he missed the whole affair by spending all afternoon with his friends down at the creek, and for weeks he pestered me to tell him every ugly detail. Robbie didn't care at all. I mourned—the loss of innocence, perhaps, or just the loss of my rabbit friend who betrayed me at a most personal level—and I learned that usually the fittest survive. Those who are different, or wounded in some way, cannot expect nature to give them a helping hand. It really is up to us.

Now I am back in the buck's hutch. My barely healed wounds still smart, and my face is once again in harm's way. I stay as still as possible, shifting only when pressure of wire on knees and palms become unbearable.

As afternoon wears on, the smell of rabbit excreta grows

overpowering. Flies buzz around my ears, landing on my eyelids and lips. Thumper turns his back to me, drinking noisily from his water bottle, then squats at his feed bowl, munching pellets. I rotate myself until I sit squat on my fanny, knees held tight to my chest, back curved, head down and eyes to the side. Now I cannot see the buck, but I hear him scrabbling about and feel his nose poke inquisitively at my bleeding knees.

"I'm gonna get you, Daniel," I whisper as the rabbit tries to burrow beneath my knees. He butts the backs of my thighs with his forehead, then retreats to his food bowl again.

Eventually, Danny returned. I heard him coming down the aisle, whistling and running a stick along the row of hutches.

"Well, why aren't ya beggin' me to let you out? Haven't had enough, huh? Or are you ready to talk?" He leered at me and rapidly raised and lowered his eyebrows, his mouth in a wide grin that showed the gaps in his teeth where new ones appeared at different stages of growth.

I squinched my eyes shut tight so as not to see him when I answered: "Please, Danny. Let me out."

Danny dropped his stick and squatted down beside the hutch so he could look me straight in the face. He batted his eyes. "I said, are you ready to talk?"

"Look, Daddy'll be home pretty soon. He'll take you to the woodshed if he finds me locked in here."

Danny laughed and turned his back to me, then he sat down and leaned against the hutch, squirming to and fro as he scratched his back on the wooden leg. The entire hutch began to wobble. Thumper's head jerked up and his beady little red eyes latched themselves to mine. The hutch tilted precariously, cascading the now agitated buck against my bare legs.

"Stop!" I shrieked in terror. "He's gonna hurt me, Danny!"

The hutch ceased its seesaw motion and Thumper backed off, shaking his head while he contemplated his next move.

"Ya gonna tell?"

For a split second, I remained silent, then Thumper began to advance on me—his long, yellow chisels hideously exposed in his gaping mouth. I covered as much of myself as possible with crossed arms, pressed my hands against my face, and screamed.

"Danny, puh-leese! Let me out and I'll tell you everything. Just hurry!"

Daniel stood up leisurely and opened the hutch but blocked the doorway with his body as I leaned hard into him.

"You cross your heart and hope to die?"

When I promised, he stepped aside and watched me fall sidewise onto the hard-packed dirt breezeway.

The plan didn't seem so wonderful to me, anymore. Ashamed of my weakness, I reluctantly confided the details to Danny. His face lit up with delight.

"I'm in," he cried gleefully. "Gaw, Leah—what a neat idea. Too bad I didn't think of it first. This is gonna be fun!"

For the rest of the day, I listened (agreeing in my silence) as Danny developed a strategy of carefully escalating terror. Robbie was in for a rocky summer, and so was my conscience!

At supper, Mama seemed pensive. Robbie woke from his nap reluctant to join Danny and me in play, instead spending the afternoon at her side helping her (sort of) set out bedding plants—a most unusual occupational choice for an active three-year-old. Danny and I chattered about our afternoon, carefully omitting any references to the rabbits. My knees still smarted, and I felt sure that Mama had doubted my sketchy explanation of blackberry vines and sharp grass as she patched up my numerous scratches.

As she poured more coffee into Daddy's cup, Mama cleared her throat and spoke. "Something odd happened this morning."

She paused, her gaze taking in both Danny and me. "Robbie seems to have the impression that the witch from *The Wizard of Oz* lives in our creek. I'm sure he just fell asleep and had a bad dream, but something about his story bothers me. He's absolutely convinced she chased him. He says you told him her name is Hatchet Annie."

Mama looked directly at me as she refilled her own cup. "Do you kids know what he's talking about?"

Danny and I shrugged and denied any knowledge of such an event. I professed shock that Robbie would implicate me in his fantasy. Daddy leaned forward on his elbows, listening closely to our protestations of innocence. He had a way of piercing right through my façade, his blue eyes probing my green ones with questions. Instead of lowering my gaze, a sure giveaway to my daddy that I was withholding information, I closed my eyes and blinked as if to clear a bit of grit. Daddy smiled and ruffled my hair, then tenderly wiped away the tear (of terror, not pain) that emerged at the corner of my eye. I turned away, unable to meet his gaze.

"Well, if you remember anything, anything at all, please come and tell me, will you?" Mama returned the pot to its place on the back burner of our old grumbly kitchen range.

We both agreed with nodding heads and "yes, ma'ams." Again, I shook off that nagging guilty feeling and risked a quick glance at Daniel. He winked at me and continued enjoying his pot roast. Daddy gazed at me a little longer, then withdrew behind his dinner plate and began telling us about a new ship in the dry dock, and how the tugboats had problems maneuvering it in. I relaxed a little, relieved that I had not been caught.

I lie awake this night in late spring when the longest day of the year is near and peer out under the shade pulled nearly to the sill of the window next to my twin bed. Danny lies sleeping in his matching bed against the west wall of our shared room. It has no window, but if he is careful and Robbie and I are quiet, he can hear the grownups in their grownup talk in the adjoining room. Robbie shares our room now, his crib on the south wall, snuggled between Danny and me, his head at Danny's feet. I hear him snuggle in his blanket at night and slurp on his thumb for comfort as I still use mine for the same. I wonder if he rubs his nose with his forefinger as I do, but do not rise and creep to his side to look. I do not want to know. His comfort is his alone, and mine is private, too. Danny snores gently with his face in the pillow. He has had his tonsils and adenoids "out" as OurGrandmother refers to it. They sit in their little green bottle in the kitchen window of our house in town until Mama accidentally upsets it into the sink, where the bottle shatters and sends pieces of Danny down the drain.

Although I am happy on the farm, I miss the chestnut tree at our house in town. Sometimes when I am at Sunday school across the street, I visit it if I have the time before Mama collects Robbie and rounds up Danny. The tree is my beginning. *Danny's was in the little cottage on McCall Boulevard, and Robbie's is here, at Daddy's farm. These are the places of our earliest memories. And on this night, as Danny's plot weighs heavy on my heart, I lie abed, remembering, remembering...*

CHAPTER 3
In Which The Stage is Set

When I was three months old, my biological father had his girlfriend tell my mother that he wanted a divorce, but that Mama should be reasonable and allow all of us—OurFather, the girlfriend, Mama, my nearly three-year-old brother Danny, and myself—to live together until the divorce was final. Mama, being the "emotional" and "unreasonable" person that she was, said, "No—HELL no!" so OurFather and his girlfriend, who had been hired by him to take care of my mother after my birth, moved out. I don't know where the girlfriend, Gemma, went, but OurFather moved in with my maternal grandmother, who did her best to help him patch things up with Mama.

Mama didn't get along very well with OurGrandmother (always capitalized in my mind) who adored Mama's older sister Auntie Nor and her husband (and later their children), but for her to take Danny's and my father's side against her own blood wounded Mama to the very core. Although OurGrandmother had divorced Grandpa Stevens and charged him with adultery (a "crime" resulting in two additional aunties), she seemed adamant that Mama should not take

OurFather's "little indiscretion" to heart.

Mama was very ill after my birth, having contracted staphylococcus infection in her breasts while still in the hospital. OurFather worked long hours at the shipyard because we were at war, and God knows OurGrandmother couldn't help Mama, even though she, herself, was a practical nurse who had supported Mama and our Auntie working at the county infectious diseases hospital (referred to locally as the bug house). Consequently, OurFather hired Gemma to take care of Danny and me while Mama fought the staph infection. A visiting nurse from Olympic Hospital came in every day to change the dressings on Mama's abscesses; Gemma prepared my formula (since I couldn't nurse) and helped Mama with Danny's and my care. Apparently, she was also assisting our male parent with his "needs," as my grandmother referred to them. "AND," Mama continued, "Where was HE when Hal brought Leah and me home—playing footsy with his floozy?"

He hadn't shown up at the hospital when Mama was released. Instead, he sent his best friend, Hal, who helped Mama from his 1939 wine red DeSoto and, cradling me in his arms, assisted us into the little McCall Boulevard cottage my parents called home.

"Now, Mayleen," OurGrandmother expounded, "a man must have his needs satisfied, and you are in no position to fulfill them for your husband at this time." Mama grimaced and pursed her lips.

"Don't give me that face!" exclaimed OurGrandmother. You know that I'm telling the truth here, and certainly you are in no condition to take care of two little children, one an infant, on your own."

Mama retorted, "You are surely not telling me anything I don't already know, Mother, but I don't see how I can overlook the fact that he's been carrying on right under my own roof while I'm so sick. You'd think he'd have the decency to go somewhere else to shack up with that woman."

"Men don't often see things the same way we do, my dear," OurGrandmother replied. "Where would you have him go? There is a war on, and all the rooms are filled with servicemen."

"...And their floozies—ANYwhere but here, Mama!"

OurGrandmother harrumphed in her throat—a universally disapproving sound that still makes the spot between my shoulder blades go icy cold and my shoulders hunch up.

Danny listened, wide-eyed, from behind Mama's chair as she fed me a bottle. No one noticed him, so he stuck his thumb in his mouth and hunkered down in silence. He had seen things in his three years—things that made him cry quietly at night—things that forever changed the direction of his life. But that is Danny's story, not mine. He experienced—firsthand, as a toddler—things that I saw as a much older child from a disparate household, so our perspectives differed. He loved "OurFather" as we came to call him in later years (not to be confused with OurFather up in Heaven) in a way that I did not. He was Danny's daddy, but never mine.

Danny had seen OurFather throw things at Mama—coffee cups, tableware—and had suffered the consequences of the back of his daddy's hand when he came to his mama's defense. But he was still Daddy's little man and the light of his father's life.

I, on the other hand, was the requisite daughter, dutifully provided by Mama for his perfect family, but not to be held in such high esteem as the child with the "spout." As Danny's daddy put it to his buddies in the shipyard, "Any old mechanic can kick a hole in a can, but it takes a real machinist to put on a spout." I didn't "get it" the first time Danny threw this little gem in my face—not until another little boy was born into our family. This spout apparently was so important that the first time Danny witnessed Mama change my diaper, he was aghast that I did not have one.

"I go phone Dr. Haller, Mama," he exclaimed. "He fix Leah and give her a spout!" Mama had a difficult few moments explaining that little girls didn't have spouts. (In later years, bless his heart, my big brother Danny did his best to try hooking me up with, in his opinion, the finest spouts in town. I, however, preferred to choose my own!)

"Now you listen here, young lady," grumbled OurGrandmother. "This is no time to get your dander up. No one wants a divorced woman, especially a sick one with children, to boot. You pull yourself together and tell him you won't give him a divorce. This will pass and you and the children will be taken care of."

"Is that all you care about," replied Mama bitterly, "that someone will take care of us and you don't need to worry? Well, I have worked before and I can do it again—as soon as I'm back on my feet!"

"And just when will that be?" replied OurGrandmother tartly. "Don't look to me or your sister for help, and your father is worthless."

Our Aunt Noreen (affectionately called Auntie Nor by Danny and me) worked at Woolworth's downtown by the shipyard, and her husband delivered mail. Mama's father, our Grandpa Stevens, lived with his wife and family a long way off. Danny had met him once or twice and liked him very much. OurGrandmother had divorced him when Mama was a little girl. Ironically enough, he had fallen in love with another woman. He would have stayed for the sake of his two children, but OurGrandmother would have none of it. She never forgave him and made Mama suffer for being his favorite.

Mama didn't say a word as her mother stalked out of the cottage and slammed the door.

My parents were officially divorced by summertime. Mama struggled to pay rent on the cottage and OurFather took up residence with his newlywed Gemma in Port Orchard, taking the little walk-on ferry across the bay to the Bremerton Navy Shipyard every day.

Whenever he got a day off, OurFather's best friend Hal came to visit Mama and play with Danny and me. Once a month, Danny stayed the weekend with OurFather and Gemma, according to the divorce decree, but I was not included in the deal. I was too young and too much trouble to take care of.

Actually, the first person I called Daddy was Hal—and when I was fourteen months old, it became the truth. War or no war, MY mama and MY daddy married on Valentine's Day. When they returned from their weekend honeymoon, we moved from the little cottage on McCall Boulevard to a two-bedroom stucco house on Stewart Avenue, a nice house on a corner lot with a huge horse chestnut tree in the front yard.

CHAPTER 4
In Which I Learn that Life is a Bumpy Ride

For that brief, few days of our parents' nuptials and weekend together time, Danny and I went to stay with OurGrandmother. She lived in an old Victorian house in the south end of our town. It rose from fifteen cement stairs above the bumpy cement sidewalk to a generous front porch. The house inside was dark and musty-smelling, much like OurGrandmother, herself. The shades seemed permanently drawn so that no one could look out onto the tiny late winter yellow grass fitfully holding on to life in the sparse dirt contained by the cement retaining walls rising from the sidewalk, and no one could look in to see the old, dusty overstuffed furniture and the wilting cabbage rose carpet in the tiny living room. At street level and adjacent to the alley running behind, a second door opened into the basement apartment OurFather had rented during the divorce. It was currently occupied by a young married couple, both of whom were employed at the Shipyard. She worked the day shift, and he was on graveyard, requiring Danny and me to be **as quiet as possible** so he could sleep during the day (emphasis provided by OurGrandmother).

OurGrandmother usually wore black—a black and white striped matching skirt and top, for instance, with mid-heel black ankle shoes with black laces. Her stockings were either black or white cotton concealed from view by the length of her skirt and held up by the garters on her whale-bone corset, laced tight across her ample body and bosom. She wore her black straw hat with its matching veil at all times when not inside and carried a black leather handbag the size of a small traveling case filled with her pills, potions and hankies for all that ailed her. She (and for that matter, the whole house) smelled of lavender with undertones of some salty and slightly nasty odor that I later identified as Epsom salts.

Grandmother had retired from her position at the "bug house" after Mama's marriage to OurFather, and now devoted her time to taking care of other people's grandchildren, but she had agreed to take Danny and me for this one short weekend so that Mama might make an honest woman of herself. Consequently, Mama and Hal had brought us over on Friday morning, along with clothing, food, and toys, to be collected no later than Monday at noon so that OurGrandmother might not miss her Tuesday session carrying for the small child of one of Auntie Nor's co-workers from Woolworth.

"My gracious, Mayleen! The children are not moving in with me on a permanent basis, are they? You have brought enough things to staff a small orphanage!" she snorted as Hal struggled up the stairs with my tricycle, a birthday present from OurFather's family. Mama was not thrilled with that particular gift, but I had been walking for months and had easily mastered the skill of pedaling, even if I did not have the commonsense God gave a mouse. Mama had let me pedal about on the back lawn at home, where if I catapulted off, my landing would be fairly soft, at least.

Mama eyeballed the fifteen steps and motioned for Hal to put the tricycle back into the car. Grandmother intervened by taking the offending vehicle from Hal's hands and placing it firmly on the front porch.

"Stop worrying, for Heaven's sake," sputtered OurGrandmother. "Don't you think I am capable of monitoring her activities for the short while she is here?"

Mama sighed, looked at Hal, and decided to let the matter drop. "We need to be off—it's a long drive to Tacoma—and we don't know how long we'll have to wait for a ferry. Now you kids," she squatted down between us and gave us both a squeeze, "you behave for your grandma, you hear? We'll be back in a few days. When we get home, we'll be a real family." Then she and Hal waved good-bye and got into Hal's old Model A. Since he was now going to be a family man, he had traded in the DeSoto for a vehicle more suiting a new wife and her children, not to mention wartime gasoline rationing.

I held Danny's hand tight as we watched the little bottle-green car with the black top chug off towards Tacoma. There went all the stability our lives had ever known—Mama and Hal. OurGrandmother was an unknown quantity. We had never before spent the night under her roof and in her exclusive care.

As the car rounded the corner and drifted out of sight, OurGrandmother opened the screen and yanked us inside. She slammed the front door and threw the bolt. "Now Danny," she snapped as she pulled him around to face her, "you watch out

for your sister and make sure that this door! stays! shut!"
Danny flinched as if he had been slapped. OurGrandmother let
loose of his arm and Danny dropped my hand.

She turned to me, bending ominously over my head, and
told me to mind my manners. I hadn't a clue what she meant
and had to ask Danny when we were finally alone. "I don't
know," he answered in a whisper. "Jeez, Leah! I'm just a little
kid—maybe she means not to wet your pants!"

That was not so easy. Sometimes I wet the bed at night,
although I never had an accident in the daytime.

"Don't worry about it." Danny leaned over and whispered
in my ear. "I won't let her do anything to you. Besides, Mama
wouldn't have left us here if SHE was gonna HURT us!"

Danny scrounged around OurGrandmother's living room
for a magazine. When he found a *Good Housekeeping*, he sat
down beside me on the scratchy horsehair sofa, and we looked
at pictures together. After a while, Danny slipped down and
retrieved his soldiers and tanks from our toy bag and we spent
the rest of the afternoon playing war, pretending
OurGrandmother's dusty cabbage rose carpet was Europe. We
were little kids—infants by today's standards—but we knew all
about the war.

As dusk gradually filled the already dimly lit room,
OurGrandmother escorted us into her brightly illuminated
kitchen. She had a light supper on the table, chicken noodle
soup and soda crackers and a small glass of milk for each of
us. Danny struggled manfully up to the table, balancing on his
knees on the hard wooden chair, in order to reach his food.
OurGrandmother motioned me to a pyramid of Montgomery
Ward (never Sears, my dear—we don't do Sears) catalogs

balanced one atop another in the chair next to Danny's. She hoisted me up and plopped me on the pile, then strapped me to the chair back with a tea towel around my waist.

Danny adroitly handled his soup and crackers. Grandmother handed me a spoon with a bent handle with which I chased noodles around in the greasy broth until I caught a few, lifting them up to my mouth smoothly, if a little sloppily. My spoon splashed down into the bowl as I used both hands to raise my milk to my lips. Grandmother made a snorting noise under her breath and retrieved it from the soup, wiping off the handle on her napkin.

"Eat more neatly, Cookie," she muttered smartly to me.

"Gosh," whispered Danny almost to himself. "She's only a baby, after all!" OurGrandmother gave him a fierce look and Danny shut his mouth so quickly he bit his tongue. He surreptitiously wiped a little blood from the spot with his napkin, showed it to me, then folded the offending red smear to the inside, glancing sideways to see if she had noticed. He winced a little as the salty broth from his next bite smarted.

As soon as we finished, OurGrandmother got us ready for bed. Danny and I shared a twin bed in the spare room. One side was shoved up against the wall and under the window. I had that side so that I wouldn't fall out in the night, according to OurGrandmother. Danny clung to the open side, hoping I wouldn't shove him out onto the braided rag rug providing the only cushion between the floor and him.

"And don't pee your pants," he growled at me after OurGrandmother left the room and turned out the light. "I figure she'll give ya a real whuppin' if you do."

The room is musty with disuse and stuffy, as the window

is tightly closed and Danny cannot unlock it. We try to settle down, but I miss my own crib and have never spent time away from Mama before. Danny is slowly getting used to one weekend a month with OurFather and Gemma, but he says he does not like going there. I plop my thumb into my mouth and suck it hard, for comfort, although I miss my special blanket with the soft, satin binding that I rub between the thumb and fingers of my other hand. Mama has packed it, but OurGrandmother has not given it to me before bed. After a while, Danny pokes me in the ribs and tells me to quit slurping in his ear. I try my best and manage to make it through the night with dry panties!

Saturday went fairly well, no unpleasant surprises from either Danny or me. Since it rained all day, we stayed inside and used OurGrandmother's furniture pretty hard, according to her. Auntie Nor came over after work and we were joined by our uncle at dinnertime. Bedtime came early again, as the grownups wanted us out of the way, which did not bode well for the prospect of my poor bladder making it through another night. OurGrandmother left the bedroom door open a crack, so Danny and I lay awake listening to the adults talk about Mama and Hal and their wedding. OurGrandmother was still unhappy that Mama had thrown OurFather out of the house and was making it abundantly clear that she disapproved of Mama's remarriage.

"The only good to come of all this kerfuffle," she commented to Auntie Nor as our uncle read the paper and drank an after-dinner beer, "is that HE is financially able to take care of Mayleen and the children. God knows, she hasn't two pennies to rub together!"

Auntie Nor took Mama's side. "It's not as if Al is waiting in the wings to take her and the children back, Mama. He married Gemma as soon as the divorce was final, and I don't notice him paying his child support."

"Would you pay for a dead horse, my dear?" retorted OurGrandmother. "None of them do!" She was bitter about men and didn't mind letting it show. Our uncle rustled his newspaper and took another sip of beer. Auntie Nor made a little noise in her throat but didn't answer.

"And that little girl—it is downright unnatural, the way she walks and talks at such an early age." OurGrandmother harrumphed and the kitchen went quiet. We could hear the continued rustle of our uncle's newspaper.

Danny punched me in the arm. "Golly, Leah—she's talkin' about you! You can't help it if you're smart. And SHE thinks there's something wrong with you." He started to get out of bed, then thought better of it and pulled the covers up around his ears, as if he didn't want to hear anything more from the kitchen.

After a moment, Auntie Nor murmured softly, "It's not her fault, Mama. She's just a very bright and wonderful baby. You should be proud of her."

"On the contrary," snorted OurGrandmother. "She gives me the willies with that big vocabulary and her knowing eyes. She's no more a baby than I am!"

"Don't you listen to her, Leah," my big brother whispered softly. "SHE don't know nothing." I didn't know whether to smile at Danny's encouraging words or to cry from my grandmother's hurtful ones. My big brother was both my tormenter and my savior, and though we often fought like tigers, I thought the sun shone out of his eyes. As if he had read my mind, his arm shifted gently across my back and he pulled me close. Finally, the conversation from the kitchen switched to the war, and Danny and I drifted off to sleep.

Unfortunately, even advanced motor and verbal skills cannot overcome an immature bladder. I wet the bed, waking us both. We squirmed around, trying to find a dry spot on sheets slipping about on OurGrandmother's rubber mattress cover. Danny finally gave up and rolled off onto the scatter rug that sat beside the bed. "Now don't fall off and make matters worse," he huffed.

In the morning, OurGrandmother was quite displeased with me. She had not planned on doing laundry on Sunday, but the soiled bed linen couldn't wait. Consequently, fault for the following events fell solely on Danny and me.

Although the day is misty and cold, OurGrandmother bundles us up and sends us outside to play while she takes care of the problem created by my lack of proper bladder control. Danny and I play on the porch for a while, then go up and down the sidewalk as far as the corner. Finally, I decide to ride my tricycle that sits temptingly on the porch next to the door. Danny balks at getting it down the stairs for me as he figures OurGrandmother would blame him if I were run over by one of the occasional cars that trundle by. He picks up a small rock and throws it at the telephone pole on the corner, where it bounces back onto the sidewalk.

I scale the steep cement stairs leading to the front porch, pull my little tricycle away from the wall, and carefully climb on. The floorboards creak under me as I slowly pedal across the length of the porch. I ride back and forth several times, eventually becoming bored with such a confined space. On one of my trips across the porch, I stop at the stairs, considering whether I should try again soliciting Danny's help.

Down on the sidewalk, Danny no longer tosses the rock but begins kicking it up and down the skinny brown parking strip of lawn between the sidewalk and the street, intent on ignoring me when I call down to him.

"Look at me," I shout, and for some unknown reason, or for no reason at all, I ride straight at those tempting steps.

"Leah, stop!" Danny screams at the top of his lungs, but his cry comes too late. As desperately as I wish to recall my action, the front wheel crosses the point of no return and I am committed to the ride of my life.

I held on pretty well for the first four steps, then lost control completely. Tricycle and self became one small package, hurtling to certain doom.

Danny flies toward me, arriving just as the tangle of child and metal connect with the sidewalk. My head snaps forward with such force that when my face connects with the handlebars, my two front teeth are driven through my upper lip. I catapult onto the sidewalk, further abrading my lip, nose, and forehead. Stunned, I lie like a dead thing on the sidewalk, unable to move, the breath driven from my small body. Danny screams my name, attempting frantically to disentangle me from the wheels and metal bars pinning me to the ground.

Apparently, Danny's screams roused our grandparent, who arrived on the scene and disengaged me from the ruins of my vehicle.

"Well, you have certainly made a spectacle of yourself, young lady. And you, Daniel—what were you thinking, letting her ride that thing down those stairs!" Her eyes flashed with annoyance as she pulled me upright. "Let me have a look at your face."

OurGrandmother takes me inside and applies ice to my forehead, wipes the blood from my lip, and examines the damage. After swabbing peroxide and iodine on each and every scrape and cut, and forming the opinion that my lip will heal without stitches, albeit somewhat scarred, she pronounces me fine. The fact that I have neither opened my mouth to protest the prodding, poking, peroxide and iodine nor spoken a single word since the incident bothers her not a bit. I sit, still and flaccid as a rag doll, my eyes refuse to focus, and the ringing in my ears keeps me from hearing anything either Danny or OurGrandmother says to me. Then, without warning, I bend over my little scuffed white high tops and deposit my breakfast all over OurGrandmother's squeaky clean kitchen floor.

For the rest of Sunday, I sat like a zombie on the kitchen linoleum, a towel around my neck and a bowl beside me, with instructions to Danny that if I vomited again, he should make sure that I hit either the towel or the bowl. Danny obliged, his face almost as white as mine. He sat next to me with my poor, throbbing head and face nestled on his shoulder until dinner time, when Grandmother insisted that he eat. She fed me some ice chips, looked closely into my still-not-quite-focused eyes, and harrumphed. "You look quite a sight, Leah. Your mother will likely pitch a fit when she sees you. Are you proud of yourself?"

I don't remember much of the night that followed, other than Danny shaking me at intervals to wake me up and my head hurting horribly. By morning, my head felt a little better, but I still couldn't focus my eyes very well and my face felt as wretched as it looked. Danny and I sat on the front porch waiting in silence for Hal's old Model A Ford to sweep around the corner and rescue us from OurGrandmother's tender care.

By late afternoon, both of us were tired, cold and, in Danny's case, hungry. Auntie Nor had come by at lunchtime and brought Danny out a sandwich. The look on her face as she tried to smile at me made my stomach lurch.

"Poor little Cookie," she murmured as she brushed the blonde bangs back from my battered forehead, "What were you thinking, riding that thing down all those stairs! It's a miracle that you are alive."

I still had not said a word, but my eyes must have told volumes, as Auntie Nor sat down on the cold cement steps and put her arm around me.

Mama and Auntie Nor are sisters, and sound alike—but she does not smell like my mama. Auntie Nor does not wear Evening in Paris perfume. She snuggles me for a short time, then picks up Danny's nearly untouched sandwich and disappears back into OurGrandmother's house, leaving us to sit and wait in silence.

Finally, when we are nearly frozen lumps of little girl and little boy, Mama and our new daddy puff around the corner in the familiar bottle green and black Model A. The car pulls up to the curb and Mama jumps out, her arms wide open and a smile on her face that abruptly changes to a look of horror when she catches sight of mine.

"Oh my God, Hal!" she screamed. "Look at Cookie's face. What has happened here?" She swooped me into her arms, barely noticing that I flinched as she hugged me close, and for the first time since I looked down that long row of steps and engaged the pedals on my tricycle, I began to cry.

I don't remember much about the rest of that day. Mama must have spoken to OurGrandmother, but if they had words I was oblivious. The only thing I cared about was that my mama had me in her arms and I was safe again.

My new daddy had to go to work the next morning, so Mama took Danny and me on the bus into town to the Scott Medical Clinic. We sat in the waiting room, Mama holding me on her lap. Danny wandered about, peering at the other people sitting and reading their magazines, and occasionally talking to the receptionist. Every few minutes, a nurse appeared at the inner door, beckoning to one of the waiting people.

After what seemed forever, Dr. Scott strolled through the waiting room. Danny's face brightened and he waved at the familiar smile on our family physician's face. I was still trying to get used to him, as Dr. Haller, who had delivered Danny and me, had left the practice and returned to medical school to become a pediatrician.

"Hi, Danny," exclaimed Dr. Scott. "What brings you to see me?"

"Mama's here with Cookie," replied Danny, hands on hips. "Guess what, Dr. Scott—betcha can't guess what!"

"You'll just have to tell me," prompted the doctor.

"Well," chortled Danny conspiratorially, "Mama got MARRIED this weekend!"

Dr. Scott pulled himself up to full height and put his hands on his hips in imitation of Danny. He turned dramatically, catching the attention of the whole waiting room, and gestured towards Mama and me.

"Well, indeed, young man." He winked at Mama, then said, "And it's ABOUT TIME, too!"

The waiting room erupted into laughter. Even my mama laughed, but Danny's face turned a deep crimson.

The doctor motioned for Mama to bring me into the examining room, and we followed him through the door into the clinic's inner sanctum.

I had already seen too much of this clinic in my young life, but today the nurses oohed and aahed at the sight of my cuts and bruises. Dr. Scott commented on my luck at surviving the fall with such relatively minor damage. The cuts through my top lip were healing and he did not want to suture them as too much time had passed.

"Her bruises will heal, Mayleen. And so will the cuts. She has had a concussion, of course, and hopefully, that will not leave her with long-term problems, although I can't rule out the possibility. Let's see how much scarring she has on the lip—she's so young that the scars may be minimal."

Mama promised to keep a sharp eye on me for the next few weeks and to return immediately if I manifested any worrying symptoms. We hurried out into the brisk February wind that drove the light rain almost sideways. Fortunately, we didn't have to wait long for the bus that took us home to our new daddy and our new life.

The scars on my face faded, with time, and the concussion healed, albeit leaving me with headaches and some vision problems that hung around for several years. My grandmother's attitude towards me did not fade, however. No matter how hard I tried, she always acted cold and aloof. No hugs, no special little grandmother-granddaughter talks. As the years rolled along, she managed to toss all my siblings into the same bag she had unceremoniously placed me in so long ago, although they probably didn't give her "the willies!" At night, I sometimes felt for the little white lines across my upper lip, rubbing them gently as if to make them disappear. Eventually, they softened and became nearly unnoticeable. Unfortunately, there was no way to erase the scar that OurGrandmother had seared across my soul with her hurtful words, but I guess those scars don't count as long as no one can see them!

CHAPTER 5
In Which My Brother is Purloined

The first house I clearly remember sat on a raised corner lot facing Stewart Avenue—a cozy one-story beige stucco with a composition shingle roof and a huge horse chestnut tree that spread her leafy branches over the entire northeast corner of lawn that ran from the Tennis's house on the south, round the corner, and ended at the fence separating us from the Camerons' house to the west. Seven steps led up from the city sidewalk to the ribbon of cement that traversed the lawn and connected to the three steps rising to the front porch. Danny had made friends with the two Tennis boys who were approximately his age. Unfortunately, I was the only little girl in the neighborhood, so I was stuck with Johnny Cameron on the west, who teased me unmercifully and tested my patience.

Daddy works long days at the shipyard, making gun sights for the huge warships helping to keep us safe from "the enemy." Mama washes and cleans and tries to cook nutritious meals with her slim rations of meat, flour, sugar, and butter. Sometimes, she sends me to the little store at the end of the block past the Coca-Cola bottling plant with a list of what to buy, and I grasp the precious coupon book, or the tokens tied tightly in the corner of my handkerchief. Mama stands on the sidewalk with baby Robbie in her arms, watching as I run at a headlong dash towards the market, admonishing me to watch my step. The storekeeper fills my mama's list and sends me on my breathless run home.

Across Twelfth Street on the north side of the corner lot is a large barrage balloon, manned by sailors in their smart uniforms—blue bellbottom pants and white blouses with the "sailor collar" in the back. The huge balloon, held down by strong cables, is supposed to keep enemy dive-bombers from taking out the huge ships being repaired and outfitted at the shipyard, according to Danny, who is an expert in all things military. I am mostly interested in the guards and secretly lust after their uniform blouses. I linger as close to the guards as possible in hopes that one of them will realize my longing and pluck the item from his person as a gift to me. Mama takes cold drinks over when the weather is hot, and once, when Pathé News (the eyes and ears of the world) is in town, she is filmed climbing over the fence with a plate of cookies for the boys!

This bit of cinema made the cut and was shown in theaters all over the country, including my grandparents' small local theater in Puyallup. Daddy's mama, my Gramma Vanac, jumped to her feet in the middle of the newsreel and announced to the whole theater that the woman was her daughter-in-law, much to the embarrassment of her daughter and grandson, who sat next to her.

Shortly after Danny turned four, Mama and I drove over to Port Orchard in my Great Aunt Alma's car on a sunny Monday morning to retrieve him from OurFather's house, where he had spent the weekend. Usually, OurFather brought

Danny back on the foot ferry that connected the county seat with Bremerton. On this particular morning, when the ferry arrived, Danny and he were not among the passengers. At first, Mama thought she had missed them, but as time passed and Danny did not turn up, we walked to my great aunt's house on Eighth Street not too far from the ferry slip. OurFather's relatives—my grandparents and great aunts—were none too happy with his choice of lifestyle. They assisted Mama whenever possible, and had, in fact, helped her with finances during her difficult struggle prior to her remarriage, a fact that greatly annoyed OurFather. They were good, Midwestern farm folk relocated to the Pacific Northwest, with good, Midwestern values that did not include dumping one's wife and children for another woman.

Aunt Alma seemed as puzzled as Mama at OurFather's failure to appear on the foot ferry. She put on her best face, however, and offered to go with us. "Then, he'll play the real fool trying to put one over on you, Mayleen. He knows I will have no problem telling him what I think of his behavior. Just say the word."

Mama politely refused, although she would have liked both the moral support and the company. OurFather was her problem, after all, and she hated to pull family members into this child visitation tug of war. Both families were delighted that Mama had custody of us, although no one really trusted OurFather to play by the rules.

The little bungalow looked oddly deserted as Mama and I pulled up in the driveway.

"Stay here, Cookie," she commented brightly. "I'll be back in a flash with your brother. We'll go into town and have an early lunch at Perkins Café."

Danny and I loved eating out, something we seldom did, as Daddy worked long hours in the Shipyard due to the war. Gas rationing kept us walking most places, and Perkins Café was more blocks from our house on Chester Street than Mama and Daddy cared to travel with two little kids. I sat there in the front seat anticipating the treat and watched Mama as she walked boldly up the front steps, pulled open the screen, and rapped on the wooden front door.

No one answered, so Mama knocked harder, waited, then pounded with both fists so fiercely that the whole door vibrated and its little window rattled. Not a peep from inside. She stood on tiptoe and peered through the frosty pane, then repeated the pounding, all the while shouting for Gemma and OurFather to relinquish Danny before she called the police.

When no amount of pounding, shouting, or combination of both produced her son, Mama began stalking around the house, looking through each window she could reach. After a few minutes, a short, stout, grey-haired woman appeared in the drive. She stopped beside the car and smiled at me through the open door, then called out to Mama as she rounded the house towards the driveway.

"Are you looking for someone, dearie?" she inquired politely.

"Yes," replied my mother, "my little boy. He was visiting his father this weekend, and no one brought him home."

"Oh, yes—that nice little couple who lived here. They moved away on Friday night, just after the mister came home with the child. Hauled up a trailer, he did. They put in their things and were gone by midnight." She paused for a moment as if weighing her next words with care. Finally, her eyes met Mama's and she continued. "He said something to my husband about a new job out of state."

Mama let out an anguished scream. Even though I was barely two, I could feel her pain—the agony of something inside breaking—like her heart, or maybe her last illusion shattering and shards sharp as glass piercing her very soul. She shuddered, then dropped like a rock to her knees, crossed her arms over her chest, hands clenched, and began rocking back and forth, back and forth, sobbing all the while.

I remember climbing carefully down from the front seat of the car and squatting beside my mother. Whether she heard me or just felt the warmth of my body as I pressed close to her I don't know, but she reached out and I took her slender hand in mine, raised it to my lips, and kissed her knuckles.

Time stands still with Mama and me in a warp where Danny is still inside the house and the door needs only to open so Mama can take his little bag in her left hand and Danny's hand in her right and walk to Great Aunt Alma's car. She will put Danny and his ditty bag, as our Grammy B calls the little canvas bag with the drawstring top, in the back seat, close the door firmly, and walk around to the driver's side. She will work the gear shift on the floor with her right hand, manipulate the clutch and the brake pedals on the floor, then maneuver Auntie Alma's car out of the driveway. We will have our special lunch out, then go home to dinner with my new daddy. But Danny is not in the back seat and Mama is not in the seat beside me and we are not going home anytime soon. My brother is gone, and my mama is now silent beside me on the hard, hard driveway of OurFather and Gemma's rented

Port Orchard house.

We stayed like that for what seemed forever before the grey-haired lady spoke.

"The Masons next door have a telephone—I'll just run over there and call for the police if you would like me to." Mama nodded an acknowledgement, and Mrs. Grey Hair left.

Mama sat up, wiped her eyes on her brown and white striped tee-shirt, then fumbled through her pockets for a hanky, eventually blowing her nose on a transient piece of tissue. By the time the police arrived, she was dry-eyed, although her cheeks and nose were still red and her eyes swollen.

The police put out bulletins, local and statewide, but by the time anyone knew that OurFather had stolen Danny, he was long gone, and the trail was cold as my mama's heart had become. In due time, Mama went to court where Judge Slayton declared OurFather in contempt.

Back in those days, stealing one's child was not considered kidnapping, as it is now, and the police and courts were much more lenient, tending to look the other way and leaving such issues to the parents involved and the civil courts. Being in contempt, however, did have some teeth—it meant that OurFather dare not step foot in the state unless and until the judge lifted the contempt citation. Otherwise, there was little that either Mama or the courts could do until she found out where OurFather had taken Danny.

Eventually, Gemma, Danny, and OurFather surfaced in Oakland, California where he worked for the Navy at Mare Island. Mama returned to court and obtained papers proving that she had custody of Danny, and although she was three months pregnant with my brother Robbie, she left me in my new daddy's capable hands and set out to retrieve her stolen child.

Mama's older sister Mary Anne lived in Watsonville, close enough to the Oakland-San Francisco area of Northern California so that Mama set up temporary headquarters there, and either Uncle Philip or Aunt Mary Anne used their precious gas coupons to take Mama back and forth to her Superior Court appearances. OurFather allowed Mama limited visits with Danny, who had grown thin and introspective.

San Francisco, like our town, was filled with soldiers and sailors preparing to board ships and leave for the war, or in the process of waiting for their ships to be repaired. Mama suffered from morning sickness, and the long rides from Watsonville left her pale and drained of energy. Even so, she received her share of wolf whistles as she climbed the steps to Superior Court. OurFather greeted her inside the door, grinning, as Aunt Mary Anne later said, like the cat that ate the canary. Mama was on his turf, and he was used to winning, no matter what the rules. Danny sat forlornly on the cold granite bench next to Gemma. He smiled wanly at Mama and tried to get up, but Gemma snatched him back so hard, she left red marks on his skinny pale arm. "Sit down," Gemma hissed, "and don't squirm!"

Mama glared at Gemma and motioned for Danny.

Danny cautiously raised his eyes to Gemma, then rose quickly and flew into Mama's arms. "Take me home, Mama— PLEASE take me home! I don't wanna stay here anymore. Daddy told me it would be fun, just a joke, but it's not funny at all! He says you don't want me anymore 'cuz you have Leah and Hal. Mama, is that true?"

"No, Danny, I want you home more than anything. Leah misses you, and so does your new daddy. That's what Mama is going to see the judge about, honey—you coming home."

While Daddy and I wait for Mama to return with Danny, I am alone most of the time. Daddy still works in the shipyard from early morning until after dark and almost every weekend; I spend the days with OurGrandmother or Auntie Nor, who will soon have a baby of her own. Sometimes Mama's younger sister stays at the house with Daddy and me on the weekends, although I think she finds playing with Daddy a lot more interesting than playing with me. She is in high school and wears her hair in little snails secured with bobby pins. She covers them up with a scarf tied at the top.

Most mornings, Daddy drops me off at Auntie Nor's apartment. It smells funny and Daddy tells me that Auntie Nor's stove burns gas and the smell comes from it. Auntie Nor's stove has holes in the funny round plates on the stove top. She lights them with a match and blue flames flare up, then settle down and lick around the pots that she puts on the little racks over the burners. Our stove at home uses electricity and the burners are red and very hot. Auntie Nor's kitchen is dark and a little damp, not all bright and airy like Mama's kitchen. Maybe that is why she works during the day at Woolworth's department store downtown near the shipyard.

My uncle wears a blue uniform and delivers the mail. He doesn't talk much, and when he comes home in the afternoon, he smells like the beer with foam on the top that he drinks out of tall glasses. Sometimes he drinks it right out of the funny little bottles he calls "stubbies," but OurGrandmother and

Auntie Nor do not like him to do that. OurGrandmother says it is crass and she laughs at me when I ask her what that means. "Like your new father," she says as she looks down at me with a smile on her mouth. Her eyes do not smile, though.

Grandmother spends her time taking care of Auntie Nor's apartment and doing the laundry. She tells me that as soon as Auntie Nor has her baby, I will not be coming to stay. Someone else will have to look after me until my mama comes home. OurGrandmother is this little baby's grandmother, too. She already seems to like it a lot better than she likes me—and it isn't even born! Daddy says that is because the new baby will be small and will need lots of taking care of, but his eyes don't tell me the same story. Daddy thinks I will have my feelings hurt if he tells me that OurGrandmother does not like me. I know that, but it is nice of Daddy to spare me the rebuff.

I spend many hours outside Auntie Nor's apartment in the little fenced yard in front with her dog named Snuffy. He is big and has medium brown hair that is stiff and pokes my hand when I try to pet him. He growls a lot and smells bad, especially when it rains. I don't like Snuffy, but I play with him anyhow. I prefer playing by myself, but OurGrandmother thinks that I am being "sneaky." She pokes her head out of the window or pops out the door to check up on me. I don't care—what can a little girl and a big dog do for mischief in such a tiny yard?

On the weekends when Mama's little sister is around, she reads to me from her magazines and we listen to Frank Sinatra on Mama's radio that sits on the windowsill over the kitchen sink. I think he sounds squeaky, but I don't say anything to her. I like Bing Crosby, especially when he sings "Daddy's Little

Girl." This is just a waiting time—waiting for Mama to come home with Danny, waiting for Auntie Nor's little baby to be born, waiting to spend my days anywhere else than that tiny, dark, smelly apartment with a grandmother who does not like me petting a dog who does not like anyone in a yard too small to play in—waiting for my new sister or brother to come. (Will OurGrandmother come to stay when Mama's new baby is born? Somehow, I do not think she will.)

My room at night is lonely without Danny—my only companions are my teddy bear and my imagination. My teddy bear is silent, but my imagination tells me that OurFather will not let go of Danny without a fight. Just a little more waiting time, Daddy tells me, and Mama and Danny will be here.

But the judge did not agree. Although he acknowledged Mama's legal custody, he refused to return her son, remarking that OurFather had now established a home in California, that possession was nine-tenths of the law, and our state had no say over Danny's custody since he now legally resided in Oakland with his father. On the other hand, if Daniel's mother wished to move to California, the court might reconsider its ruling.

Mama fled the court in tears.

"Well," muttered Judge Slayton when Mama called him at our home state courthouse, "so that's how they want to play the game, huh? Well, two can play as well as one. Mayleen, you need to get your boy out of that state. No, I don't want to know the details—but once he passes California's borders, the papers you have establish your exclusive legal custody of the boy. Sooo, ball's in our court, now. Let the games begin."

Mama put down the phone with the fire back in her heart.

Now she knew what to do—but the how would take a little luck and a lot of planning!

For this particular court date, Mama had stayed up in San Francisco with our new daddy's sister Marie and her husband Bill. They had a little girl the same age as Danny and couldn't imagine how much Mama must be suffering at the loss of her son. If the problem were getting Danny out of the state, Uncle Bill thought he might have a solution. To help Mama in this regard, it was not safe for anyone that OurFather knew. He would suspect Aunt Mary Anne and Uncle Philip—he might even know about Aunt Marie and Uncle Bill since my daddy Hal was (at one time) his best friend, but he would never suspect that Uncle Bill's best friend was a taxicab driver who had had a similar experience with his children. His ex-wife had taken them to another state and retrieving them had proven very difficult. If strangers hadn't helped him out, he might never have seen his children again. Now, if Mama could convince OurFather that he had won, she might have a chance to be alone with Danny. They could take this opportunity to travel straight east over the mountains into Nevada and down to Reno, where Mama could try for a train ticket home. For enough ration coupons to take care of the gas, he volunteered to drive.

And so, on a rainy Sunday morning in February, Mama and Aunt Mary Anne drove up to OurFather's Oakland house and received permission to take Danny out to lunch for the very last time. Mama wore a bright red pajama suit, black patent leather high heels, and a classy red hat, and she carried a shiny black purse. The bump that would become a brother or sister in due time didn't even show under the peplum of the jacket. No one could possibly forget what she was wearing that day as she mounted the steps and knocked at OurFather's door.

"You win," she sighed deeply. "I can't stay here and fight you any longer. I need to be home with Leah and Hal, and the new baby is coming in June. I have a bus ticket for tonight." Mama flashed the ticket at OurFather, then placed it back in her purse. "Just promise me that you'll be good to our boy."

"I'm glad that you finally see reason, Mayleen—you have Cookie and I have Danny. That's only fair, after all. Gemma will be a good mother to him, you'll see, and when I feel I can trust you, maybe you can come and visit him—and bring Leah to see her real father."

Gemma trotted back and forth in the background, trying to stay out of Mama's sight but remaining close enough to hear her surrender. She had a smirk on her face that told Mama volumes.

If Gemma wants a son, Mama thought to herself, let her get one of her own.

"You don't trust me?" Mama asked OurFather in an appropriately soft and conciliatory voice. "I already promised to have him back by four o'clock. I just want to take him to the store after lunch and buy him a toy—after all, he never got his Christmas presents."

After a few moments (as if deliberating the possibility of Mama having ulterior motives) OurFather—smiling like a Cheshire cat—grandly escorted Danny and Mama out to the curb.

OurFather eyed the car and Aunt Mary Anne, then walked around to the back, looked at the license plate, and noted the number in his little pocket notebook. He touched the pencil to his tongue and wrote with great care the make and model of the vehicle, all the while making sure that none of this passed Mama's notice. Danny fidgeted and Mama patted him comfortingly on his shoulder. She grinned at OurFather with as much sincerity as she could muster.

"Well, you better make sure he's home on time—" OurFather's voice drifted off menacingly and he gestured for Mama to go.

Mama helped Danny into the back seat and settled him in. She shut the door firmly, then got into the passenger seat beside her sister, smiled at OurFather, and waved good-bye. As Aunt Mary Anne backed down the driveway, OurFather stomped up his front steps, turned, and shook his finger at Mama.

"Say good-bye to California, Danny," said Mama. She smiled at OurFather as Aunt Mary Anne drove slowly down the street, "and wave one last time to your father. We are going home!"

In the back seat, Danny exhaled deep and long, as if he had been holding his breath since well before Mama closed the door and the little automobile started down the long residential street away, away from OurFather and Gemma's bungalow.

Aunt Mary Anne drove straight to the Greyhound station in Oakland, dropped off Mama and Danny, and headed home. She could honestly say later that she didn't know where they were. Mama took a locker key out of her purse and retrieved her suitcase. In the ladies' room, she changed into dark slacks and a sweater, bobby sox and penny loafers, and changed purses. She pulled up her dark shoulder-length hair into a ponytail and put a scarf over her head. Danny changed into clothes Mama had bought the day before. When they were ready, the bright red outfit, high heels, hat, and purse went into the locker, along with Danny's discarded outfit. Mama tossed the key into the nearest trash bin and, suitcase in tow, took her son's hand and strolled out the back door. Uncle Bill's best friend was waiting—not with the taxi, but with his family car and his two little girls.

Mama's eyebrow raised.

"I thought that no one will be looking for a man and a woman and three little kids travelling east. Your sister-in-law sent along some food, so we can get started for Reno straight away." He stashed the suitcase in the trunk and settled Danny between his daughters, then motioned for Mama to get in— and with a wink at the kids in back and a smile for Mama, they headed for the highway.

OurFather gave Mama until 4:30 to return Danny; when she didn't show up, he drove to Watsonville and busted down our aunt's front door while she stood laughing in her living room.

"By this time, she's over the state line," Aunt Mary Anne gloated, "and safe from you!"

"Don't laugh, Mary Anne, just don't laugh!" OurFather shouted as he shook his fist in her face. "No woman gets the better of me—you tell that sister of yours to watch out—I'll get even!"

Two months later, he kidnapped Danny and me right off the sidewalk outside of the bakery on Callow Avenue.

CHAPTER 6
In Which I Am Tossed Out with the Trash

Mama and her friend Anna had gone window shopping in Charleston, walking back and forth on the Avenue with Danny, me, and Anna's children Kathryn and Geordie. Geordie and I were ensconced in strollers to curtail our propensity to dart into streets. Mama was quite pregnant but contented with life in general and today in particular. The sun shone warm on this bright springtime morning, and the two friends had had little time together since Mama's return triumphant with Danny.

Since the Callow Avenue Bakery had no room for four rambunctious children, two strollers, and several adult shoppers, Mama and Anna left us outside at the door, Danny minding my stroller and Kathryn minding Geordie's. We were all looking in the window at the displayed goodies, laughing and pointing at the ones we wanted our mothers to buy, and didn't notice the strangely dressed person inching carefully towards us.

Suddenly the figure pounces, grabbing Danny by the arm, then snatches him up into strong arms like iron bands. She (he, it) darts north up Callow Avenue with the frantically struggling Danny and stroller with me careening crazily in tow. "Drop the handle, Danny," the figure hisses in his ear. "We don't want her." Danny holds on tighter than ever, all the while kicking whomever it is as hard and as fast as his Buster Brown oxfords can move. They drum against ribs and back as he screams for help.

The kidnapper—let's call a spade a spade—half dragged/half carried the onerous burden of small boy, stroller, and little girl (now adding her strangled sobs to the commotion) down the narrow space between two buildings and into the adjacent alley. There sat OurFather in an automobile, motor running, doors open.

"I said, drop the handle, Danny!" Gemma makes no attempt to disguise her voice here. Danny does as he is told, and Gemma shoves him into the back seat and slams the door shut. She thrusts my stroller between two huge garbage cans and then hurries around to the passenger side of the waiting car. OurFather almost strips the gears as he slams the transmission into first and steps on the accelerator. I sit there, frozen in my stroller, still screaming, and watch as OurFather and Gemma disappear down the alley, again carrying away my brother, Danny.

As fate would have it, the police chief was getting his hair cut in the local barber shop when the hullabaloo began. He ran out of the shop with the sheet still draped over his clothing and his sideburns half trimmed.

"It's that damned ex-husband of yours, again," he retorted to Mama when he heard what had happened. "At least the little girl is safe!" he exclaimed when a bystander reunited me with my mother. She snatched me out of the stroller and held me close, soothing my sobs as she smoothed my hair.

"I'll never forgive him for this," she hissed, "never—as long as I live!"

"We'll get the little boy back for you, too," the chief declared. "He can't have gone far."

They called Daddy out of the shipyard to take Mama and me home. Before he arrived, the police had an all-points bulletin out on OurFather and his carload, but OurFather dressed Danny up as a little girl and headed for the Canadian border. A week later, the all-points was cancelled and OurFather headed south to California.

"Let that be your lesson, Mayleen," OurFather gloated on the telephone to Mama. "No woman ever gets the best of me— especially not you!"

Those days before OurFather sent Danny home were lonely. It was during this time that I discovered the art of hidden listening. If I was very quiet and, preferably, went unnoticed behind the furniture or under a table, then the grownups might forget that I was there. I learned the value of keeping my own council and did not often tell Mama and Daddy what I did those long hours I played alone outside. Although my brother Danny has always accused me of remembering being in the womb, it was this hidden listening skill acquired while he was gone that made me so aware of the family dynamic.

I lie awake in the dark in my room with the empty twin bed next to mine and the crib in waiting for the new baby coming soon. We are waiting for two births, actually—the baby and, with the return of Danny, the rebirth of our family. I listen to my mother and father talk in whispers that creep through the thin, uninsulated walls between my bed and theirs. I listen and remember so as not to say or do something that causes Mama more pain. She is fragile, now, with the baby's birth so near— more fragile than she was the first time Danny disappeared into thin air. Until OurFather sends Danny home, we are fractured.

I wasn't in school yet and often played outside on the lawn that stretched from the Tennison house on the south to the Cameron house at the west, forming a half-circle around our white stucco home that squatted atop the bulkheaded corner yard. Ten steps led up to the cement walk leading to our front door. Around the side that fronted Twelfth, the street sloped slightly up hill so that the side yard had only eight stairs terminating at the little back stoop off the kitchen. Splendid in the corner spread our lovely old horse chestnut tree.

One had to be careful beneath those wonderful spreading arms with their full-blown leaves like huge green hands in the summer and soft, brown ones that fell in the autumn winds. The horse chestnut gives up its fruit unwillingly, surrounding each nugget of potential life in a prickly green package that starts out soft, but eventually turns hard and painful when someone (Danny) flings them full-tilt into your unsuspecting back. I loved that tree, and of all the memories of my early childhood, the days I spent playing with my dolls under her shielding branches are my sweetest.

It is here I find the bent spoon and the aggie marble in an old tin (Pastiglie Menta Leone) with a sturdy lid buried between two roots. I do not know these words, but the tin smells of mints. Danny is gone with OurFather God only knows where and I am digging to China in search of him when my little hand spade strikes something hard. A few more scrabbles and some scooping with my hands and I pull the old tin loose of its hidey-hole. I am on my knees trying hard not to get mud on my pants—the new ones with the flannel lining and the roll-up cuffs that Mama makes me wear so I won't get sick. I get sick a lot, and that makes Mama and Daddy worry. If only Danny were here, I think, they wouldn't have so much time to think about me. I pry the tin open carefully as if it were some Pandora's box from which magic might leap and further destroy my world. The lid sticks for a moment then gives way so suddenly that its contents flip out onto the scabby under-tree grass. I fumble frantically for a few seconds, then retrieve them.

It is here that I discover a huge snake ball in the early spring when hibernating things begin to awaken and tiny green tips form on the branches of my tree. Up against the top rim of the bulkhead sit rough-hewn rocks with smooth tops where I sit precariously, back straight and fanny hanging over the edge. During the winter, rain has exposed a tree root that grows close to the stones, revealing, on this blustery spring morning full of rain spats, the entrance to snake city that undercuts the tree. Garden snakes, brown and green with racing stripes in red and black and dark blue down their sides, writhe about in a huge tangle. I scream and run for the house— five stairs up to the front porch—and trip, skinning my knees (and my pride). Mama runs to my side. I point out the snakes to her, and she gets that light back in her eyes for a moment before her grief at Danny's absence flicks it out again. It is a snake ball, she tells me, and says Daddy will explain it when he comes home (if he is not too tired from his long hours at the *shipyard). Even though I know the snakes cannot hurt me if I leave them alone, I am both repelled and drawn back to the spot where the snakes live.*

In the morning, the snakes were gone, either returned to their home underground where Daddy explained they had wintered or gone on to have babies of their own in some other, more private snake nursery.

For years after, every picture I drew of houses—every one of them—had a little brown snake curving gently up the front walk, head lifted, eyes looking forward, neatly forked tongue gently tasting the air. It became my signature piece until I learned that snakes have hidden (Freudian) meanings. But, to paraphrase Groucho Marx, sometimes a snake is just a snake.

Not to say that life didn't go on while Danny was missing— it did. Mama and Daddy kept up the image; Mama attended church regularly and Daddy joined her when he had a Sunday off from the shipyard. It was both easier and harder this second time around. Mama had lost faith in the government. She no longer believed that the courts would bring her son home. She was in no condition to travel again to California and battle it out with OurFather, nor did she believe he would return Danny voluntarily. She had a sadness about her that never quite went away. Even when she was laughing with Daddy at some silly radio program or at something I had done, the laughter never quite reached her eyes.

Two weeks before Robbie's birth in June, OurFather sent Danny home on the Greyhound bus accompanied by our Aunt Mary Ann. Danny and I didn't see OurFather until Judge Slayton finally lifted the contempt of court order after WWII ended, and at our mother's request. In the end, she couldn't find it in her heart to keep him from his children forever—but she never trusted him again.

In the future, it weighed heavily on me that one of my parents—my biological father—felt so little for his toddler girl child that he would abandon her in a back alley next to the rest of the trash. Perhaps in his mind, it was not practical to take both of us; and, perhaps, his partner didn't want the burden. I always felt that OurFather's reason for taking Danny and leaving me in that back alley was because of some deficiency in me—probably my lack of a spout. Whatever his reason, it created a sense of insecurity that took me nearly a lifetime to overcome.

CHAPTER 7

In Which I Learn That Life is Unfair and Girls Don't Count for Much

Life settled into a pattern after Robbie was born. Daddy still worked long hours in the shipyard making gun sights and other precision instruments for the warships and planes, helping in his own way the war effort that dragged inexorably along. Robbie kept Mama busy making formula, sterilizing bottles, and pureeing baby food. Danny made friends with the Tennison boys who lived next door to the south, and I met Frankie Cameron, the new boy from the brick house to the west, who became my nemesis.

I am outside in our backyard, climbing on the wooden fence that separates us from the Camerons' yard. Frankie is digging in the little flower bed on his side of the fence. He is filling up a little pail—the kind you take to the beach for sand—with dirt and small rocks and old leaves from last year's flowers. Mama has sent me out to dry my hair in the sun. My hair is fine and platinum blonde, and I hate having it washed by Mama. She dips her long, rat-tailed comb into the green Wave Set bottle. The stuff looks like slickery lime Jell-O and reminds me of the egg whites Mama separates from the yellow yolk when she bakes. I squirm as she smooths the green slime through my clean, wet hair and rolls strands of my Dutch bob onto curlers that snap with a rubber band and pull out my little neck hairs. It takes forever for the smelly slime to dry in my hair and help the curlers to produce tight little pretend curls that fall out of my hair the minute Mama finishes combing it. I hate the smell and the feel and the nasty metal curlers. Mama smacks me on top of my curlers with her comb and sends me out to dry in the afternoon sunshine. And now I am rocking back and forth on the fence, hanging over and watching Frankie dig with his little shovel, and now I am watching Frankie stand up with his little bucket full of dirt and pebbles and little bits of dried up flowers, and now Frankie upends the pail onto my head of curlers and Wave Set and little rubber bands that pull out my hairs. I hear someone screaming. It is Frankie. He is screaming because I am holding his head with both my hands and my teeth are sunk deep, deep into his left ear. I can taste the salty blood that bubbles from my lips and runs down my chin. Mama is prying my teeth from Frankie's ear and is asking me "Why are you biting him, Cookie?" and I lift my hands up to my head and point to the rocks and the dirt and the little dead leaves. She doesn't say a word. She just looks at my hair, sighs deeply, lifts me up, and carries me back inside. Frankie and I are not friends anymore. I have my hair re-washed and he has three little toothmarks on his ear.

During this time, Mama became a broker of sorts. One of her sisters had a friend who was desperate for a child and couldn't get pregnant (a little morsel I divined by sitting quietly under the table in the kitchen alcove), and another sister had a family member by marriage who had more children than she could care for and was pregnant with another. Her husband, I gathered, was "at sea" and may not have been the coming baby's daddy. Heady stuff for a three-year-old; nonetheless, I kept my mouth shut and my ears open. The things one hears when one's head is down!

I sit hunkered next to the wall and under the kitchen table. Carrie is with me as we listen to her mommy talking with my Auntie Noreen's best friend. They are discussing Carrie's new baby sister or brother who will be born a few weeks earlier than my own coming sister or brother. Carrie is a couple of months older than I am. She has tears in her eyes as her mama talks about the new baby going to live with another family. "What if she wants to give me away?" Carrie whispers in my ear. Then Mama hears us and makes us go outside to play "while the grownups talk."

Mama never asked me about what I overheard under the kitchen table. I think she pretended that I couldn't possibly understand the nuances because I was just a little kid, and that was okay with me; but sometimes, I ached to ask her what was really going on.

In the next few weeks, the ladies met again at Mama's kitchen nook to work out the details of transferring Carrie's now newborn baby brother into the loving hands and home of Auntie Nor's best friend.

"Mama named him Joey," Carrie confided in me as we sat under the branches of my horse chestnut tree. We were picking up freshly fallen chestnuts in their prickly green cases and piling them into haphazard pyramids. "She says he looks just like my daddy." Carrie sighed and closely examined the horse chestnut in her hand, brushing her fingers back and forth across the soft, green bristles.

Carrie's mama had come this morning with the baby, a suitcase full of clothing, and a diaper bag. We could hear the ladies talking clear out at the tree because all the windows were open to let in what small breeze stirred in the unseasonably hot, late spring air. We quietly crept up under the open kitchen window to better make out exactly what they were discussing. At present, there seemed to be some kind of disagreement going on.

"But you agreed to the infant." Auntie Noreen's voice had an edge to it.

"That's okay," interjected her friend. "Let's hear what she has to say."

I could hear Mama clear her throat; the heat and pollen of this unusually warm spring day had stuffed up her head. "So, now that you have no doubt about the boy, you want to keep him and give his sister in his place, did I understand you correctly?" Mama sounded exasperated.

"Yeah! We always wanted a son, and Carrie was a big disappointment to her dad. We already have the two other girls living with his parents. I don't mind her goin', and Joey more than makes up for any problems her dad might have."

Carrie gasped, her face turning as white as the clouds that drifted lazily overhead in the blue, blue late springtime sky.

"You can take her today if you want. I have her stuff all packed up in the suitcase," Carrie's mama continued. "We can send along her toys, later. She actually don't have much—and you won't have to get up at night, or potty train her and all that real baby stuff."

Carrie's eyes filled with tears that began rolling down her

cheeks. She wiped them off with the backs of her hands as quickly as they appeared, drying her hands on her dress front, then lifting them back to her eyes as if to stop any new tears. Her grubby little fingers left dirt marks on her cheeks and I used my apron to try to clean her face. She buried her now red face in her hands and sobbed noiselessly.

"Well, bring her in here and let me take a good look." This was from Auntie Nor's friend. "I can't make a decision until I talk with her."

We heard rustling as the women scooted off the benches that were built into the kitchen nook and provided seating at the table. The only chair sat at the open end and was usually reserved for Daddy. Presently the back door opened, and Mama stepped out on the little porch. She glanced around the side yard, then spotted the two of us.

"Carrie, your mama wants you to come in for a few minutes, honey." She nodded to me. "You can wait for her on the steps, Cookie. I don't think she'll be long." It was obvious that Mama wasn't going to let me follow her into the kitchen. Carrie wiped her eyes on her sleeve, took Mama's proffered hand, and they disappeared into the kitchen, Mama closing the door firmly behind them. A few seconds later, the kitchen window closed, as well.

I trotted quickly around the side of the house and up the front steps, quietly letting myself in through the front door. It took both hands to work the thumb latch, but I had learned the trick from Danny. Mama didn't think I could get in this way, so she wasn't listening for me. I walked as quietly as possible to an undercover spot closest to the kitchen and hunkered down.

Mama was talking quietly, but I could still make out her words. "It's okay, Carrie, don't cry. This nice lady just wants to ask you a few questions. Can you answer, honey? Can you do that?" Carrie must have nodded her head because I heard her blow her nose, then Mama continued; "Her name is Mrs. Cramer and she's really nice."

Carrie snuffled a little and I could hear her squirming around in Daddy's big kitchen chair that sat at the end of the long wooden table in the alcove. Then Mrs. Cramer must have stood up because I could hear unfamiliar feet shuffling around in the kitchen, searching in cupboards for something. Mama came into partial view. She reached into the cupboard over the sink and got out a glass, filled it with water, and handed it to someone behind her.

I wished with all my might that I could be with Carrie and hold her hand as she answered questions for this unknown lady, but Mama was there, and I didn't think she'd let anything bad happen. I had faith in my mama.

"Do you know who I am?" I heard Mrs. Cramer ask. Carrie probably just nodded her head. "I came here to take your baby brother home to live with me and my husband and to be his mama and daddy. Did you know that?" Again, she must have agreed.

"Well," continued Mrs. Cramer, "now your mama wants to keep the boy and give us the girl instead. Do you understand what that means?" Carrie started to cry again. I could hear her making great gulping sounds. As quietly as possible, I crept around the corner and tried to make myself into the smallest of packages to conceal beside the refrigerator.

Mama knelt next to Carrie, holding the sobbing little girl's head to her chest and making sh-sh-shing sounds into her mussed hair. I could just barely see Carrie's mama where she sat breastfeeding little Joey. Carrie's tears seemed to have no effect on her.

Mrs. Cramer continued. "You will have a good life at my house. You will have a new name and a new family—your own room. Maybe, even a pet—a kitten."

Carrie looked up at her mama, but her mama didn't look back. She just shook her head "no" and kissed Joey's forehead.

I sit there, hidden by our old, grumbling refrigerator, staring at the dust bunnies stirring at the back where the coils that keep the insides cold protrude out into the room and prevent the fridge from snuggling close up to the Dutch blue wall with bright white trim that Daddy has painted the kitchen in his spare time. How can this happen? Mamas and daddies don't give their children away in the blue-painted kitchens of friends and relatives, do they? But I can hear Carrie sobbing, and I can hear Mama soothing her, and I do not hear Carrie's mama saying a word. It is apparent to me that Carrie will go to live in a new home with new parents and she will never see her brother Joe or her sisters again. And it makes me afraid, deep down inside afraid—that maybe all moms and dads don't think that little girls are as good as little boys—not just OurFather. But what if the new parents don't want her? What if Mrs. Cramer tells her she does not want to take her home? And I stand up beside the grumbling refrigerator and I step out into the kitchen—blue and white and clean as my mama likes it, and I run to my mama, where she kneels beside Carrie, and I hold my mama's legs tight. What if the Cramers want to take me instead of Carrie? Will my mama make me go away?

"Cookie, what is this!" exclaimed Mama. "You shouldn't be here, listening to this grownup talk."

"You won't make me go away, will you?" I mumbled into her legs.

"Silly girl—of course not!" whispered Mama in my ear. "Daddy and I love our little girl very much."

"Then can Carrie come and live with us? At least she knows who we are."

Mama hugged me closer to her without letting go of Carrie. "I don't have any control over Carrie's mama, Cookie. That's up to her. But maybe it will be for the best if Carrie does go to a new home. Maybe this is a blessing in disguise for her."

Mama had a look of disgust on her face that she failed to conceal from me. I guessed that she was as unhappy as Carrie and me over this whole mess. "Now you go back into the living room, honey. I mean it! This is for us grownups to sort out. Hurry now, you hear me?" She patted my fanny and aimed me back towards the archway that led into the living room. I did as she asked and retreated, but not as far as the archway. I detoured at the refrigerator, hoping that Mama wouldn't notice. Either she didn't or decided to ignore my disobedience. I squatted back down in my hidey-hole and waited.

For a few minutes, silence reigned in the kitchen, punctuated only by Carrie's muted sobs. Then Mrs. Cramer knelt beside Mama and put her arms around Carrie. "You will be my daughter," she whispered in Carrie's ear, "and no one will take you away from me. Will you come to your new home with me?"

I heard a tiny mewling sound from Carrie, then her little voice said "yes."

"So, let's make the arrangements," sighed Mrs. Cramer. "Come sit on my lap and we'll get to know each other."

Auntie Noreen made a nervous giggle, and suddenly everyone started to laugh. Everyone, that is, except Carrie and me.

We look at each other—and between us passes an unspoken message about growing up girls in an uncertain world. If we can't trust our parents, who can we trust? She is coming to live in my town, and she will have a new name. When we meet in school, we will avoid each other because of this day in my mama's Dutch blue kitchen with the white trim. Our friendship is nipped in the bud before it can properly begin, and when we officially meet again in our twenties, we will never speak of this day.

CHAPTER 8
In Which I Confront the Specter of Death

When Robbie was learning to crawl, Daddy brought us a cocker spaniel puppy, a beautiful floppy-eared red male Mama named Spunky. Nominally, he belonged to all of us, but he was Danny's dog in every sense of the word from the moment they set eyes on each other. He followed Danny and his buddies everywhere, deigning only to give me notice when Danny was in school. Robbie pulled on his ears and the little stub of a tail attached to his constantly waggling rear end, but Spunky never growled or protested. He would slip quietly out of Robbie's reach and ask to be let out of doors, where he would wait patiently at the corner for Danny to come home. Spunky listened to every word Danny spoke, and it was to the dog that Danny poured out his hurt at OurFather's treachery. Spunky put a smile back on my brother's face and a spring into his step—I wouldn't have cared if Spunky never came to me. He was Danny's best medicine.

It is early spring and Danny is at school half of every day. He doesn't ride the big yellow school bus that I secretly covet as it picks up and drops off the big kids in our neighborhood. Danny goes to a school close by, so he walks there in the morning and is home by lunchtime. The bus comes early in the morning and in the afternoon, but sometimes on special days, it comes by while Danny is still on his way home. I wait on this day on the long front steps that lead down to the sidewalk. Spunky waits with me and lets me slick back his forehead hair and run my fingers down his silky leg feathers. I love this dog, too, and we sit in the weak noontime sun, sharing our warmth, Spunky leaning into me and I into him. Danny is coming down Twelfth Street and has to cross Stewart at the corner. Spunky leaps to his feet in delight and jumps the short distance to the sidewalk. As he runs across to meet Danny, the yellow school bus rounds the corner. In a split second, I see the bus and the dog, and Danny is shouting "NO, NO" at the top of his lungs, but I do not hear the sound. I only see the look on his face and his mouth open wide and his eyes open even wider. I shout to Spunky, but he does not stop, and the bus hits him hard and spins him into the air, where he flies over the top of the bus and comes to rest in the intersection. My shrieks mingle with Danny's screams, which brings Mama outside, and she sees the dog and me and Danny and says "Oh, my God, why THIS dog? Why THIS dog?" and the bus, the yellow school bus I want to ride so badly, just drives on up the street like nothing has happened.

Spunky was gone. Mama lifted his broken little body in her arms. Tears streamed down her cheeks and dropped on his head—an offering of her grief that could in no way bring back his life. We waited until Daddy got home from the shipyard and then buried him in the flower garden by the back porch. Mama planted sweet peas over his grave. Danny retreated back into himself, although sometimes, at night, when he thought the grownups couldn't hear, he would tell me some of the things he had told to Spunky, although I knew it wasn't the same. But we shared a history, and even though we often disagreed, as all siblings do, he was my big brother and my protector, and I would always be there for him.

A short time after Spunky's death, I learned to read. The local newspaper came late in the afternoon, and on days when Daddy was home in time for dinner, he would hold me on his lap and read to me out of *The Sun*. It was our time together while Mama cleaned up dinner things and prepared the baby for bed. I would follow along as Daddy's low, gentle voice with its ever so slight Czech accent (Bohemian, according to his mama, my grey-haired chubby dumpling of a new grandmother whose soft arms held me close while she sang to me in another language and I snuggled in her spacious lap). I would point to the words as he read slowly enough for me to drink in this wonderful new way of communicating. Within a few weeks, I astonished Mama and Daddy by working my way through a front-page story. Now I had something to lord over Danny! He turned six in July and was preparing for first grade in September.

"It isn't fair," Danny whined to Mama. "She's still a baby and now she's readin' the paper and she hasn't even gone to school yet." Danny sat on the floor zooming his big, metal B-29 airplane back and forth, back and forth, all the while beetling his brows at me every time I passed by. Mama stood, or rather, half-leaned against the kitchen wall while she talked on the telephone. Her legs were crossed at the ankle and she casually swung her top leg back and forth with the ebb and flow of her conversation.

Now Danny widened his area of attack, pretending to rev up the motors and making striking motions towards me. I fled into the kitchen and stood behind Mama, who was becoming increasingly annoyed by our squabble. Finally, as Danny swooped the airplane past her legs and into the kitchen, she reached out with her swinging foot to shove it out of Danny's hands.

Smack! Mama's feet shot out from under her.

I watch in horror as Mama, in slow motion, hits the freshly waxed floor flat on her fanny, legs turned awkwardly outward—a horrified expression on her face. The phone flies out of her hand and swings, dangling from its long, black cord, back and forth, back and forth, occasionally bumping into the kitchen cabinet adjacent to its wall box—some woman's voice calling frantically from the receiver. She slides across the floor until her legs fetch up short on the opposite wall, then collapses onto her back, splayed out like the Raggedy Ann doll that flops on my bed. For a moment, she lies there in shocked silence, then a low ungh, ungh noise issues from deep in her throat.

Danny drops his B-29 and kneels beside Mama's head, afraid to touch her. I capture the still swinging telephone and hear my Auntie Nor's voice demanding to know what is happening.

I hear my voice tell her that Mama has fallen down and is lying on the floor. Auntie Nor tells me to take the telephone to Mama, but when I try to hand her the shiny, black receiver, her hand will not close around it. "Tell her I am hurt, Cookie," she whispers between the funny noises she is making. I say to my aunt that Mama cannot take the phone; that she cannot get up off the floor. The telephone goes "click" and before I can hang it up on its cradle, the operator breaks in and asks "number, please." I would like her to call Daddy in the shipyard, but I do not know the number, or even if there IS a number. Carefully, I hang up the receiver.

Mama now lay with her head in Danny's lap, totally silent. Her eyes were closed, and little beads of sweat dotted her forehead. Her lips were so pale in her ashen face that they seemed blue to me. Danny looked up with eyes ready to panic.

"What're we gonna do, Cookie?" I just shook my head, squatted down by Mama's side, and took her hand in mine.

It is cold and limp—like some little dead animal, her carefully painted nails red and bleeding wounds. I have seen death. Spunky, hurling through the air, live one minute and gone the next; our kitten, cold and stiff in the street with its head crushed by some uncaring automobile trundling too fast in the early morning mist—the neighbor's dog, dead from unknown trauma, buried in their backyard with a crude wooden cross to mark the spot—the little red squirrel, limp and bloody with holes where its eyes used to be before crows peck them out. Dead things are cold and quiet. Like my Mama. My heart quivers—a terrified little bird, thumping wildly inside its chest-cage.

Then Mama's eyelids fluttered and she made a little mewling noise. She was alive! From the bedroom, I could hear Robbie fussing in his crib, awake from his afternoon nap. Mama's fingers tightened around mine as she struggled to rise.

"Robbie!" she gasped. "Cookie, go see to the baby."

I shook my head. Robbie would be all right in his crib for the moment. It was Mama who was in danger—a danger neither Danny nor I knew how to resolve.

Danny rose to the occasion. "Leah, you go next door and ask the sailors for help," he directed. I didn't want to leave Mama, but we had no other choice. Danny couldn't get up without dropping Mama's head on the floor. Like a shot, I leaped up and headed for the back door.

For as long as we had lived in this house, the Navy had had a barrage balloon facility stationed on the vacant property directly across Twelfth Street from our side yard. All day and night, the huge balloons floated above us, tethered on their cables as thick as Daddy's wrist, to keep enemy planes from diving low over the shipyard where men and women repaired and readied our huge warships for duty. Mama often took cookies to the sailors, and once, was actually filmed by Pathé News delivering a batch. The footage ended up on the newsreel at movie theaters all over the country.

But now, Mama needed help.

I scurried out the back door, not taking the time to run down the long set of stairs, but instead jumping from the bulkhead to the sidewalk below. Without more than a cursory look at the street, I darted across, fetching up breathless at the high chain-link fence that surrounded the lot.

"Please come help my mama," I gasped as I rattled the fencing. "She fell down in the kitchen and she's really hurt!"

A nice-looking young man in navy dungarees and blue shirt, his white cap perched on his curly black hair, squatted down to my eye level.

"Are you serious?" he queried. "You come from across the street, don'tcha."

I pointed back towards the house, still gulping in air.

"Hey, Chief Ginty," he shouted to the other sailor. "The little girl says her mama fell down and needs help. Whaddaya think we should do?"

Ginty, who was older and kind of wizened up, trotted over to where we stood on opposite sides of the fence.

"That so, girly? Your mama the one'ta bring us the cookies?"

I nodded,

"Well, get on over there, son, and find out what's goin' on. I'll cover for ya here."

The young sailor sprinted for the gate further down the fence line, fumbled with the padlock for a moment, then swung the gate open and moved through, closing it firmly behind him.

"Okay, kid," he called, motioning to me, "let's go take care of your mother."

By the time we reached the backyard, we could hear Robbie screeching at the top of his lungs. Danny still sat with Mama's head in his lap. Mama's eyes were open, although a little glazed, and she had some color back in her cheeks.

"Hey, kiddo," the sailor said to Danny, "I'll take over, now." He motioned in my direction and sent me for a throw pillow from Mama's platform rocker. After placing it under Mama's head, he directed Danny to attend to Robbie in the bedroom and sent me to fetch a blanket.

"Good job, kids," he smiled at Danny and me when we returned. He covered Mama with the blanket, then took her wrist and felt her pulse. He smiled down at her. "You got good kids here, ma'am," he commented as he appraised her condition.

Danny held Robbie in his arms, attempting in his own, big brother way to soothe the sobbing baby. Without being told, I trotted to the ice box and retrieved a bottle of formula and turned on the hot water at the sink, as I had seen Mama do so many times. I opened the cap, took out the little hard plastic disc that blocked the nipple hole, and inverted the nipple. A little formula spilled as I manipulated the nipple into its proper spot and screwed it back onto the bottle. Carefully I held the bottle under the running water to take off the chill as I sucked the sweet formula from my hand.

Behind me, I could hear the sailor asking Mama questions, and finally, her voice, weak and very soft, answered him back.

"I can't feel my feet," Mama whispered, "and it feels like electricity running down my legs." She raised up on one elbow, gasped, and dropped back flat on the cold, kitchen linoleum—all browns and reds and black like little bricks running across the floor. My eyes met Danny's as I handed him the bottle. He sprinkled a few drops on his arm, then plopped the nipple into Robbie's greedy little bird mouth. Robbie immediately stopped fussing and set to draining the bottle. He was almost old enough to hold it for himself, but as Danny steadied it, Robbie gazed up adoringly at his big brother.

I worry that my mama cannot feel her feet. I do not think this is a very good thing. I look at my own feet, secure in their sturdy Buster Browns that are so ugly, and try to imagine how I would feel if I could not sense my feet. Could I stand up and walk? Can Mama still walk? I lose myself in Danny's eyes, eyes that hold the same questions. What will we do if Mama cannot walk? She is everything to the three of us. In my mind, I see Mama in a wheelchair, Daddy pushing her slowly down the street, Robbie sitting in her lap, Danny and I trudging along behind. Maybe OurFather will come and take Danny away again and I will be left alone to be Mama's feet.

Before my imagination could take me further down this path, I heard the sailor tell my mama he was going to call for an ambulance. Mama sputtered and tried to sit up again. This time she was more successful and got herself up on both elbows.

"No, I don't think it's that bad," she whispered. "I think I'll be okay in a few minutes. I just need to rest, that's all."

The sailor's face didn't look like he agreed with her, but before he could protest, the door flew open and Auntie Nor dashed in, practically pulling OurGrandmother behind her.

"Mayleen, just what is going on in here," OurGrandmother demanded. Auntie Nor took Robbie and his bottle from Danny and pulled up a kitchen chair to sit in. The sailor from across the street stood up and addressed OurGrandmother as if she were an officer.

"She fell down, Ma'am. The little girl came to us for help and the Chief sent me right away. She's hurt her back, I think. I was gonna call an ambulance to take her to the hospital when you came in."

OurGrandmother snarled at him. "Just where did you get your medical degree, young man? I am a nurse and her mother, and I will decide if she needs an ambulance. You can return to your post, now."

The sailor seemed to melt right in front of my eyes. That OurGrandmother could do that to anyone—even someone as brave as a sailor—amazed me. He dropped his eyes, took his cap in his hands, and backed slowly towards the door. "I'll be goin', now." He looked towards me and nodded his head. "If you need any more help, just come 'n get me again, okay?" Danny and I nodded to him as he reached the back door, pulled it open, and bolted down the stairs.

"Well!" huffed OurGrandmother. "He couldn't wait to get out of here, could he? He could have offered to help us get Mayleen up and walking." Mama paled again at the thought of standing up. "Give that child back to his brother, Noreen, and give me a hand."

Danny started to protest, but OurGrandmother withered him with a look. I didn't even try to stop her, more to my shame, but I was smaller than Danny, and if he couldn't stop her, I surely had no chance.

Our auntie hands Robbie back to Danny and rises to help OurGrandmother. She reaches out a hand to her sister, then stops. "Are you sure this is a good idea?" she asks OurGrandmother, but she is defeated in an instant. OurGrandmother has Mama halfway sitting as Auntie Nor grasps her other hand. They pull Mama to her fanny and I can hear the air come out of Mama's lungs in a huge gasp as they plop her none too gently on the floor. Her eyes close and little beads of sweat form on her forehead. I lean down and push the hair away from her face where it swings back and forth, back and forth, sticking to the sweat. OurGrandmother and Auntie Nor pull her to where she can rest her back against the kitchen cabinet. I see that the little silver-colored knob on the door under the sink is sticking into her back and is making her wince, but I do not say anything. What can a little kid say to the grownups?

After an eternity, Mama relaxed a little. "I think it's better, now," she told her mother. "Maybe I can get up and sit on the chair."

"It's about time," snorted OurGrandmother. "This escapade has disrupted the day for long enough. Pull yourself together, Mayleen. It was just a little fall, after all." I could see in Mama's eyes that it took all her courage to let them draw her to her feet and sit her down on the kitchen chair.

"You're right, Mama," she replied bitterly. "What was I thinking? But then, I didn't drag you into this, after all." Her eyes met her sister's. "It's probably time for the both of you to go home. Hal should be along any time, now. I heard the shipyard whistle blow just before you got here."

Auntie Nor summoned up a little spunk. "We'll stay until he gets here, May—I can start some supper for you and Mother can change the baby." She turned towards OurGrandmother. "Right, Mama?"

OurGrandmother harrumphed once, then took Robbie and headed for the bedroom. Danny crept up to Mama and laid his hand on her arm. "Are you really okay, Mama?" he whispered. She shook her head almost unperceptively. Danny and I exchanged glances, but before either of us could speak, the back door opened and Daddy swept in.

He immediately took charge, as he always did in times of crisis, sending OurGrandmother and Auntie Nor home. He helped Mama to bed, laying her flat on her back, fed Danny, Robbie, and me, and put us all to bed. The next morning, he called in sick and took Mama to the clinic in town.

We made quite a parade into the clinic: Daddy helping Mama, Danny carrying Robbie, and me trooping along behind with a stroller filled with coats, diaper bag, and Mama's purse.

Dr. Scott came to the reception area and waved at us. We knew all the doctors and nurses here. These doctors had delivered all of us kids and provided medical care for our whole family for many years.

We waited as patiently as three little kids can possibly wait while the nurse took Mama back to see the doctors and Daddy went along for moral support. Robbie fussed and the receptionist took him behind the desk and rocked him until he fell asleep. We waited for what seemed like hours until Daddy finally reappeared with Mama, holding her by her arm.

When we were all settled into our old Model A Ford Elizabeth, Daddy remarked that Mama had dodged the bullet, as he put it, this time.

"Kids, she's got a badly sprained back, and possibly some damage to her tailbone. Sooo," he dragged out his voice, high and then low, like the whistle when a train passes by, "we all have to jump in and help her as much as possible until she gets better. Can you and Cookie do that?" He directed his words to Danny.

We both nodded.

Mama finally healed, to a degree, but she wasn't quite the same after her fall. Now she grimaced when she picked up Robbie if she thought no one was looking. Danny ignored it, but I kept an eye on her and tried to anticipate her movements, picking up things before she could get to them. With time, we all settled back into our routines.

The war slogged inexorably onward, further trapping Daddy in its claws. He worked longer hours as summer dragged into autumn and Danny returned to school. I turned four in December and spent the long winter months helping

Mama with Robbie. We attended the Presbyterian Church faithfully, even though the pastor, whom we all referred to as "The Reverend Mr. Schaffe" scared the living bejeebies out of me. He was short, dour of complexion and temperament, and had a mass of stiff, grey hair that tended to stand up on his head, especially when he wound himself up for his hellfire and damnation sermons. His massive eyebrows met at the bridge of his nose, giving him the look of a mad schnauzer dog, and his choppy, darting motions emphasized the comparison.

Daddy often worked on Sundays, making it difficult for us kids to attend Sunday school, so we all sat at church services with Mama as quietly as possible, through every description of dangling on slender threads over the fiery pits of Hell. Danny laughed under his breath and nosed through the literature filling the backs of the pews. Mama held Robbie firmly in her lap to keep him from squirming loose now that he was walking and struggled manfully (or womanfully) with her Bible and the hymnal. I sat, terrified, certain that every threat issuing from The Reverend Mr. Schaffe's schnauzer mouth was aimed directly at me. Consequently, I was very relieved when Mama decided that logistics and gas coupons dictated that we change churches. A month before Christmas, we began attending the Lutheran church on Eleventh Street, just a short walk up Stewart Avenue from our house.

My new Sunday school was a delight! The teachers used felt boards to illustrate stories like Jonah and the Whale, Noah's ark, and Jesus teaching the children. To top it off, the Sunday school "nursery" area had (among other delights) an indoor sandbox designed to keep little kids happy while their parents attended sermons in the sanctuary upstairs. The sandbox stood on legs and was just the right height for play without soiling Sunday-go-to-meeting clothes and shoes.

I loved it! My class learned Christmas carols to sing at the Christmas Eve celebration—"Away in a Manger" and "Silent Night"—and Daddy found the time to attend and hear me sing. The older kids did a live nativity with Danny playing a rather fidgety shepherd dressed in old gunny sacking with a tea towel around his head. Daddy had found the time to make him a shepherd's crook, so he would look the part. Robbie sat between Mama and Daddy trying to pay attention to the program going on around him. When it came time to light the fourth candle on the advent wreath that hung from the church ceiling on a long chain, he was delighted, clapping his little hands in excitement.

After services, we all walked home, Mama and Daddy singing Christmas carols and popular Christmas songs, holding Robbie's hands between them and occasionally swinging him up in the air. Danny and I trotted along behind, content in the knowledge that our family was intact.

In April, Mr. Roosevelt, the president, died. That spring, construction had started on a new church across the street from us. Danny came straight home from school, and after he changed clothes and had a snack, we ran across the street to play in the piles of sand left there for mixing foundation cement. We could hear music coming from some neighbor's radio, and Danny and I hummed along as we built highways for his metal cars and trucks. The sound of a door slamming shut broke my concentration. I looked up and across the street towards our back door. Mama was sitting on the back steps, her shoulders hunched up and her hands covering her eyes.

She was swaying back and forth, back and forth as if she were rocking herself.

"What's the matter with Mama?" I asked. "Look, Danny, she's crying!" Danny raised his head as I left my place at the sand pile and ran across the street, wiping the sand from my hands.

"Mama, what's the matter?" I whispered softly as I squatted on the step beneath her feet.

"Oh, Cookie," she sobbed, taking her hands away from her eyes and reaching for the hankie she always carried in her apron pocket, "the president is dead. What is our country going to do without him?"

In all of my short life, I have known only one president and nothing but war. Family members and friends are fighting on ships in the Navy and units in the Army all over the world. Some of them are never coming home again. Perhaps she hides her tears from me at these sad deaths, but I do not think so. I have seen her cry just once since OurFather moved away and took Danny with him, which now seems so long ago. I cannot understand why the death of someone so far away should make her cry now. But I put my hand in hers and hold it to my cheek as I had that awful day in Port Orchard, and let her tears fall hot and wet on my arm. Danny finally gathered up his trucks and cars and came home to see what all the fuss was about.

"Wimmin!" he exclaimed. "You guys cry every time sumthin' happens. You got leaks in your eyes?"

"Honey," Mama exclaimed. "Someday you'll understand why this is such a sad day for our country. You're just a little boy and you have had your own burdens to carry. Don't worry about me, I'll be okay in a minute." She stood up, wiped the last of her tears away, and put an arm around each of us. "Let's go into the kitchen and have some cookies and milk. I don't care that it's close to dinner. We can sit around the table and tell stories and laugh until Robbie wakes up and Daddy comes home from the shipyard."

And we did.

In early May, when victory is declared in Europe, we rejoice. Mama and Auntie Nor sit in Auntie Nor's little kitchen in the apartment on 7th street while Danny and I watch and the two cousins, Robbie and Auntie Nor's little boys, play outside with Snuffy. Danny and I say nothing as Mama and our aunt celebrate the end of this part of the war with toasts, drinking amber-colored liquid over ice from tumblers kept on the shelf over the kitchen sink. When the time for us to go home comes, Danny carries Robbie and pushes my stroller while Mama stumbles along beside, still singing and dancing.

Most of our family was in the Pacific theater on ships, or on the ground in the islands near Japan waiting for the big invasion. In August, the new president gave his orders, and the Enola Gay took flight to deliver a crushing blow to the Japanese at Hiroshima. In mid-August, the war was officially over, and Mama and Daddy celebrated in the streets along with all the other families in our town who worked so hard to support the war effort. Sailors and civilians danced together, hats flew into the air like confetti, white and tan and brown against the blue summer sky. In the shipyard, whistles on ships and cranes and supply trains all blew simultaneously and singly, creating an afternoon and night of joy that spilled over even into our staid little neighborhood.

Now, perhaps life could return to normal, as Mama and Daddy desired. My normal was gone, and I only hoped that what my parents could see coming in the future would be better than the past. All the pain and misery Mama had endured, all the bad times and bad memories inflicted upon us by OurFather and the war, could just fade into a distant mist and disappear from our consciousness forever.

CHAPTER 9
In Which We Get Back to Basics

On the first day of summer in 1947, Daddy came home from the shipyard with an announcement: "We are moving," he spoke with a flourish, "moving back to our roots! Enough of this city living. Mayleen, we are going back to the farm!"

Although Mama became a city girl with the divorce of her parents, she had lived until then in one rural area or another, mostly on the small dairy Grandpa had owned on the Olympic Peninsula up north. Daddy's parents still farmed near the little town of Sumner in the Puyallup Valley, raising strawberries, green beans, lettuces, and beets for sale in the city. They had a few dairy cows as well as a steer for beef, and chickens, hogs, and rabbits for eggs and meat. Gramma and Grampa offered a few animals to get us started on the little place Daddy had found west of town.

"Don't frown, honey—I'll keep my job in the shipyard, at least until we get things going. Kids, this is what life's all about, raising our own meat and growing our own vegetables. We can sell eggs and..." Mama stopped the rush of words as she wrapped her arms around him and kissed him smartly full on the lips. "I'm not worried about the job—I'm just thrilled to see you smiling!"

Daddy hugged her close, his face beaming. Then he held out his arms to the three of us and we melded into a huge ball of united family.

We moved to the little farm on the outskirts of town, clearing out our home on Stewart Avenue across the street from the new church, and began settling in by early July.

Our new home sat on fifteen acres abutting a large, wooded area of mixed trees that separated us from the low-income housing of Park View at the bottom of the hill. During the war, this area had housed the families of enlisted men, allowing the sailors to reside with their wives and children while their ships were being fitted or repaired in the Navy Yard. Now, the families residing there consisted mainly of single mothers and their children, or families displaced by wartime and unable to find jobs. State and federal subsidies of rent and food helped them survive, although most people tended to view Park View as charity.

After Danny made a rude remark about some kid's clothing when we were at the little IGA market in Park Wood, our nearest grocery, Mama commented that we should treat everyone with respect, regardless of address or income, and that sometimes really nice people, through no fault of their own, fall onto bad times. He made a face behind her back and muttered to me that he wouldn't want any friends that lived in such a place.

I loved my new home from the moment we stepped out of our Model A Ford Elizabeth into the little yard between the house and the barn. Someone had swept the bare dirt clean of twigs and debris, and the steps leading to the closed back porch were freshly scrubbed. Daddy held the screen door for Mama, who rose the four steps and peered around the corner.

"Hal, it's perfect," she laughed.

"You haven't seen anything but the mudroom, honey— wait until you see the fireplace!" Daddy laughed in chorus and motioned us kids to follow as Mama began her walk-through.

Daddy's mudroom spilled us into a large kitchen. Plenty of cupboards both above and below the long linoleum-covered counters that lined the entire east wall provided ample storage for dishes and pots and pans. Mama could prepare meals here with ease. A double porcelain sink stood on its own legs halfway up the counter, its old-fashioned double faucets mounted on the wall above. To the south sat the cookstove, not wood-burning as Mama had expected, but electric, with four burners and a griddle on the side. Not new, but in good condition. The refrigerator, old and grumbling but family-sized, sat between the porch door and the countertops at the north. To the west sat an old kitchen table long enough to seat eight.

Beyond the table, a door opened into an ample bathroom with claw-foot tub, modern toilet, and sink with a shelf above and a mirrored cabinet for toiletries. Shelving for linens lined the wall adjacent the kitchen. Danny took a peek and beamed at the size of the tub. He liked water up to his neck, especially as he now was allowed a bath by himself. I wasn't too keen on the size of the tub, as I had almost drowned and didn't like water of any kind near my face.

Adjacent to the kitchen was a large general-purpose room in which a squat dark brown oil heater crouched next to the south wall. Through an archway, we could see the living room and the doorway to a bedroom. A huge fireplace nearly covered the west wall—the entry was so large that Danny and I could stand almost upright in the opening. Daddy said it was a circulating fireplace, explaining to us that fans took the heat generated by logs and pushed it to every room in the house.

Next to the living room and opening off it was a small dining room with French doors opening onto a small cement patio. Adjacent to it and to the west was a second bedroom with entrance to both the dining room and the large central room with the oil burner. To the north of the central room was a smallish room with two glass-paneled doors—obviously some kind of salon or formal library. I knew without saying that this would eventually become my bedroom. All in all, quite a pleasant and reasonably modern farmhouse, Mama opined with delight.

While Mama brought in a few kitchen things and arranged them conveniently for preparing a quick lunch, Daddy took Danny, Robbie, and me down to the barn and chicken coop, pointing out the fenced-in pasture to the east and a large garden plot on the west. Our new dairy cow, a sweet-faced Jersey, pale fawn with darker brown face and legs, looked up from the small cross-fenced pasture portion nearest the barn and eyeballed us with curiosity. The chicken coop held ten Rhode Island Red hens and one cocky rooster, who strolled about bullying everyone. In a pen behind the barn, a Chester White sow resided, hugely pregnant, according to Danny, who thought he knew everything. Actually, he had overheard Daddy and Mama talking and had picked up that little tidbit.

As we walked slowly back to the house, Mama called us in for lunch. Daddy took Robbie up on his shoulders as he pointed out the Hereford steer grazing further down the pasture towards the trees. "He'll supply us with meat this winter," Daddy explained. "And the sow will farrow soon. We'll sell the shoats and keep one for ourselves. Bacon and ham to go with our own eggs! Not much of a garden this year, but just wait'll next summer! We'll have our own lettuce and tomatoes and vegetables enough so Mama can set them up in quarts for winter. Cookie, I know you'll help, and Danny and Robbie will be old enough to pull a few weeds." Daddy's voice shone bright with pride. Danny didn't look as thrilled as Daddy, but the thought of learning to preserve food sounded interesting to me.

We settled into our new home. From the beginning, it felt comfy, like old slippers after a day of new shoes. Danny and I learned to feed and clean up after the livestock; I became adept at coercing our hens to give up their eggs without too much damage to myself. The rooster learned to stay away from me when I had a bucket or a stick, although he still attempted behind my back maneuvers designed to inflict as much harm as possible on me and still permit him to retreat before I could react.

Mama planted a late garden, aided by Robbie, who puttered about behind her, patting seeds into the soft, dark loam. I helped her battle the army of early rising weeds, keeping them from pushing out the young shoots. Daddy worked each day, rising early to milk our cow, then driving to the shipyard for his shift, returning in time to supervise the evening chores. Danny was not nearly as eager to learn milking as Daddy was at teaching him this task, but in time, he took over total care for Blossom. By the time school began,

I felt as if I had never lived anyplace but this farm. I was home!

And so it came to pass, as the Good Book says, that I found myself down by the creek in position to do a little sisterly spying upon my older (but not always wiser) brother. That I had made the acquaintance of an (in my opinion) interfering old hag set in motion a life-changing period.

CHAPTER 10
In Which Danny Gets the Upper Hand

In the days following my incarceration in the rabbit hutch, Danny and I developed a routine of alternately spying on Hatchet Annie and delivering carefully worded intelligence to fuel Robbie's rapidly growing terror.

The old lady spent her days picking berries, foraging for mushrooms, gathering firewood, and selecting a wide variety of greens, seeds, flowers, and leaves, which she placed for safekeeping in the covered basket she usually carried. We would follow her about, skulking behind bushes and creeping up through long grass and shadows. Occasionally, she indicated her awareness of our watching, once approaching me silently from behind.

"Little girl, listen to me a moment." I glanced back over my shoulder. She hunched down beside me, a look of concern on her face. "Thy brother and thee are not doing God's work. Remember, what thy sows, thy reaps!" When I ignored her and did not speak, she shook her head sadly and left.

Usually, she paid no attention to us.

Twice we tracked her up Quaker Hill, stopping at its crest to watch her below at her cabin, hanging laundry or gathering eggs. Actually, her cabin looked inviting: path swept smooth, smoke curling gently from her chimney. When the soft summer breezes blew from the west, we could smell baking bread and brewing coffee. For me, it became more and more difficult to attach sinister meanings to her activities. Danny managed quite well, however, and I went right along with his agenda!

"Robbie," Danny would whisper at night. We all slept in the same room, Danny and I in twin beds, Robbie in his crib (even though "I'm a big boy, mommy" had become his nightly protest).

"Robbie, did'ja know?" Danny would whisper. "They say Hatchet Annie killed her husband and little baby boy just your age. She cut 'em up into itty bitty pieces and threw 'em in Chatham Swamp!"

"Yeah," I would add, "They say she killed a neighbor kid. Everyone thinks he ran away, but really Hatchet Annie fed him to her pigs!"

If Robbie started to cry, Danny would silence him, placing his hand over Robbie's little mouth, and whispering "Shhh, did you hear that? I think that's her outside the window now! Quiet down, Rob—she'll hear us!"

Actually, we didn't want Mama and Daddy to know what was going on—we were having too much fun! Well, to be honest, Danny was. As the summer progressed, my conscience bothered me more than I wanted to admit. I loved Robbie and regretted greatly my weakness that day at the rabbit hutches. I should have let the buck shred me rather than reveal my wickedness to Daniel.

If Mama coaxed Robbie outdoors when she worked in the

garden and yard, Danny and I usually managed to separate him from her side for a little additional torture. One afternoon, we spied Annie at the creek and lured Robbie down on the pretext of picking berries. He loved blackberries!

Annie knelt, her back to us, across the creek, searching the dark, moist layers beneath the trees for mushrooms. At first, Robbie didn't see her, intent as he was on finding berries. Much to his dismay, hard green knobs and withering blossoms covered the blackberry vines. Robbie had weeks to wait before the berries ripened.

"Where's the berries, Cookie? You guys said there was berries down here. Did you get 'um all?" Robbie sounded exasperated. He stood before me, hands on his hips, and stamped his bare right foot on the grass. Robbie's overalls, legs rolled up to the knee, covered most of his striped tee shirt. He looked like a little denim-covered Hobbit, although it would be years before I read the epic novel introducing me to Middle-earth and the little ones of the Shire.

Danny poked his head around the berry vines, his forefinger crossed over his lips in a gesture of silence. He motioned toward the creek, pledging Robbie to muteness with his eyes. Robbie pursed his lips so tightly they turned white. His eyes followed Danny's, widening to owl-like proportions, pupils dilating in response to his first glimpse of Annie, still unaware of our presence, on the east side of the creek. Rob's expression of stark terror brought me a physical twinge, but Danny's swift pinch squelched my feelings of guilt.

"Know what I heard?" Danny looked solemn. "The older kids taught me this poem about her. Listen careful, Robbie. I wouldn't want YOU to disappear!

Robbie's eyes pleaded with me for protection. "What'd they say, Danny? You gotta tell me!" Danny cleared his throat and whispered:

"Hatchet Annie, Hatchet Annie
Sneakin' through the trees,
Searching for a victim,
Sniffin' at the breeze.
Little boy walkin' by
Doesn't have a care.
Little boy, little boy—
Now he isn't there!"

Even though I had authored this deplorable bit of doggerel, I winced as Danny recited it, sing-song fashion.

"What happened to the little boy, Danny?" Robbie's eyes, impossibly, widened further.

Daniel motioned toward Annie's back. His meaning was obvious. "She got him, Rob." After a suitable pause, he leaned closer to Robbie and whispered low: "Let's hope she don't get you!"

Robbie shot forward in utter silence. Danny reached out and grabbed him by his overall straps as he passed. They both sat down hard on the creek bank, Danny's hand covering Robbie's mouth.

"Don't you dare tell Mom," he warned. "She won't believe you, anyhow."

Robbie wrenched himself free with one huge forward lunge that unbalanced Danny, sending him flat on his back. Robbie streaked back up the trail towards the barn, whimpering to himself, with Danny, out for revenge, in close pursuit.

Annie looked up from her mushroom picking, attracted by our creek side commotion. Her eyes, as they met mine, held such sadness—she shook her head gently in admonishment. I hung my head, lowered my eyes, and backed slowly up the trail.

Robbie no longer slept well; he grew pale from staying in the house whenever possible. He even stopped reminding Mama about being a big boy—the bars on his crib gave him a feeling of security. Mama took him to the doctor, who pronounced him healthy as a horse and sent him home with orders to play outside in the sun.

Poor Robbie! He dogged Mama's every step, finally refusing to go outside even when Mama held his hand. My parents were stumped, but eventually chalked it up to "going through a phase." I was greatly relieved when Danny decided to terminate Robbie's torture. My conscience needed a break!

As June turned into July, a warm one that year, Robbie slowly permitted Mama to draw him out of doors. Soon his color improved, along with his appetite. Mother professed relief but remained puzzled about the cause of his fear. She had her suspicions, I knew, because she occasionally tossed out little inquiries that I had to field. Eventually, I put the whole thing out of my mind, as only children can, and vowed to make amends to Robbie. Daniel, on the other hand, had other plans.

CHAPTER 11

In Which the Tables are Turned and I am Hoisted on my own Petard

I cannot be certain just when I became the victim of my own hoax. Perhaps the old adage about saying something often enough and it will come true has basis in fact. More probably, Danny was finally exacting revenge for my spying eyes. When Robbie ceased to be a viable victim, Danny turned on me, planting little seeds that subtly changed my focus on Annie. At his suggestion, I began to imagine she was following me through the woods, and I startled at every breaking twig and dropping leaf. By August, I was ripe for the picking.

"I was over by her cabin yesterday." Danny walked up behind me quietly and stuck his cold hand on my back above my sunsuit top. I froze in place, holding my breath.

"I saw her dancing around the yard with her goat. She had a broom in her hand." His voice lowered, conspiratorially, "She was chanting!"

"Did ya hear what she said?"

"Yeah!" Danny squinched up his eyes and grinned malevolently.

"Blonde boys and towhead girls
Eyes of blue and teeth like pearls
Catch them fast and cut them up
And on their blood and guts I'll sup."

"You're making that up," I gulped.

"Oh, no! I heard her say it, all right. Why would I joke about a thing like that?" My big brother's eyes implored me with innocence.

"You like to tease me, that's why." Common sense returned. "Besides, you know what we've been sayin' to Rob is baloney. We just made that stuff up."

"True, true, but ya' know, she's awful mad at you 'cuz you told lies about her to Robbie." For a moment, he seemed seriously concerned for my welfare.

"You don't really think she'd hurt me, do you?"

"Well," he smirked, "I guess that's a chance you'll just have to take the next time Mom sends you to the dairy."

That summer, Mama had begun trusting me with a major responsibility that took me away from home. Twice a week (ever since our cow dried up) she loaded a battered milk can into our little red wagon for me to pull over Quaker Hill past Hatchet Annie's house and down the far side to Smith's Dairy. I'd watch Mr. Smith fill the can with fresh, foaming milk from one of the tall cans in the dairy's cool room. He would cover our can with clean cheese cloth tied down with white string and carry it back to the wagon.

"Pray you take care not to tip the can," he'd warn me solemnly. "Your mother be waitin' for this milk."

I took great pride in not spilling a drop!

These trips quickly became the high spots in my week,

allowing me time to practice my "imaginings" while I ferried the milk can back and forth between dairy and home.

I pretend to be alone in the wilderness, carrying food and medicine to pioneer families trapped by rising floods. I am the Pony Express, galloping down southwest canyons between Indian infested cliffs, delivering the United States Mail. I am the cavalry rescuing a beleaguered fortress. Twice a week, I free my vision and let it take me far away from brothers and farms and my guilty conscience.

I liked to tell Mama about my trips to the dairy. She'd laugh and applaud my make-believe, often commenting on my wild imagination.

"Just remember, sweetie," she'd caution, "imagination is a two-edged sword!" She explained to me what she meant by the saying, but I could not believe that something as wonderful as my ability to dream with my eyes open could possibly backfire.

Now I know! Where once dreams walk with me, nightmares now dog my steps. Now I travel through the world of Annie and her little hatchet! Now I walk the hill in mortal danger!

What had started out as harmless amusement had taken a Draconian turn.

Tuesdays and Fridays were dairy days. I had gone on Tuesday, just yesterday, and had a wonderful adventure there and back. When I passed Annie's cabin, I hid for a few minutes behind a clump of wild lilac and watched her weeding her carrots and peas, laughing to myself and thinking up new stories with which to amuse Danny. Today, the thought of passing Annie's cabin turned my blood to ice. I shuddered despite the warm day, remembering all the times she had shaken her head at me in disapproval. It didn't take much imagination (and I had plenty of it) to turn her sad eyes and stern looks into eyes plotting sweet revenge against an upstart liar, especially since my brother took every opportunity to remind me!

Just then, Daniel reached behind me and grabbed a handful of hair. "Betcha can't wait 'til Friday—maybe she'll scalp ya!" He tugged sharply, making a slicing sound as he drew his finger across my brow, and dashed for safety before I could respond.

By Friday, my apprehension had turned to dread. Mama would surely want an explanation if I declined to make the dairy trip, and as much as I wanted to, I couldn't tell her the truth! This was all Danny's fault, I reasoned! If he hadn't teased me, I wouldn't have made up Hatchet Annie to scare Robbie. Now he'd had his fun with Robbie and had the pleasure of torturing me, as well. This was not fair! How could I turn the tables on him?

"Mama, I've been thinking." I stood beside the kitchen counter, absently dabbling in a water spill, my damp finger drawing little stick figures on the old linoleum overlay.

"'Bout what, sweetie?" Mama stood at the ironing board smoothing starched pillowcases fresh from the line. She had sprinkled and rolled them earlier, and now expertly maneuvered her hot iron over a particularly pretty embroidered case. I liked watching Mama iron. She worked in swift, gliding motions over flat surfaces, then with exquisite delicacy used the iron point to pick out lace and ruffles. Sweet-smelling steam rose from the iron's path, scenting the air.

"Well," I began, "I have such a good time goin' to the dairy, it doesn't seem fair. Danny should have a chance to get the milk for a change. He deserves to have some fun!" My water doodles took shape. I stopped and wiped the last one away with my shirt sleeve when I realized it was a hangman's noose around the neck of a little stick figure girl.

"That's a very sweet gesture, Cookie," Mama responded, nodding her head, "but I gave the job to you. Daniel has his own chores, and if you've found a way to have fun while doing yours, that's nice. Now, don't worry about your brother—run along to the dairy. I need milk for dinner."

"But—" I protested.

"No buts, honey. Just get going."

Mama seemed a little impatient as she turned back to her ironing.

"Can I take Robbie along for company?"

"No, Leah, you may not. For some reason, he's afraid of that lovely woman who lives over the hill. For the life of me, I can't understand why!" She turned towards me and pinned me with her eyes. "Now, quit stalling, young lady—or is there some problem I should know about?"

"No, ma'am," I muttered, "No problem at all."

I knew when to leave well enough alone.

I ran like the wind to Smith's Dairy, the wagon making occasional side trips as it hit rocks and ruts so hard it threatened to vibrate into pieces. As the wagon and I crested Quaker Hill, the milk can flew out. I watched in shocked silence as it bounded gaily toward Hatchet Annie's cottage.

"Oh no!" I moaned under my breath as I darted after the errant can, snatching it at the last possible moment before it bounced through shrubs and weeds into Annie's yard. I sat down hard, clutching the can in a death grip. After my breathing returned to normal, I carried the can back to its berth in my wagon and continued with greater caution to the dairy.

Mr. Smith was waiting for me by the gate. Mr. Smith had a peculiar way of speaking—he and "the Missus," as he referred to his wife, were originally from someplace in England. He had a funny first name—Fender, or Hubcap—something like a car part. "You've come for tha' milk, I see."

"Yes, sir," I stumbled over the words. My jaw was so stiff from clenching my teeth in anticipation of Hatchet Annie's swift vengeance that it actually hurt to talk. "Yes, I've come for the milk."

"Come into the kitchen for a minute, dearie, won't you? I've some fresh cookies, still warm from t' oven. Oh, do come have one while Axel fetches your milk." Mrs. Smith waved me into her cozy little kitchen.

I liked Mrs. Smith. She often slipped me little treats to eat on my walk back home. I forgot my still impending death and followed her inside.

Presently, Mr. Smith's cheerful red face poked itself in at the opened kitchen door. "Milk's in t' wagon, girl. Best get tha goin' afore your ma calls after ya." I dragged myself from the house with reluctance, saying thank you and good-bye to these kind people I would not see again. Hatchet Annie and my fate awaited my return past her cottage.

Time stretches out in a thin line, one end attached to my little white farmhouse, the other tied to a wooden gate at the Smith Dairy Farm. Step by step, I climb the hill. I do not see

Annie's cabin as I pass it. I do not see her weeding in her garden, nor hear her chickens chirruping as they scrabble for the worms and bugs in the little turned-out holes where weeds used to be. I exist only to pull one little red wagon that carries one beat-up milk can over one hill to home.

I was on the downward slope when reality re-emerged. From somewhere behind me, quite close, a soft voice called out.

"Girlie, oh little girl!" I froze.

"I say, girlie!" My hand gripped the wagon handle so tightly that my knuckles turned white.

"Please, little one. Come here, I say!"

The voice took on a commanding quality that almost made me turn, but at the last possible instant, I found my legs.

I lurch forward, yanking at the handle so hard that the wagon rises like a rearing horse. The unseated milk can flies through the air, spewing milk in a wide arc, hits the ground, and bounds down the hill before me.

I followed, almost keeping up with the runaway milk can until the wagon flopping behind clipped me smartly on my heels and ankles. I turned loose the wagon, abandoning that faithful old toy to Hatchet Annie, and ran Hell for leather home to my mother.

Mama had spent the afternoon washing the kitchen floor and was applying a second coat of wax when I skidded into the room. Startled, she jerked upright, stepping aside as I swooshed across the shiny linoleum. She snagged my arm as I shot past her, stopping me flat.

"Whoa, sister, what's the matter here? Mama dropped her wax applicator. "You look like you've seen a ghost. Did something happen to you?"

I cannot speak. My terror is so great it paralyzes my vocal cords. My mouth tries to obey, opening and closing the way our little guppies gasped the time Robbie took them out of their bowl to pet them. Mama squats down to my level, takes my shuddering shoulders in her strong, warm hands, and looks me eye to eye.

Something she saw there frightened her. "You are scaring me, Cookie. Tell Mama what's the matter!"

She wraps her arms close about me, pulls me into her warm haven of safety, and brings me back from that tiny corner of my being where I cower in terror.

"Oh, Mama!" I began sobbing. "You're gonna be so mad at me. I lost the milk—I couldn't help it. Oh, no—she has my wagon! Oh, Mama!" I wailed; a soggy little lump of misery puddled at my mother's feet.

Mama lifted me up and carried me into the playroom. Cradling me in her arms, she sat down in the rocking chair and held me close, humming and rocking. The combination of sound and motion soothed me, and after a few moments, the story erupted.

I told it all—from its inception in June, through the hot days of July when the tables turned on me, until the tale culminated in today's encounter on Quaker Hill. (Or, as my older brother later taunted in mixed metaphor, I spilled my guts and sang like a canary.)

"Well," Mama mumbled. A strangely strangled sound escaped through lips held tight between her teeth. I thought for a moment she was laughing, but it wasn't possible. *(Was it?)*

"That is certainly some tale, Cookie. You are telling me that you made up stories about that nice old woman to scare your brother, then hoisted yourself on your own petard? Oh, my!" She made that strange noise in her throat again.

I would not read Don Quixote for several more years, but somehow the sense of Mama's phrase penetrated my shell. I guessed she meant that two-edged sword thing. She was probably right, although I had had my older brother's help. Ahead of me loomed the matter of punishment.

"Are you gonna tell Daddy?" I could feel my lower lip begin to quiver.

"No, honey. You are going to tell him yourself." She smoothed my hair back from my sticky forehead.

"What're you gonna do to me?" I shuddered and dug deeper into Mother's lap.

"I think we'll hold off on that until after you talk to Daddy," she said firmly.

This was terrible—the old "wait 'til your father gets home" thing that every little kid fears most. Daddy would hear my tale of treachery and deception from my own lips, and when I was finished—not a doubt remained in my mind, I was still going to die today, just not at the hands of Hatchet Annie. My mother pushed me gently from her lap and stood up. "Now," she spoke firmly, "Let's go find the milk can and your wagon."

While Danny stayed with a napping Rob, Mama dragged me reluctantly towards Quaker Hill. To my surprise, the wagon sat upright at the foot of the hill, and inside sat our milk can—filled to the brim. I could not believe my eyes. I had seen milk spewing out as the can rolled over and over until it took one final bounce and slammed to a stop abut a large rock. I had actually stepped in that milk as I rushed past.

"Oh, that sweetheart!" Mama smiled. Shielding her eyes with one hand, she gazed uphill, then raised her other hand to wave. I refused to look and buried my face in her skirt. After a moment, she took the wagon handle and placed it in my hand. "Come on, let's go home. It's almost suppertime."

Mama waited until after supper to mention the day's events to my daddy. Daniel could hardly contain himself during mealtime, almost spilling the beans until Mama pierced him with "the look." He continued to squirm in his seat, hoping Daddy would ask what was wrong. Daddy chose to ignore him, focusing instead on my uncharacteristically subdued demeanor.

"What's with Miss Chatterbox tonight?" he finally asked. Mama glanced my way, took a bite of meatloaf, and commented that I had had an interesting day. "She'll tell you all about it after we finish eating." Daddy tossed me a quizzical glance, one eyebrow raised. I pushed the food around on my plate and tried to look cheerful.

Eventually, everyone finished eating. I offered to clear the table, wash and dry the dishes. Mama thanked me for my kind offer and excused me from dish duty, reminding me that I had something to tell Daddy. She then dragged Daniel into the kitchen and enlisted him for KP. He shot me a dirty look, warning of retaliations planned for later. I mugged at him and scooted from the kitchen barely in time to escape the towel in his hand. My brother had perfected the dishtowel snap by his fifth birthday; he loved to hone his skill, using me as a most unwilling target!

Daddy was nowhere in sight as I tiptoed between kitchen

and playroom. If I could avoid him for one more hour, I might put off the coming inquisition until tomorrow.

Daddy spotted me as I attempted to slip past the living room door. "Cookie, I'm waiting," he called out. "Come on in here and let's talk."

I suspect that Mama had already filled Daddy in on today's excitement. He seemed remarkably calm as I stumbled through my narrative; his face betrayed no emotion but bemusement. Occasionally, he harrumphed to himself or cleared his throat.

"That's quite a story." Daddy took his favorite pipe from its rack and reached inside the humidor for his Prince Albert tobacco.

I liked watching Daddy fill his pipe. First, he took his reaming tool from its usual place in his pocket, and carefully cleaned charred tobacco from his pipe bowl. He scraped these ashes into the ashtray, then tapped the bowl on the palm of his hand to knock out any remaining tobacco crumbs. Daddy filled the pipe with fresh tobacco, gently tamping it into place. With the pipe firmly clenched between his teeth, he struck a kitchen match, applied flame to tobacco, and sucked. Daddy made a slickery sound as he drew smoke into his mouth. After his first puff, he turned his attention back to me.

"Yes, quite a story. What d'ya think we should do about it, Little Beaver?" Ever since my two top front teeth had grown loose and Daddy had finally plucked them out with his needle-nose pliers, some perverse sense of humor had caused him to refer to me as Red Ryder's small Indian sidekick.

"A trip to the woodshed," I whispered. "I bet it's a trip to the woodshed." Danny must have been listening from behind the door. I heard him laughing.

"I don't think so, honey. Not this time. I think you've been punished enough. You must've spent a few miserable nights and days, lately. Have you learned your lesson?"

I almost fainted with relief. "Yes, Daddy. I promise you—I'll never ever make up stories like that again."

"And what about teasing your little brother?"

I hesitated a breath before answering.

"I promise I'll try, Daddy. I promise I'll try *real* hard."

"I guess that's all any of us can do, Little Beaver." He gave me a squeeze, carefully turning his pipe away from my face. I felt his whiskery cheek rough against my own. "I love you, Daddy," I whispered into his ear. "And I love you, too, my little girl," he replied, his words muffled against my hair.

The following Tuesday, Mama loaded Robbie into the wagon along with the milk can, we packed a lunch, and all of us walked the hill to Axel Smith's Dairy. Before Friday, our cow freshened with the birth of her calf. We no longer needed dairy milk—we had our own again.

CHAPTER 12
In Which I Learn that No Good Deed Goes Unpunished

That summer, we had company. Mama's oldest sister, Auntie Mary Anne, and our cousins Amanda Sue and Little Philip (named for his father and diminished to avoid confusion) came up from California for a visit. I gathered from listening in on grownup conversation from my vantage place beneath the living room window, opened, as usual, to channel the late afternoon cooling breezes through the house, that my aunt was unhappy. Amanda informed me that Big Philip (her daddy) had stayed behind in California to play house with his girlfriend. Amanda was older than me by a year and was sophisticated beyond her age according to Mama. Danny said that meant that she was too big for her britches and thought she knew everything. She was conceited, as well, as she had minced out of the car on her arrival, put her hands on her hips, and recited, in a sing-song high-pitched voice:

"*Hubba-hubba, ding ding—*
Baby, I've got everything!
And she did.

Amanda had huge sky-blue eyes fringed with long, black

lashes set into her peaches and cream face, and raven hair that hung down her back in natural curls—the huge, sausage-shaped kind that I secretly coveted. I had baby fine blonde hair flat as a thread and not inclined to curl no matter how many times Mama tried to bend it to my desire, worn in a short Dutch bob that framed my rather wide face.

I had green eyes—the kind that grow up hazel—and freckles on a button nose that burned bright red in the summer sun. Amanda wore frilly little blouses and pleated skirts with suspenders. On her feet were white bobby socks and patent leather Mary Janes.

I usually wore blue jeans rolled up mid-calf and a striped tee shirt. Although summer seldom found me with shoes on my feet, this particular year I had come into possession of a pair of secondhand cowboy boots, found, to my surprise, in the hand-me-down basket at church. My Sunday school teacher Mrs. Pool, the minister's wife, said I could have them if Mama agreed. They were brown and had inset red rosette trim and I took them off only to bathe and sleep. Daddy joked that they had probably grown to my feet by now, but Mama was not amused. On more than one occasion, she had had to prevent me from wearing them to Sunday school with my blue-dotted Swiss dress.

Amanda noticed them the minute she walked through the door.

"Wow, those are super-looking boots," she gushed. "Are you gonna let me wear them while I'm here? Auntie said to make myself at home." Amanda knew the house rules—guests pretty much got what they wanted around my mama.

"Now, Cookie," she'd say, "you know that (insert name of

guest) is only going to be here for a short time. Let (her or him) play with (wear, etc.) that item. You wouldn't want your (auntie, cousin, friend, or whatever) to think that you are selfish, would you?" As a general rule, I agreed with Mama and didn't mind sharing, but I had learned early on that Amanda tended to "play rough" with things that didn't belong to her. As I searched madly for some reason to deny her my boots, I realized that her feet were bigger than mine by at least two sizes.

"Sorry," I answered with obvious delight, "you won't fit into 'em. Your feet're too big!"

Amanda Sue pulled her eyebrows down severely, squinched up those beautiful blue eyes, and pursed her perfect little bow lips. Her peaches and cream face turned the color of tomato soup (the kind I liked for lunch that Mama made with milk, not water) and she pulled back one of her shiny black Mary Janes and kicked me smartly in the shin.

Tears appeared in the corners of my eyes and I had to bite my lips to prevent attracting Mama's attention.

"That hurt!" I whispered through clenched teeth.

Amanda got a sly look on her face and hissed in my ear that she'd have the boots, one way or another. In my heart, I knew that the boots were a little large for me, and, although still too small for Amanda, with some little effort she could have shoved her feet into them.

"And when I go home, they'll be in MY suitcase, **Cookie**," she snickered. I didn't like it when she used my nickname—she made it sound like a joke.

Daddy took a few days off from his job at the shipyard to show his sister-in-law and her brood a good time, he explained to Mama when she objected.

"I'll take the kids fishing so you can talk with your sister," he exclaimed. "I can see she's got some problems on the home front and needs to talk to someone!"

I liked going fishing with Daddy. He had rules, though, and I thought that Amanda Sue and Little Philip were unlikely to follow them. As soon as we were old enough (by Daddy's standards—Mama disagreed with him but lost the argument) he taught us to bait our own hooks and to clean our own fish— with supervision, of course.

Daddy waked us before the sun was up and he tasked Danny and me with digging the worms. We stumbled out into the clear, pre-dawn morning with shovel, tin can, and flashlight to dig in the compost heap beside the barn. Danny turned the rich dark brown soil to expose the wriggling, damp night crawlers illuminated by daddy's camping flashlight. We retrieved them before they could disappear into the soil and decomposing kitchen trash, snatching them by their fat, slippery bodies, and tugging them free.

We squat there, the backs of our legs and our fannies wet with dew, filling our coffee can with worms and earth to keep them alive until their ultimate sacrifice on the end of our hooks to lure fish from the water to fill our stomachs. Fish scales and innards become part of that same compost heap. We are too young to see the cycle, but even so, there is rightness to our quest, amid the squabbles of who picks the most and whose worm is the largest. Daddy interrupts us with a call to breakfast and we trudge back to the house, our captives finding comfortable spots in their coffee can prison.

Danny usually carried the worm can after I nearly severed

the tip of my little finger on its razor-sharp edge the year before.

We departed after breakfast, Daddy and his gang of fisher-children, armed with rods and reels, hooks and sinkers, lines and leaders, and a can of freshly captured night crawlers, to our favorite fishing hole.

The fishing went rather well, I thought. Robbie and Little Philip sat astride a log on shore, dangling their baited hooks in the water and splashing with their bare feet—a move that practically guaranteed their bait had given up its life for nothing! No self-respecting fish would come within a mile of those two, but they had a lot of fun and kept out of Daddy's hair as he assisted Amanda. Danny and I baited our hooks and walked upstream from the novice section to test our luck. We fished for a couple of hours, arguing back and forth about whose catch was the largest, when Daddy called us back. Amanda and the little boys were all fished out, according to him, and it was time to pack it up for home.

On the ride back, Amanda sat in the front with Daddy and Little Philip. She chattered on about fishing and how life in Washington on the farm was different from her city life in California. Daddy nodded absentmindedly as she droned on. I looked out the window and ignored the front seat chatter until her announcement that she'd always wanted a pair of cowboy boots made me perk up my ears.

"You know, Uncle Hal," she confided in her silky voice, "Cookie hasn't once let me try on her boots, even though I asked as nicely as I could." She swiveled her head around and fixed me with a truly evil grin. "We're not gonna be here much longer, and I would really like to see how they look on my feet." She sighed and slumped melodramatically in her seat.

Daddy cleared his throat a couple of times and sucked on his pipe stem. "Well, Amanda, those boots do belong to Leah, and it's up to her whether or not she lets someone else wear them."

I smiled to myself—at least Daddy was on my side.

Amanda persisted; "Well, Uncle Hal, it's not as if someone else hasn't worn them before—after all, they were used when she got 'em!"

"It's between you and Leah, Amanda. That's all I can tell you—you'll have to ask her again."

Amanda's shoulders hunched together, and I could almost hear her scowl. I hoped that she would drop the subject before we got home—Mama might not see Daddy's point of view.

As Daddy guided our sturdy little Ford down the long, rutted drive to the house, I could see Mama and my aunt waving at us from the back steps that led into the mudroom off the kitchen. In the front seat, Amanda muttered under her breath—probably planning her next move in the ongoing struggle between me and my boots on the one hand (foot) and her on the other.

As the car came to a halt, Amanda opened the door and bolted towards her mother, holding her right arm close to her body. "Mama, look what happened to me when I was fishing with Uncle Hal!" She brandished the cosseted arm towards her mother, pointing in Daddy's direction. Daddy, who was helping Little Philip out of the car, whipped his head around with a puzzled look on his handsome face. Danny poked me in the ribs and gave me his quizzical "what's up" look. I shrugged my shoulders—any injury to Amanda was as much a mystery to me as it apparently was to Daddy. Danny whispered in my ear; "I bet she's makin' up something to get outta cleanin' the fish."

Danny was probably right. Everyone who went fishing with Daddy knew that if you caught it, you cleaned it, except for little kids like Robbie and Philip. He had reiterated that rule earlier today, including Amanda Sue in refreshing the fishing-with-Daddy rules.

Mama raised her palms in Daddy's direction. I could see him shaking his head in denial as Auntie Mary Anne examined her offspring's supposedly damaged limb. Daddy stomped over to Amanda and glanced at her arm. He eyed her with skepticism. She turned that peaches and cream face towards him and flashed a smile that failed to include those bright blue eyes so dramatically fringed with dark, heavy lashes.

"I don't blame you, Uncle Hal—but that fishing rod was so heavy! My arm is *aching*, and I really need to rest it. Can I go sit in the shade over there on the side lawn? Cookie and Danny can have my fish."

She turned toward us and smirked. "Thank you for showing me how to fish. I had a really good time!"

Daddy mumbled something about how he reckoned we could take care of her fish, gesturing vaguely in my direction, then attended to the fishing gear. Mama and Auntie Mary Anne settled Amanda on the lawn with cookies and lemonade, then took the little boys into the house for a cleanup and naps. Danny and I followed Daddy towards the outside tap where we always cleaned our catch.

"Hey, you two, take off those shoes before you get 'em wet. Mama'll have your hide if you mess 'em up." Daddy motioned towards my boots and Danny's everyday shoes. I didn't suppose she'd mind if the boots were ruined, but I did. I carefully removed them and placed them on the grass next to the back stoop, then turned to the task at hand.

Daddy, Danny, and I squatted on our haunches side by side at the water bib cleaning fish and tossing the guts into the compost bucket provided by Mama. I was halfway through my pile and reaching for another trout when something up by the stoop diverted my attention. Amanda was no longer lounging on the grass eating cookies and drinking lemonade—she now sat on the back stoop right next to my boots. I rinsed my hands under the stream of water from the open tap and wiped them on the sides of my jeans.

"I'm thirsty, Daddy—how about you? I'll get us some of that lemonade Mama made, okay?" Daddy barely raised his head from the fish but grunted his assent. "Bring some for me, too, will you, Leah?" Danny asked as politely as any big brother can. He was careful not to let in any of the demanding tone with which he usually prefaced his "requests" as Daddy was clearly within earshot.

As I made my way towards the kitchen, I snatched up my boots with my left hand and carried them past Amanda Sue into the mudroom. Mama intercepted me and directed me back outside. She carried a tray with glasses of lemonade and a plate of freshly baked cookies.

"Don't bring those boots in here, honey, you'll need them when you're done cleaning fish. Just leave them outside where you can put them on at chore time. Here!" She handed me a glass of lemonade and put a cookie into my mouth, effectively cutting off the protest rising to my lips. "I'll just take this stuff out to your daddy and brother." Resigned to the inevitable, I followed her out the door and down the steps, depositing my boots as far from Amanda as possible and as close to my work area as practicable. I sat down next to Daddy and ate the cookie, still warm from the oven.

The lemonade seemed especially tart after the sweetness of the cookie, making my mouth pucker and bringing tears to my eyes. As I wiped them on my shirt, I saw Amanda eyeing my boots. I opened my mouth to protest when a large, angry-looking wasp bumbled down into the hollow of the right boot.

Time slows down. The wasp leisurely slips out of sight, dodging into the boot toe, and making (to my ears) an angry buzzing sound that almost drowns out the voice in my head that says no, no, Amanda—there is a wasp in the boot as I see her hand reach oh, so slowly out toward my boot and I see the smug look on her face as she smirks at me with those blue lash-fringed eyes and that little, bow mouth, and the creamy skin with no freckles. My mind screams at her as she flips the shiny black curls away over her shoulder and takes the boot in both hands and pulls it over her toes. My mind screams no, but I hear my voice, very slow and very low, saying "That's okay, Amanda—you can try them on. Pull it on, Amanda. Pull the boot on tight." I watch in horror as she crams her too-big foot deep, deep into the boot until it makes contact with the angry wasp crammed between her toes and the boot end. Slowly her mouth opens—over-wide to match the huge eyes that bug out of her face and threaten to pop right out of their sockets. The sound of her scream speeds up time and her frantic call to "pull it off, pull it off" hits my ears like the sound of a gunshot.

POP! I snapped out of my altered state to watch my cousin

doing what would later be called the funky chicken across the grass and into the driveway, frantically trying to yank off my tan cowboy boot with the red rosette inserts.

Daddy leaped over me as I sat in morbid fascination, eyes glued to that boot toe and its hysterical gyrations. I felt a combination of elation and guilt as Daddy captured the screaming Amanda and attempted to wrench off the offending footwear. As hard as Daddy yanked, the boot would not budge. Amanda's eyes were now red with salty tears that streamed down her cheeks, making clean furrows as they went, her nose gushing mucous as she blubbered onto Daddy's shoulder. The boot might have succumbed to Daddy's struggle if Amanda's foot had not been damp from the grass, or if she had had on socks. As if was, her foot refused to budge. Eventually, Auntie Mary Anne held her by the shoulders as Daddy continued his heroic struggle with Amanda stretched between them as the object of a frantic tug-of-war.

After what seemed like a lifetime, Daddy called for Danny to bring him the gutting knife he had thrown down next to the fish. With sudden insight, I realized exactly what Daddy had in mind. He was going to cut my boot from Amanda's foot! Part of my mind gibbered at Daddy to cut off her foot instead and save my boot, but, thankfully, some internal censor stopped my lips from moving. I watched in horror as the gutting knife sliced down the boot side, through that lovely red rosette inset, down to where the shank met the shoe.

When her foot remained trapped, Daddy reached for his wire snips and, with an apologetic glance at me, cut through the shoe portion, as well. With one last frantic yank, boot separated from foot and flew in a high arc across the driveway, ending up near the irrigation ditch in the neighboring field, looking for all the world like a gutted animal.

We stared in awe as Amanda's foot emerged, wearing a still very much alive and furious wasp with its stinger imbedded deeply into her big toe. Daddy flicked the insect onto the grass, where it buzzed crazily in a circle before it flew off towards the bucket of raw fish innards.

"Wow!" Danny whispered in admiration. "Did'ja see the size of that wasp? That's one tough sucker!"

Mama arrived with ice for Amanda's foot, which had now swelled to twice the size of its mate. I slowly separated myself from the battlefield ministrations and trod in misery towards the remains of my precious boot now resting ingloriously in a cowpat.

Daddy raised his head and gazed solemnly in my direction. "Sorry, Cookie," he muttered apologetically. "There was nothing else I could do. Too bad you didn't see that wasp before Amanda got her foot in there." He paused for a moment. "You didn't see it, did you?" he asked with just a touch of suspicion in his voice.

I turned and looked at my daddy and slowly shook my head. I hated to lie to him, but the head shake seemed to let me off the hook. *One more entry in my ever-growing book of lies, I think silently.* Tears streamed down my cheeks as I retrieved what remained of my most prized possession.

Mama and Auntie Mary Anne cosseted Amanda, settling her in Daddy's living room chair and elevating her foot on Mama's special pillow—the one Uncle Jerry brought her from the Philippines—with an ice pack on her swollen toes.

Daddy tried to fix my boot. He sewed up the shaft with his

curved needles and the heavy tan thread he used to repair halters and bridles, taking care to match the red rosette insert as best he could, but even the most artful stitching couldn't make the boot functional.

Danny said that I would get over it—after all, they were secondhand—and perhaps someday another pair would come my way. I didn't think so—very few church clothing baskets had hardly ever worn cowboy boots almost my size in them. Besides, it was my own fault that the boots were ruined. Perhaps if I had warned Amanda about the wasp, things would have turned out differently. I knew in my heart, however, that she would have given me that evil, smug grin of hers and forced her foot in even harder.

I know I shouldn't have, that Mama said we must forgive those who trespass against us (it's a Bible rule or something) but sometimes, late at night when I couldn't sleep, I lay awake reliving the moment when Amanda Sue got hers. *"Just another entry in the Book,"* I think to myself, *"but this time, maybe it was worth it."*

CHAPTER 13

In Which I Learn Not to Judge a Book by Its Cover

After the cousins went home to California, Mama sent Danny, Robbie, and me out to Wildcat Lake for swimming lessons. When I was four, I had almost drowned Mama and myself in an unfortunate accident at this very same lake. My parents and a group of their friends were spending a pleasant Sunday afternoon picnicking. Danny and I and the other kids were playing around the edge of the lake while Daddy kept an eagle eye on Robbie, who was confined to an area designated for toddlers. Those who could were swimming back and forth between our picnic area and the float anchored offshore, where Mama was sunbathing. When Danny tired of me tagging along, Uncle Matt, one of Daddy's friends, took me up on his back and ferried me out to the float. I lay there with Mama, side by side, being one of the big girls, until Mama noticed my bright red skin.

"Good Lord, Cookie, you look like a boiled lobster!" She cast her eyes around searching for something to cover me up, but the float was bare. Only my mama and I were still out there—everyone else was on shore either setting up the picnic food or waiting around to eat. We could see Danny and the other kids splashing around near shore, and Daddy had Robbie in his arms waving at us and calling for us to come in.

"Well," said Mama, motioning to her back, "I suppose if Matt brought you out here, I can take you back. Climb up, honey, and hang on tight." Mama sat at the float's edge, her legs dangling into the water.

I did as she suggested—clambered up on her back and wrapped my arms around her neck as Mama slipped off the float. The instant that cold lake water touched my burned skin, I felt as if I had been thrown into a freezer! My teeth began to chatter uncontrollably, and I lost my spot on Mama's back. Instinctively, I tightened my grip. Mama was a strong swimmer, but she was small and had never fully recovered from the bad fall she had taken a few years before. Even though she later had surgery and spent nearly a year in bed, her spine would always be delicate.

Mama reached one arm back and tried to reposition me, but I flinched as her hand struck my blistered skin and slipped even further. Suddenly, Mama and I were face-to-face, and I had a stranglehold around her neck. For one paralyzing moment, our eyes met before we sank beneath the water like two millstones lashed together.

I panic! As the murky, green lake water closes over my head, I climb right up Mama's torso, scrabbling for the elusive surface that lies a fingertip's length above me. Mama gives me a feeble shove as she tries to pry my arms from their death grip around her neck—but I will not let go. As I struggle for air, I find myself standing on Mama's shoulders, forcing her further down into the water. It is as if Mama and I are alone in the lake, except for fishes swimming by with bemused grins on their little fish lips. The water is an eerie cartoon green color, and I can see bits of leaf and grit and grass floating down past my face. I see a slow-motion gush of bubbles from Mama's mouth and her eyes bulge out like the eyes of those grinning fish. Do my eyes look like Mama's eyes, I wonder as I watch my arms reaching for the surface way, way above my face. My hand breaks through, waving wildly, and Mama shoves me hard, momentarily pushing my head up and beyond the hand so that I can grab lungs full of air and water. I see people on the shore laughing and pointing at Mama and me as we struggle to live—Mama and her four-year-old anchor, dragging her inextricably down, down to the squishy, mud bottom and the weeds and snails. We sink again and Mama strips my hands from her face and shoves me hard upward, and this time we both surface, Mama spewing water and gasping for air. We thrash for a moment as I re-establish my handhold, then we sink once more, eyes wide open, face-to-face—my mama mouthing something I cannot understand. She pries my hands free and uses all her strength to propel me towards the surface, then sinks, sinks towards the bottom below as my upward momentum pushes her downward.

This time when I surfaced, Daddy was there, his strong arms reaching out to hold me up.

I breathe in huge gasps of air and water and weeds as I struggle to rid my lungs of water. "Here's Cookie," I hear my daddy shout. "Take her, Matt, while I go after Mayleen." Daddy passes me off and is gone, gone away beneath the surface in search of my mermaid mother silently drifting towards the muddy lake bottom. I no longer struggle as Uncle Matt's strong, hairy arms hold my limp body close to his own, transporting me slowly to shore. He lays me on the sand and holds my head while I cough out lake water and force air, which feels like acid, into my lungs. I want my mama—I want to feel her arms around me, holding me tight and telling me that we are safe.

After an eternity, Daddy pulled Mama, barely breathing, onto the shore. Daddy found her crawling towards shore on the lake bottom, dragging herself along from weed to weed. It didn't occur to me for a long time that if something had happened in the lake—if Mama had drowned before Daddy got to her, it would be my fault!

In the following days, I developed an absolute terror of water. Mama recovered without consequence, but I dreamed of drowning nearly every night. It became almost impossible to wash my hair, as the thought of water coming anywhere near my face sent me into a panic and I bathed with only a few inches of water in the tub. Mama and Daddy gave me what they thought was ample time to recover, but as time passed and my fear failed to lessen, they sent me to the YMCA's Learn to Swim program.

I refused to enter the pool. When no amount of encouragement from the instructors—or watching my friends learn to dog paddle and then advance to beginners—alleviated my fears, the instructors suggested that confronting the place of the trauma might make a difference. Accordingly, here we were at Wildcat Lake.

Robbie and Mama hurried off to his group of pollywogs— those kids who already had the fundamentals of swimming down, and Danny joined his group of intermediate swimmers. I sat on the shore next to the mudpuppy beginner group, just watching them splash around in the ankle-deep water. My instructor was a very nice lady who suggested I watch for the first day. Secretly, I hoped she would feel that way tomorrow and for the rest of the summer!

I grew bored after a while and wandered up the grass towards a little boy lying on his stomach on a blanket. At first, I thought he was asleep because he lay so still, but to my surprise, his huge, dark brown eyes were open wide and fixed on my face.

"Hi," I chirped, squatting down on my haunches, "My name's Leah, but my friends call me Cookie. What's yours?"

"He can't talk—he's a dummy."

I raised my eyes to a long-legged young man with insolent eyes seated in the shadows of an alder tree, leaning back against the trunk and sucking on a long strand of grass.

I glanced down at the little body lying on the blanket and saw pain in those huge, brown eyes.

"But he does have a name, doesn't he?"

"Yeah—it's Johnny, but he don't know it."

The brown eyes squinched a little and the mouth twitched. I leaned over and looked straight into his eyes. "Hello, Johnny. You wanna call me Cookie?"

A faint smile curled his lips. I could see him trying to say something. His arms and legs made swimming motions on the blanket and those brown eyes smiled, even though his face couldn't.

I looked up at the young man. "So, are you his dad?"

"Naw, he's my youngest brother. I'm watchin' over him while my mom helps a couple of the other kids with swimmin' lessons." He reached down and poked Johnny in the back with his long, skinny pointy finger. "Ya can't swim, can ya, huh John? Ya can't even float! Six years old, and ya just lay there like a sack o' potatoes, dontja, kid," and he poked him again.

The way he talked to his brother made me mad inside, but I was just a little girl, not much older than Johnny, and what could I do?

"Do you mind if I talk with him?" I asked, hesitantly.

"Na, go right ahead," said his brother. "I'm gonna go over to the concession stand and get me a big soft drink." He poked Johnny with his bare toe and asked if he wanted something, then threw back his head and laughed as the little boy squirmed. "Speak up, boy. No? Be right back." He aimed the last at me, his finger cocked like a gun barrel and made a clicking sound with his tongue. He rose to his feet and left.

Johnny raised his head a couple of inches off the blanket and looked me in the eye. "Coo-kee?" he mumbled around his tongue that kept getting in the way. "Coo-kee!"

And so it began. Every day, I ducked out of getting into that terrifying lake, and every day, I searched out Johnny on his blanket. I usually found him under the same tree with some relative, not always his older brother, keeping an eye on him—as if he could go anywhere, I thought. I could see the light come on in his eyes when he saw me trekking across the ragged grass. Johnny was in there, all right, but nobody else cared to look!

I brought books and read to him and we had conversations. Well, I talked to him and he answered back with his eyes and what little use he had of his mouth. His arms and legs were useless, for the most part, as his condition left him without control, but he could sit if tied in his special seat—

sort of a modified highchair, or in his wheelchair. By summer's end, we were fast friends; although I hadn't learned a swimming stroke, or for that matter, even put so much as a toe in Wildcat Lake, Johnny had learned two more words. He could now say "Hello" and "Mama," and I was pretty sure that he had also learned to read.

"What is he gonna do without me?" I tearfully asked Mama on the last day of swim lessons. "Nobody else talks to him—or even cares."

"You have been very kind to him, Leah, but he has his family, and I'm sure they love him." Mama turned her attention back to the old, dirt road as we drove home from the lake. Danny and Robbie squabbled in the back seat while I sat up front with Mama. "You might like to know that I have invited his parents to attend our church. They've promised to bring Johnny to Sunday school with their other children. Maybe you will see him there."

Mama gave a grunt as she put one foot on the brake pedal, one on the clutch, turned the wheel, and changed gears simultaneously. I didn't think I'd ever learn to drive like my mama did. She seemed to maneuver Elizabeth, our old Model A Ford, without effort—coaxing her around sharp and hairpin turns, weaving between cars in traffic and parking with ease. When Mama could take a little attention from the road, I asked her if she knew what was wrong with Johnny.

"He has cerebral palsy, Leah. That's the official name, although most people would say he is spastic. I guess he was born the way he is. No one seems to be able to help the poor little boy. It's nice that you paid attention to him this summer." She pulled into the driveway and stopped the car, then turned to me.

"Even if you didn't learn to swim a stroke, I guess you learned something more important." I waited for her to tell me what that lesson was, but she just gave me a smile and opened the car door. Danny snickered under his breath in the back seat. "Yeah, she learned how to be friends with a spaz! Good goin', Leah!" Mama leaned over the seat back and stared in shocked surprise at her eldest son.

"That was very unkind, Daniel. Do not repeat it."

Danny sneered at me as soon as Mama withdrew her head and opened the car door, mouthing "spaz" in my direction, then whispered softly so Mama wouldn't hear him. "Takes one to know one, I s'pose. That's you, Leah the spaz! 'Fraid of the water and friends with losers!"

Johnny showed up at Sunday school the following week. His mother brought him in and parked his wheelchair next to me. I smiled at Johnny and patted his knee. His eyes were a little fearful—I guess he hadn't been to Sunday school before.

"Don't worry, everybody's nice here," I assured him, and I held his hand while the teacher spoke about Jesus healing the sick. Johnny's face lit up and he whispered something under his breath—something only he could understand—but I got the sense that he wanted Jesus to heal him.

"Do you know how to pray?" I inquired. His big brown eyes said no, so I promised to pray for him, and I did.

I guess God didn't hear my prayers, or maybe when you pray for someone else it just isn't the same, but nothing seemed to change for Johnny. He came to Sunday school all that autumn, and although the other kids teased him occasionally, for the most part, he got along okay. His face always glowed when he saw me, and that made my heart feel good. I don't think Mama really understood the friendship that Johnny and I had. He couldn't talk, but that didn't mean he didn't understand. Even his family didn't know that. They never seemed to try, and his mama had a handful of little kids to take care of. I guess she didn't have the time to look into the heart of one little boy and see the light that shined inside him, even though it burned bright enough for me to see.

One Sunday morning in early December, Mama woke me. She sat on the edge of the bed and took my hand in hers. "Leah, I have some bad news." She whispered softly so as not to wake the boys. "Johnny won't be at Sunday school this morning."

I sat straight up in bed. "What happened," I squeaked. "Is he sick?"

"No, Cookie—there was an accident last night."

"But he's gonna be alright, isn't he?"

Mama's voice sounded funny, like she was having trouble getting the words out. "I don't know how to tell you this, but Johnny's gone."

"Gone? Where'd he go, Mama—is he coming back soon?" I had to ask, but somewhere, deep inside my heart, I knew that Johnny was never coming home.

"He's not, honey. Last night"—Mama made a funny little noise in her throat, not quite a cough—"while he was in the bathtub—Oh, Cookie! I don't know how to say this! He drowned, in two inches of water. How does that happen to a little boy with cerebral palsy! Don't people care?" Mama turned her head to the side, but I could see the glimmer of tears in her eyes.

"I care, Mama. The cerebral palsy is what kept him trapped inside his head so that he couldn't even scream." I was quiet for a moment, then asked my mama if Johnny was in the bathroom alone.

"His big brother was supposed to be watching him, honey. I guess he stepped outside for a moment (goin' to get me a big soft drink) and Johnny slipped out of his seat. His mama heard him calling for her, then he called your name! Damn it!" Mama's words exploded from her mouth along with little blobs of spit. "Two inches of water!"

My stomach feels like I have swallowed a big chunk of ice and little streams of fire are creeping down my cheeks—tears of fire, burning, burning into my face and my soul. I have let him down, somehow. Johnny needed me, and I was not there. My arms and legs start to shake, sort of like Johnny shakes when he is trying to reach for something—correction—how Johnny used to shake. He is gone and I cannot control myself and I cannot make Johnny come back. Did Johnny's brother just step out for a soft drink like he did that first day at the lake? Or did Johnny's big brother let him die on purpose? Will anyone but me miss him? For a moment, just the tiniest fraction of a moment, I wonder if MY big brother would let me drown if I had cerebral palsy. Would he look at me with his scornful Danny eyes and laugh and call me spaz as I breathe water and soap into my lungs? Would he?

Mama took me in her arms and gave me a quick squeeze. "Now, get up. It's time to get ready for Sunday school." Sunday school! Mama actually thought I could go to Sunday school?

"I can't go today, Mama. How can you make me go today?"

"It's just where you need to be, Leah—with your friends."

I cross my arms over my stomach with the ice block still in it, hoping they will help the lump to thaw before Mama wants me to eat breakfast. She tenderly wipes away my scalding fire tears with her thumbs, smearing them across my cheeks to dry tight and salty on my skin. Later, I look in the bathroom mirror while I brush my teeth and think how lucky I am. Johnny could not brush his own teeth or wash his face or sit on the toilet without help. I look at our bathtub—at how deep it is as it stands there on its little claw feet. I know how it feels to sit inside those slippery, shiny white porcelain walls and slide on my fanny up and down the slick, soapy bottom. I remember sliding so fast once that I upend and whack the back of my head hard on the tub bottom and see sparkly stars in front of my eyes. I remember how it felt that day at Wildcat Lake when Mama and I almost drowned. I remember how it feels to breathe in water like fire and my lungs hurt and hurt and all I can do is scream inside my head.

Is that what happened to Johnny when his brother wasn't watching? Or did he slip forward out of his tie-in chair and slide face down in the water, calling for his mama and, in the end, calling for me?

That morning in class, our teacher told everyone about Johnny's death, and we talked about heaven and that you got there by believing in Jesus and that he was your savior. One of the kids who sometimes teased Johnny asked if Johnny would go to heaven.

"I don't know," answered our teacher. "It's hard to tell if Johnny ever let Jesus into his heart."

I sat at the back of the room, wanting desperately to say that I knew Johnny was in heaven. At first, I thought I had prayed in vain for Jesus to heal Johnny's legs and arms and bobbly head and inability to speak. At first, I thought Jesus had failed my friend. Then, I realized that Jesus did answer Johnny's heart and my prayers.

He is in Heaven with Jesus, I think, and he is running and laughing and telling Jesus all the things he ever wanted to say. I do not care if the stupid Sunday school teacher is unclear on the concept—Jesus loves the little children, and that includes Johnny.

I would always miss Johnny, would always remember the lesson I learned from him that summer at Wildcat Lake. It's not what's on the outside that counts—when the heart lights up and shines in a person's eyes, that is his soul shining through. Johnny's soul was all the colors of the spectrum—there for anyone to see who cared to look beyond the crippled limbs—and as long as I lived, Johnny would shine for me in every rainbow. I didn't have words to give voice to the feeling inside of me. Mama said perhaps it was compassion, sympathy for the suffering of others and the desire to help, but I don't think so. In a few months, I would learn the name for this kind of listening, but for now, I let Mama pacify me with the words she meant for comfort.

I didn't feel sorry for Johnny in the usual sense—only frustration that others couldn't see the little boy trapped inside, and a sadness that so many people failed to be touched by his life until he no longer had it.

In the future, I brought home many of the broken children among my classmates, and Mama always fed them a hot meal and found something nice for them to wear. She didn't complain (too much) about my penchant for the underdogs, but Daddy really didn't understand. To Danny and Robbie, they were always Leah's pet projects, but I learned something about life from every single one of them—lessons that served me well in the years to come.

CHAPTER 14
In Which a Gift is Bestowed

When I was six years old, my Uncle Dodo came to visit. We seldom saw OurFather's younger brother, as he lived in California and rarely traveled to our rainy corner of the world. Even though Mama was divorced from his brother and was remarried, Uncle Dodo remained on excellent terms with both Mama and Daddy. He had a smiley, upturned mouth and cheek dimples that gave him an angelic appearance. His eyes always sparkled—especially when I asked to touch those dimples. Mama called them "angel's fingerprints," a sure sign the bearer was blessed. I called them face dents, similar to my own set, but deeper. Mine showed only when I smiled.

Mama called him Will—short for William, his given name. OurFather had his own brother-specific names, most of them not complimentary. They didn't get along, those two. According to Mama, they had a history, whatever that meant.

No one knows why my older brother started calling him Uncle Dodo instead of Uncle Will, not even Danny, but the name stuck! He took it with his usual good humor and came bearing gifts.

"I may have slacked off on the birthdays and Christmases

during the war, but I intend to make up for it now," he gasped as he staggered through the back door and deposited a collection of bags, bundles, and packages onto the back porch/mudroom floor. "There! When I get them distributed, we'll have a party!" Uncle Dodo had spent World War II in the Navy, stationed as a radioman on a variety of naval vessels and bases around the Pacific Theater.

Danny, Robbie, and I clustered around the heap of offerings—patting, squeezing, shaking, and making wild guesses as to contents and recipients for each. I counted nine packages, wondering silently which of us got only one— Danny, I hoped!

"Break it up, kids." Mama pulled Robbie away, pointing towards the kitchen door as she spoke. "Take all those packages into the kitchen, right now. Honestly, Will!" She turned to Uncle Dodo in exasperation. "You'll spoil us!"

"I can if I want to, Sis! I'm just thankful we're all still around to spoil. Come on, guys—let's get this booty into the house!" He laughed, throwing back his head and howling enthusiastically just as Daddy grumbled in from the barn.

"You'd all do better to get your chores done. Will! When you come, they lose their heads." He turned to the three of us. "Get to it! Danny, Cookie, scoot." Danny's eyes met mine—we bolted for the door in tandem. Danny made it through the screen door a step ahead of me. Daddy popped me on the fanny as I passed by. "Slow down, you two," he warned, "and do a good job!"

Uncle Dodo left the package collection to Mama and followed us out the door. "Wait for me, guys! I'll help!" We heard the screen door slam behind him.

At the barn, he and Danny pitched hay to the calves and carried buckets of slop to our nasty-tempered Chester White sow. I fed the chickens, carefully cleaning debris from their waterer and refilling it. While the hens remained occupied pecking scratch from their long, V-shaped metal feeder, I collected the day's accumulation of eggs, warm from the nest. Uncle Dodo watered the rabbits and replenished their pellets. He whistled as he worked, occasionally cracking a joke Danny and I didn't get. Since we loved him, we laughed anyhow.

When all the chores were done, Uncle Dodo swung me up on his shoulders astride his neck. I balanced there, laughing, as he held my legs and swung himself around until he lost his balance and dumped us both into the haystack. He sat up, covered with hay, and Danny and I tickled him until he said "uncle." Eventually, Mama called us up to dinner. We walked back to the house holding hands and swinging our arms, taking no thought to the basket of eggs I carried. Fortunately, none of them cracked!

Daddy seemed quiet at dinner, but Mama made up for his lack of conversation as she chattered brightly. We passed chicken and mashed potatoes back and forth, listening to Uncle Dodo's stories of the fabled Southern California weather.

"You guys should pack up the kids and move down there," he enthused. "Housing is cheap—you could get a brand-new house in the Valley for less than you pay to rent this place—and there's not as much upkeep! Sis," he turned to mother, "can you believe there's an orange tree in every yard—with the sweetest fruit you've ever eaten? Just reach up and pick your own."

I found that hard to believe, myself. In my lifetime, I'd had neither a tree-ripened orange nor a sweet one! The few oranges my brothers and I had seen came buried deep in the toe of our Christmas stocking, brought down the chimney by Santa. They were invariably hard, with bright orange, deeply pebbled skin—and sour! We ate them anyhow.

"There's one thing we have here that we don't have in Southern California, Will," Daddy answered, "and that's employment. At least I HAVE a job here. The shipyard's still paying the bills last time I looked."

"You wouldn't have any trouble getting a job, Hal—not with your qualifications. If not the shipyard at Long Beach, there's always the new defense plant starting up in Pomona. I'm thinking of applying there, myself."

"You finished college and got your degree. What do I have? Eighth grade, that's all!" Daddy sounded bitter. His voice had an edge to it that reminded me of the way my teeth squeaked together after I sucked on one of those sour Christmas oranges. I had never heard Daddy sound that way. Danny's eyes met mine. He continued, "You were in the service. I was frozen to my job. That doesn't give me the same opportunities as you have, Will." Daddy sighed deeply and reached for the chicken platter.

Uncle Will made conciliatory noises in his throat but had no answer for Daddy.

"Boys, boys—try and get along, will you? California sounds terrific but we like it here, don't we, kids?" Mama nodded her head, encouraging us to back her up. I nodded, of course, but California actually sounded pretty good.

After Mama and I cleared away the dishes, she brought out

her famous cherry pie. She'd baked this one especially for Uncle Dodo, in honor of his visit, and Daddy had brought ice cream from the store. Usually, we had homemade ice cream, but this was a workday for Daddy, who hadn't had time. Mama cut and served the pie, generously mounding vanilla ice cream on top. We all ate in silence, enjoying this midweek treat.

After dessert, I served coffee to the adults who sat and talked grownup stuff while Danny and I washed and dried the dishes. For once, Danny didn't try to beg off kitchen duty. He was as interested as I was in the interplay between Daddy and Uncle Will.

"What'ja think of Unca' Dodo's idea 'bout us all movin' to California?" he whispered to me as he dried glasses. I always had to wash, as Danny didn't use hot enough water, according to Mama, but I hated it! We used soap shavings swooshed up in the hot water to make suds. This mixture made everything feel slimy to the touch—a feeling that sent shivers up my back, especially when touching the silverware. Handling the slippery china became an adventure in dexterity.

"Shhh!" I hissed at him. "Don't whisper so loud. They aren't deaf, ya know!" I paused to wrestle a large platter into the rinse water side of Mama's double sink. "It might be interesting, but I don't think Daddy's gonna go for it."

"Well, maybe Mama can convince him. Having one of those orange trees growing outside the door sure sounds good to me—imagine, sunshine all the time!"

I finished rinsing the potato pot, my eyes roaming countertop and stove for any remaining dirty dishes. Only the adults' coffee cups remained. I queried Mama silently, motioning towards the cups. She waved me off, rising for refills all around from the still half-full coffee pot. Danny continued to babble while I drained the sink, sluiced away the remaining soapsuds with cold water, then carefully scalded the dishcloth with nearly boiling water from the reservoir on the stove.

"Off to bed, kids. You still have school tomorrow—and take Robbie with you." Robbie, already in his Red Ryder foot pajamas, had fallen asleep on Uncle Dodo's lap. His head rested open-mouthed on the tabletop precariously near a still full coffee cup where a little pool of Robbie drool made a damp spot on Mama's tablecloth. Uncle Dodo rose with Robbie in his arms, careful not to wake him. "We'll get to those presents right after school tomorrow, guys!" He winked at me and smiled broadly, his upturned mouth playing connect-the-dimples. "Don't get up, Sis! I'll carry this guy to bed." Danny had that stubborn, "I'm gonna argue" look in his eye, but a couple of elbows in the ribs directed his attention towards our uncle, who shook his head. He escorted us to our shared bedroom and carefully placed Robbie in his crib. I was secretly jealous of Robbie and his sleepwear, as Red Ryder was my favorite cowboy hero. Unfortunately, I no longer wore foot pajamas but took solace in my collection of Red Ryder books and comics.

"See you in the morning, kids. Sleep tight!" At the door, he paused for a second, then turned around, saluted Danny, bowed low to me, and flipped off the lights. He left the door open a crack as he exited, allowing a transient sliver of light to cast shadows on the wall.

Usually, Danny would get up and shut the door tight after Robbie was asleep, but tonight he left it open so we could listen to the grownups talk. We couldn't quite make out the words, but the tone was unmistakable—Daddy and Uncle Will were squabbling like two little kids! Finally, they went to bed. They must have called a truce because everyone was cheerful at breakfast the next morning, even Daddy, and all through our uncle's visit, not one more word was mentioned about moving to the land of eternal sunshine and trees filled with sweet, juicy oranges!

After an interminably long day at school, Uncle Dodo distributed the presents, inadvertently sending me on the first steps of a journey that lasted eight years. I have no recollection of any gift he gave that day except one—the very last box. He stepped towards me with it, this box with the big pink bow. "And last, but never least, for my niece," he said, and with a flourish, he placed it at my feet.

The box itself was the most beautiful present I had ever seen. For a few seconds, I almost forgot to breathe, then Danny bellowed out, "Well, ain't ya gonna open it? Criminy, Leah, I wanna see what's inside!"

"Yes, honey, open it up," encouraged Mama. She turned to our uncle. "I hope you didn't spend a lot of money, Will. She's just a little kid!"

Uncle Will waved off her protests. "I couldn't resist it when I saw it, Sis. It's perfect for Leah, and if she'll ever open it, I'm sure you'll agree! Go on, kiddo, have at it!"

Daddy comes forward with scissors to cut the ribbon so I will not have to spoil that beautiful pink bow. (I had it for years, that bow, first tied to my headboard, and later, when I had my own room, draped over my vanity mirror.) *Carefully, I peel off the tape and remove the box top. White tissue paper* covers whatever rests inside. I hold my breath as I tweak it aside to reveal what my uncle has brought for me.

"Jeez," snorted Danny as I pulled out the most wonderful teddy bear I had ever seen. "I thought it was gonna be something *neat!*" Daddy caught hold of his arm and unceremoniously jerked him aside.

I exhale and behold my gift with awe! My uncle has brought me a fully articulated bear just the right size to hold tight and cuddle, covered with creamy white mohair the color of the winter berries still hanging in clumps from bare-branched bushes down by the creek! Around his neck—and oh, yes, I know immediately this bear is male—is a red leatherette collar, and as I turn him on his tummy, he growls! He is magnificent!

When I could speak, I turned to Uncle Dodo.

"His name is Winter," I whispered, "Winter Bear, and I love him. Thank you, he's wonderful!" Uncle Will winked at my mother and gave me a big hug.

"Don't you think she's a little young for a toy **that** color? Will, you must have spent a fortune on it!" Mama turned to me with that stern look she reserved for her no-nonsense pronouncements. "You'll have to put it up until you're a little older, honey," and she reached for my wonderful new best friend.

"Just a minute, Sis!" laughed my uncle. "I gave the bear to Leah." He turned confidently towards me. "You'll be careful to keep him clean, won't you?"

"Yes," I whispered. "I promise!"

"I'm going to hold you to your word, honey." Mama released her grip with a reluctant nod.

Uncle Dodo went home to California a few days later, while we stayed exactly where we were. I didn't see an orange tree until I moved to California as a young wife and mother.

In the months that followed, Winter Bear became my best friend—my confidant, the keeper of my dreams. I was a sickly kid, often bedridden with croup, tonsillitis, earache, and other assorted ailments. During the long days when my brothers were at school and Mama was busy with household chores, I could always count on my wonderful, furry friend to keep me company. I read out loud to him; he joined me at a thousand tea parties, and never complained when "Pepper Young's Family" kept me glued to the radio. If I woke with nightmares, he didn't laugh or call me a scaredy-cat—he simply snuggled close. Sometimes, I swore he whispered comforting words in my ear! Danny occasionally kidnapped him for ransom or to keep me from revealing a few of his escapades. Surprisingly, Robbie left Winter Bear alone—I guess he had no use for a creamy white teddy bear with a red leather collar!

CHAPTER 15
In Which We Meet New Friends

In the spring, Daddy began talking about a new employee at work. Fritz Nelson and his family had recently moved to Bremerton from "the South," wherever that was, and Mr. Nelson had come to work for Daddy at the shipyard in Bremerton. "Honey, they don't know a soul in the area, and I'd like to get them out here to dinner some night. His wife needs someone to show her around, and they've got a couple of kids—Fritz Junior is just about Danny's age, and Cookie, there's a little girl for you!" Robbie smiled eagerly at daddy. "Sorry, Rob, no little brother."

Mama immediately invited them out to spend Saturday on the farm.

The Nelsons were from a small town in Tennessee, not exactly hillbillies, but "not far from the holler," as some of Daddy's cronies at the shipyard snickered. Mr. Nelson had apprenticed as a machinist, and Daddy said he was quite good. Daddy appreciated a hard worker who could take on an assignment and work with little supervision—it made his job easier.

It was obvious to all of us just why Daddy liked Mr. Nelson.

The man always smiled. He never raised his voice to his wife, Verna Lee, or the kids, Little Fritz and Mimi—short for Wilhelmina—a huge name for a little wisp of a girl barely four years old. Mrs. Nelson was tall and thin, with short, greying hair worn in a choppy bob that did nothing for her long, rather unattractive face. Her thick drawl was practically unintelligible. For a long time, I thought she spoke a foreign language! Mr. Nelson, on the other hand, had modified his speech to a honey-soft croon that soothed the ears! He spoke with deliberation and clarity, even though his wording and phrases differed from the clipped vernacular I had grown up with. Little Fritz, or Fritzie, was almost the same age as Danny. They shared a grade level in school, but little else.

"Jeez, Leah, he's a sissy!," Danny whispered to me in bed that Saturday night after Daddy drove the Nelsons home to their rented duplex. "He wouldn't play in the barn or go huntin' for frogs and pollywogs in the creek, or anything! And Daddy says I gotta get along with him 'cause he's new around here and ain't got any friends! I know why! He's just a darned sissy!"

Danny thumped his pillow to punctuate his point.

"Mimi's no prize, ya know," I murmured back. "She's Robbie's age, for gosh sakes, and she doesn't even talk, at all. She spent the whole day staring at Winter Bear and tearing up my paper dolls!"

"Why didn't ya just give her the stupid bear, Leah, so she'd leave your paper stuff alone?"

I didn't answer him. Danny was always trying to get a rise out of me.

The Nelsons soon became a fixture at our house. Mama

got along with Vi, as Mrs. Nelson was called for short, and even if she hadn't actually sought out the friendship, she made the best of it. The Nelsons were older than Mama and Daddy and had come to parenthood later in life. Mrs. Nelson catered to her children in a manner totally foreign to my brothers and me! We were expected to eat what was set before us, without question, especially when we were guests at another's dinner table—a rule that had had me in trouble more than once! The Nelson children, on the other hand, picked at their food, eating only what interested them. The rest lay in little piles distributed over their plates and surrounding table linen. "Our foods are new to them, honey," she explained when I complained. "They're used to different vegetables and cooking methods. You'll understand when you're a little older!"

Understanding came all too soon! During spring vacation from school, our parents went away by themselves for a much-deserved break, leaving the three of us with the Nelsons. We had hosted Fritzie and Mimi on the occasional weekend, and I suppose they were returning the favor!

All three boys bunked together while I shared a twin bed with Mimi. She glued herself to my side as I opened my small suitcase, eyeing each item with great expectations.

"I left my bear at home," I proclaimed triumphantly, as the last of my shorts and tee shirts disappeared into the drawer Mrs. Nelson had emptied for me. Mama had suggested that Winter Bear would be happier atop my bed than being dragged to a stranger's house and I agreed. Mimi shrugged her shoulders and turned away in disappointment. I stuck my tongue out at her back. When I looked up, Danny stood in the doorway, shaking his head disapprovingly. I made a silent note to catch him in some minor disobedience of his own, just to be on the safe side, and followed him outside to play.

A brief shower had sweetened the air and sharpened our appetites as we all played with enthusiasm until Mrs. Nelson called us in for lunch on that first day. I was expecting the usual toasted cheese and tomato soup type of lunch Mama always set out. Instead, I was introduced to "Tennessee holler luncheon," Nelson style!

"Y'all wash up, now," she declared, shooing us towards the bathroom. I waited in line for my turn as unfamiliar odors drifted from Mrs. Nelson's small kitchen. "What's that funny smell?" I whispered to Danny who stood, hands on hips, ahead of me. "I sure hope it's not lunch."

Danny scrunched up his nose, a look of distaste on his face. "If it is, we're both in trouble—you know what Mama said—'clean your plates and be polite.'" We lingered at the sink as long as possible before joining Robbie, Mimi, and Little Fritz at the table.

Robbie sat hoisted up to the table by a large Sears and Roebuck catalog atop a highbacked wooden chair. In front of him, a small plate contained a thick slab of homemade bread generously slathered with what appeared to be uncolored margarine. Closer inspection revealed it to be lard! Instead of glasses filled with milk, mugs of steaming coffee sat at each place. A large cream jug and a bowl of apples shared center table with a glass, restaurant-style sugar dispenser, and a similar container filled with thick syrup. Danny and I had tasted coffee only when we sneaked a sip from our parents' cups. We exchanged glances as we seated ourselves. Robbie squirmed, threatening to careen off his perilous perch at any moment. Little Fritz and Mimi dug in with gusto.

Danny lifted his bread to his nose and sniffed. "Gotcha," I whispered and poked him in the ribs. Food sniffing was definitely not on Mama's list of good table manners. He bounced a look of contempt off me but nodded in agreement— for the moment we were even! He bit into the bread slab with quasi-enthusiasm. I watched in awe as he resolutely chewed and swallowed, his face turning tomato red as he struggled for control. He grinned at me, a silent dare, and gestured towards my plate.

"Pass the jug, would ya?" Fritzie motioned with his bread towards the syrup container. He took the proffered jug and liberally applied its contents to the bread and lard. Inspired, I followed suit, grinning back at Danny as I took my first bite, expecting the syrup to cover up the taste of lard. Unfortunately, the syrup turned out to be blackstrap molasses, the sulfured variety! In desperation, I snatched up the coffee mug. Even the cream I had poured in couldn't cover the bitter taste of chicory that now competed with the lard and molasses. Danny grinned and feigned alarm at the expression on my face!

"Maybe you'd better excuse Leah from the table, Mrs. Nelson," he announced gleefully, "she's got a weak stomach." I caught a glimpse of his face as I fled. "Gotcha back," it said. "Gotcha back!"

CHAPTER 16
In Which We Learn About Trains

In late winter, just before Easter break, OurFather sent money north to Auntie Noreen along with a plea for her to intercede with Mama and convince her to send Danny and me down to visit him while school was in recess. I remember the look on Mama's face when Auntie Nor showed her the letter.

"Seems so reasonable, doesn't it?" Mama bit her lower lip, holding the side between her teeth while she reread the half plea half barely disguised threat. "He's got me between a rock and a hard spot. I've dropped the contempt, so he could come here and visit the children. On the other hand, he does have his job to consider."

Now that the war was over, returning military personnel were taking positions previously held by civilians, many of whom, like Daddy, were frozen to their jobs for the duration of the war. Daddy had tried many times to enlist and join his brothers (and OurFather's brothers) in serving our country but was refused each time. His job was considered essential to the wartime effort and, try as he might, he was there for the duration.

"I don't trust him," snorted our aunt. "He's looking for any excuse to keep the both of them down there."

Since the last time I had seen OurFather, when he was busily engaged in watching Gemma stuff Danny into the back seat of his car while I screamed for my mama from my spot next to the garbage cans, I was less than impressed with his desire to see me. Danny—yes. He had defied the law and risked arrest to have his son, but manifested, up until now, no such desire for his daughter.

I close my eyes and reconstruct the alleyway behind the bakery on Callow Avenue in town. OurFather's shiny black car with the whitewall tires spinning in place and spewing dirt and gravel while he shouts for Gemma to "Hurry, hurry before someone sees me" repeats behind my lids. I see his eyes, wild with fear (anger, danger), the whites flashing in the late morning sunshine slanting down as it rises over the two-story buildings running north and south along Callow. I see his face distorted with the shouting and Danny's face white with fear and Gemma with her hair down now and hanging in her face— and that is how I remember them, and I do not want to see either of them again. My Gramma B is his mama, and she has pictures of OurFather hanging on the wall in her bedroom. She has a picture of my mama and Danny and me, but she does not have a picture of Gemma. OurFather smiles with his mouth in those pictures, but not with his eyes—at least not in the picture where he wears the Army Officer uniform. I ask my Gramma B if he is still in the Army and she says no, that they let him out. My Grampa B says he is a coward, and the Army did not want him. Gramma says, "Oh, Andy, don't talk like that," and Grampa B says that it is the truth. But Mama is talking now, and I stop daydreaming and listen.

"Don't you think I've thought of that every second since you brought that damned letter out here?"

I was in my usual spying-on-the-grownups position, huddled quiet as a mouse between the refrigerator and the cookstove, keeping my mouth shut and my ears open. I must have reacted to Mama's language slip, as she reached over with her foot and gave me a little shove. "Out with you, Cookie. This is grownup stuff."

I reluctantly slunk around into the playroom, but as soon as Mama and her sister returned to the matter at hand, I sidled close enough to the door to resume listening.

"Apparently, he wants you to deliver them to him in San Francisco." Mama read aloud from the list of instructions included with the ticket money. "Well, that is not going to happen. IF I decide the children will visit him, I will be the one to deliver them. After Hal and I discuss this, I think I'll have a little talk with the judge."

I wasn't privy to her conversation with Daddy, but they must have decided (after a consult with the family attorney) that it was in everyone's best interests if Mama took us to California; OurFather was informed of the change in delivery plans. I did hear at least one end of the conversation, brief as it was on long distance, that Mama had with him. On more than one occasion, she held the receiver far away from her ear as he shouted into the other end. Danny and I listened with horrified fascination as he finally acquiesced to Mama's plan.

In the end, our great aunts (OurFather's aunties) tossed in enough additional money so that when Mama, Danny, and I boarded the train, we had our own stateroom with bunks for the three of us to sleep in (semi) comfort. We spent the night before departure with Daddy's mama, who lived in Tacoma fairly close to the train station. Robbie would be staying with her for the duration of our trip so that Daddy could work and take care of the home front without a small child under foot.

It is morning now, and we are all standing on the platform in the early morning, fog shifting around us in fat wisps, waiting for the sound of the whistle and the thumping of the engine. I can feel the wood beneath my feet vibrate as the train wheels, down the track and just out of sight in the swirling fog-mist, rumble the metal track and transmit up my legs to my tummy. Danny leans out over the track and Daddy yanks him back with one hand, his other keeping tight hold of Robbie's overall straps. Mama is sitting on the large suitcase that holds most of our clothes, her feet resting on the small ditty bag containing cosmetics and hairbrushes and toothbrushes. Now the fog lifts a little and pale sunshine breaks through just as the train finally pulls into the station and huffs to a stop. Wheels squeal and jets of air spout from the brake boxes and the stack on top of the huge black engine blows steam.

"Just like the movies," says Danny as he tries to pry Daddy's restraining hand from his shoulder. "Leah, did you see the engineer? He waved at me!"

I think that the engineer waves to everyone as he slows the train to a stop in front of Mama and Daddy and their three squealing children. We are alone on the tracks, our family, the only passengers waiting to climb the little ladder stairs that the man (conductor, Daddy calls him) brings from inside the train car and puts on the ground. Daddy kisses Mama and gives me a hug and tousles Danny's hair, then passes our suitcase up to the conductor. Mama pries Robbie loose from her skirts and hands him to Daddy. She gives him a quick kiss on his forehead. I do not think Robbie knows he is not going with Mama. He is being too good!

Finally, we were on the train. At the last minute, Danny hopped back down to pick up Mama's small ditty bag sitting forlornly at the foot of the stair. As he scampered back to his seat, the conductor swung up with stairs in hand and signaled our departure.

Slowly, the train pulled away from Daddy and Robbie. Mama waved frantically and laughed as she blew kisses to her boys left behind—Daddy and Robbie, left on their own while the three of us began our big adventure.

Presently, a blue-uniformed man with chocolate bar skin and shiny black eyes that smiled along with the rest of his face took Mama's bags and escorted us down the aisle between rows of half-empty seats and opened the door to the following car. This one had no seats—instead, little cubicles with curtains to shut them off from prying eyes ran down both sides. Mama said they were sleepers, little spaces for people to rest for the night (or whenever they became tired of looking out the windows). Personally, I couldn't imagine growing bored with those windows. It was as if the train stood still and a never-ending panoply of trees and fields full of cows and horses, rivers, and sounds and rows of automobiles streamed past, each with its own story to tell.

After a short walk down the aisleway, the conductor opened the door and we passed into a third car. Here, instead of curtained cubicles, doors opened on each side to reveal a small compartment with bench seats and a smaller cubicle with sink and toilet. Danny immediately began examining the fixtures in the minuscule toilet area. "Look, Leah!" He lifted the seat cover on the commode and pointed inside. "There ain't no water in here. When you flush the thing, you c'n see the track!"

I cautiously peered inside, astonished at his accuracy as he pulled the handle. Water streamed down the inside as a trap door opened. I could indeed briefly see the wood ties zipping along beneath us before the trap door snapped shut.

"You kids quit messin' with that thing, do you hear?" The porter shook his finger at Danny, and Mama snatched me back into our compartment and sat me down on the hard, shiny seat by the window. "Can't hardly keep kids from playin' around with stuff they ought not to," smiled the porter. With a tip of his hat, he backed out the door, handed Mama a little key, and departed.

Mama sat down abruptly on what served as a sofa and nearly slid off the slick, shiny green leather seat, catching herself at the last minute. She smiled up at Danny and me, gave us a thumbs-up, and sighed. "Well, we're off, for better or worse. Danny, do you remember the last time we rode on the train?" She patted the cushion next to her and Danny climbed up, snuggling close. "We were coming home," he muttered.

Suddenly, Danny bolted upright and turned to face Mama.

"I don't gotta stay down there, do I? I am coming **home** with you and Leah!" He emphasized the home part.

Mama's eyes squinched up as if she were trying to hold back tears. "You know I didn't want any of that to happen to you, honey. We are just visiting. In ten days' time, we will be back home with Daddy and Robbie and you will be doing your chores on the farm."

He sighed and sagged deeply into Mama. Then, his face brightened.

"If he wants someone to stay, we can always leave Leah!"

OurFather and Gemma were waiting trackside when the train rolled into the San Francisco station, thirty-six hours late. Mama was exhausted, as she had not slept much the night before. She shared the pullout bed with me, while Danny took the upper berth, a small bunk that swung out from the wall above us. He had taken a comic book to bed with him, ostensibly to read it from the small light above his pillow. Actually, he spent the greater part of the previous night snickering as he attempted to pelt me with spit wads that half the time missed their mark and ended up in Mama's hair.

While coming over the mountains dividing Oregon from northern California, our train had been stopped by an avalanche that narrowly missed it but took out the avalanche shed and covered the track ahead for a good quarter mile. It happened on what should have been our only night on the train. Danny catapulted off his berth onto Mama when the train abruptly shuddered to a halt, brakes screeching, on the snow-slicked track. He leaped over me, stepping on my legs in the process, and opened the pull-down shade covering our outside window. Mama put on her robe and popped her head out the door onto the aisle now filled with passengers in various stages of undress. Our porter appeared, doing his best to calm everyone so he could be heard.

"Everything's under control," he spoke in his calm and soothing tone, all the while motioning everyone to stay where they were. "Engine didn't leave the tracks and neither did any of the cars. O' course, we's all stuck here 'til the crew c'n get in and clear the snow off the track. Don't worry—we got plenty a food! Now, you all go back to your beds and I'll bring along some coffee and tea"—and, with a nod to Danny and me, he added— "and a little hot chocolate, too!"

The sun is up now, making all the snow sparkle like Mama's ring sparkles when the light dances off of it. It hurts my eyes to look out the window too long, and Mama says "Cookie, pull down that shade." Danny plays in our little bathroom, tossing crumbs from some leftover cookies into the sink and watching them drop to the track below. I wonder about using the toilet and if we are here for a long time, if Danny and Mama and I use it, will the track below fill up with poop. Mama says where is your brain, honey. We will be out of here soon. But I notice that she makes Danny stop poking stuff down the commode.

We walk to the dining car and take our turn waiting in line for a little table by the window where we can eat oatmeal with cream ("yes, Daniel, you will have oatmeal") and drink orange juice and watch the workers walk back and forth between the work train behind us and the one way down the track with their shovels and picks and implements for clearing snow and ice and debris from the demolished snow shed. Danny talks to everyone he can find and keeps Mama and me posted, as he calls it. He shouts to workers walking by from his opened window and reports what they say to everyone inside. Mama says to close the window, he is letting in the cold, but she laughs. Her laughter makes my heart fill up to the brim with happiness. Who cares how long we are trapped on this mountain in the snow if my mama is happy. Danny brings his head inside and makes gagging motions towards his now cold oatmeal. Mama says, "Mind your manners, young man. Whose fault is it that the oatmeal is cold? Eat it anyhow." Danny mumbles, but he picks up his spoon. He is happy, too. Every day we are trapped on the mountain is one less day he will be forced to spend with OurFather and Gemma.

But now we had arrived. OurFather's face reflected his surprise at seeing Mama. "I was under the impression that Nor was bringing the children, Mayleen. What are you doing here?"

"Apparently, you were mistaken," Mama retorted. "And, for your information, here is a court order, restraining you from keeping the children from accompanying me back to Washington when the visit is finished."

OurFather backed away from the proffered papers in Mama's outstretched hand as if she were holding a live rattlesnake. "If you don't take the envelope, you won't be seeing the kids without me being present. This order is from the Superior Court right here in San Francisco." Mama's voice had just a touch of satisfaction.

"Are you gloating, Mayleen? It's not becoming of you." OurFather's face had turned crimson, his eyes burning with suppressed anger.

"No, Elton. I am merely telling you the plain truth. If you do not accept the court's conditions, then you will not be taking the children out of my presence. Believe me—the state of California is fully prepared to comply with this order."

OurFather stretched out his hand and took the envelope with contempt and loathing in his eyes. It took no imagination to see that he was planning some evil reprisal for Mama.

CHAPTER 17
In Which I Meet a New Brother and Come to Terms with Gemma

Since we were almost two days late in arriving (OurFather seemed to think it was Mama's fault and could hardly contain himself), the adults determined that Danny would have the first visit with OurFather over in Oakland while Mama and I stayed in San Francisco with Daddy's sister Marie and her husband Bill. I could get acquainted with their daughter Janet, who was close to Danny's age, and OurFather would return Danny five days hence. OurFather and I would then proceed to Oakland for a shorter visit, with him delivering me to the train station on the morning of our departure. Neither Danny nor I was thrilled with the plan.

Mama was apprehensive about letting Danny go, but Uncle Bill assured her that he had taken the matter of OurFather running off with him under advisement. Uncle Bill not only had friends who drove cabs but was well acquainted with multiple members of the San Francisco Police Department, two of whom lived in Oakland. I heard him assure Mama that OurFather's house would be watched "like a hawk over a henhouse." Cousin Janet was none too happy being saddled with a cousin two years her junior but did her best to make me feel welcome. By coincidence, Uncle Bill's sister and her family had lived catty-corner from us on Stewart Avenue, and Janet's cousins Tommy and Patsy were Danny's and my ages.

The family lives in one of a row of houses rising up a steep San Francisco street, each cuddled so close to its neighbor that even a little kid like me can stand on the common walkway between them with arms outstretched, and almost touch them both. The narrow walkway leads to an equally tiny backyard where Janet and I play when it is not raining or choked with fog. Janet has a small dog that likes to fetch a ball when we throw it, but Uncle Bill says we must take care not to let the ball get into the neighbor's yard, or out onto the steep street in front.

Bulkheads, higher and thicker than the one supporting OurGrandmother's Bremerton home, hold these houses flat on the hill. Steep steps rise from the slanting sidewalk to the front porch, with just a hint of grass between the foundation and the bulkhead. I shudder when I see those steep, long steps and remember my bumpy ride. My left index finger rubs the still white and visible scars on my upper lip.

Janet's house was heated by electric wall devices that burn hot and red. Aunt Marie said to keep away as they may burn me, but I already knew about these kinds of heaters. Last Christmas, the whole family celebrated at Daddy's sister Barbara's house on their farm northeast of Tacoma. We traveled on Christmas Eve, taking the ferry across at the Narrows, and arrived late at night to beds with cousins and the pull-out sofa for Mama and Daddy. Daddy carried Robbie directly to bed with little John, and Mama hurried Danny and me to Jimmie and Jerilyn's bunks. No one took time to explain the house rules about taking care with the horrid floor furnace that provided heat to the creaking old farmhouse. Consequently, I learned about them when I woke up early on Christmas morning and ran down the hall to climb into bed with Mama and Daddy and gaze with wonder at the stockings on the wall (they had no fireplace) filled by Santa, who got in to fill them through the unlocked front door.

I run in my bare feet and flannel nighty down the long, dark hallway, ignoring the glow that rises from the floorboards about halfway down. I see the danger when I am too close to stop and try to jump over the grid that lets heat from the furnace below up into the hallway to dissipate throughout the ground floor. As I rise in the air, my brain tells me it is too far across and I will not make it. I try to skew myself so that I will land on the thin strip of hallway running adjacent to the grid. The hot air blows my flannel nighty up around my shoulders, and when I miss the wood, my feet land plop on the superheated metal strips. My feet sizzle and my body jerks them up by reflex, and I fall on my nearly bare fanny.

My screams brought Mama and Daddy on the run, incidentally, waking the rest of the family. Daddy cursed as he examined the soles of my burned feet where blisters appeared immediately in straight lines as wide as those on the grating. Mama gasped in horror at my left buttock. My panties had scooted up, and in vivid crimson on my soft white flesh, one could see the unmistakable imprint of "Pat. Pend—4709..." raised in angry comment (reversed, of course). Aunt Barb tut-tutted at Daddy's language, applying ice to my fanny and my feet. Mama soothed on Unguentine supplied by Uncle Jim. The cousins and my brothers snickered behind their hands, Danny and Robbie receiving withering looks from Mama. Daddy's hand snaked out at Danny and bopped him on the backside before he could hop aside.

"Gaw, Daddy," he retorted, "her butt looks so funny like that I couldn't help laughing."

Mama sighed, gave me a hug, and Daddy carried me to a cushioned chair beside the tree where I spent most of the day, feet up on the ottoman, sitting sideways on the right side of my fanny.

Now, more than two months later, the blisters on my feet were healed and the red stripes were fading to brown. My fanny, however, was a different matter. I would bear those scars for years.

I absently scratch my behind as Aunt Marie warns me about leaning against the wall furnace.

Aunt Marie and Uncle Bill's house had three stories, excluding the garage built into the bulkhead under it. The main floor had a hallway, a kitchen and dining room, and the living room with big bay windows that looked out towards San Francisco Bay. According to Uncle Bill, you could almost see the water (if you had a good imagination). Upstairs, the next level held the bathroom and three bedrooms—one for Uncle Bill and Aunt Marie, the center as a guest room, and a sweet little windowed bedroom overlooking the backyard for Janet. The top floor had a playroom for Janet and an area Uncle Bill used as an office. Mama and I shared the guest room. When Danny came back, he would sleep upstairs in Uncle Bill's office. I figured this would make Mama happy, as she poked me at night and told me to please stop squirming so she could sleep.

Before I knew it, OurFather arrived unannounced with Danny in tow. "I thought you would be bringing him tomorrow morning," Mama retorted as she opened the door to a forlorn-looking Danny and his rather disgruntled biological male parent.

"He says his stomach is bothering him and I don't need a sick kid right now. Where's Cookie?" He caught sight of me peeking around the kitchen door. "Leah, go get your things. You're coming tonight."

"Upstairs, Danny, scoot!" Mama brushed her lips across his forehead and directed him towards the stairs. Danny had stayed here before, and he darted beyond OurFather's reach without so much as a good-bye. "I'll get her things, El, but this wasn't the agreement. You should have called."

"Long-distance costs money, Mayleen, and contrary to your family's opinion, I am not made of the stuff. Incidentally, you can have her back in three days, not the four as planned. Something came up and I don't need her hanging around. You can pick her up?"

He framed it as a demand, not the question it appeared to be. Mama bristled, but Uncle Bill put his hand on her shoulder and assured OurFather that he would personally appear on the third day to bring me back to San Francisco.

"And we can plan a day at the zoo for the kids if the weather's okay." He winked at me and Mama heaved a sigh, softening her shoulders. She wiggled the stiffness out of them as Uncle Bill gave them a quick rub.

Danny trickled soundlessly down the staircase and gave me a quick poke in the back while he hissed in my ear to keep quiet. He pulled me around the side of the staircase away from the grownups bickering in the entryway and turned me to face him.

"Gotta secret to tell you," he whispered (as quietly as it was possible for Danny to whisper), "and I ain't supposed to tell you. But I am, anyhow, just to get even with 'em." He paused for greatest effect, then continued. "Gemma and *HIM* have a new kid." Before my eyebrows could raise any further, even as my mouth began to open, his hand covered it and he continued. "It's a boy, and I ain't supposed to tell *ANY*one about him, especially Mama. *HE* said if *SHE* found out 'cuz a us, *HE* ain't gonna pay any more money for *US*."

Danny's face screwed into a look indicating both anger and anguish. He loved OurFather, but he obviously hated what he was doing. "What do you want me to do?" I whispered in his ear, trying not to spit in his hair.

"Ain't nothin' you can do, Leah, 'cept don't let on I told'ja. Act like it's a big surprise."

Mama came around into the hall just then and indicated I should get my coat from where it hung on one of the hooks that marched in a straight row down the staircase side. I gave Danny a nod and a wink, put on my coat, and walked out to the entry hall where my little suitcase stood. Taking it up with my left hand, I surrendered my right to OurFather. Without a word, he dragged me out the door and down the steps to his waiting car.

And now I am here in Oakland at OurFather and Gemma's little white cottage surrounded by the white picket fence. It is mid-morning and I have met my new "brother" James (called Scooter by Gemma and OurFather). Scooter is almost two years old and still wears diapers that droop down to his knees and keep his plastic pants rounded out like some crazy balloon. He squishes as he moves around and smells bad. OurFather has gone off to work at the Mare Island Shipyard, and Gemma has gone back to bed after making his breakfast, drinking a cup of coffee and smoking a cigarette. Scooter is bouncing up and down in his crib and I am confined to the bedroom we share. My stomach growls and Scooter whines and throws his empty bottle at me. I duck and it hits the wall, dropping down to the wood floor with a loud thud. Gemma pounds on the wall from her bedroom and tells us to "shut the hell up" and "stop makin' so much noise so I can sleep." Scooter gets a funny, almost scared look on his face and plops down on his now poopy diaper, making a squishing sound.

I am old enough to get this little kid some milk, I think, and find a cracker or something to keep my tummy from growling, so I pick up his bottle from the floor and reach for the doorknob. It turns, but the door will not open. I try again, then put down the bottle and use both hands on the knob. It is useless. The door is locked, and Scooter and I are trapped inside the bedroom.

Now I am scared. What if the house catches on fire? Or Gemma forgets we are here and leaves us all day long? I have to go to the bathroom, and I cannot hold it much longer. My bladder is damaged from so many infections, and it is unhappy at the moment. Now that I know I cannot get to the bathroom, I have to go **RIGHT NOW!**

I turn from the door and look towards the small window on the south wall, skulking behind the dirty curtains pulled tight to keep out the light. I pull them open and let the shade *up a little, allowing bright sunlight to penetrate the darkness. Scooter laughs and reaches toward the light. I wonder why this kid has no words at his age. I do not think he is stupid—maybe no one talks to him.*

The window is shut tight and I cannot push it up as hard as I try, and I cannot reach the top of this pane where I can see a lock. Scooter and I are truly stuck here until Gemma releases us from our prison. I return to the door and knock on it as hard as I can, a rapid tattoo of rap, rap, rap, and I rattle the doorknob. From the next room, I hear someone (Gemma?) rustling around, and finally the doorknob rattles and turns. The door swings open hard, nearly knocking me down, and Gemma drags herself in. Scooter immediately reaches out, chattering something unintelligible.

"Can't you be quiet?" she snarled in my direction. "I like to sleep in. Your old man don't care, so long as I have his coffee and eggs ready in the morning. And you, young man, why're you still makin' a mess in your shorts?"

I do not wait for an answer from Scooter as I dart out the door and down the hall.

Gemma had James cleaned up before I left my hiding place in the bathroom. It seemed wise to let her calm down before I put myself within her reach. I didn't know her and didn't trust her not to make me the object of her obvious anger. The clock on the kitchen wall showed the time as after eleven in the morning when I quietly tiptoed through the open door. Gemma had Scooter in his highchair, a bowl of cold cereal, no milk, sitting on the (dirty) wood tray. Mama wouldn't approve, I told myself. Robbie's tray was metal, and it always sparkled. Scooter picked at the dry cereal with his hands, alternately eating it and tossing it on the sticky floor.

"You wanna bowl of Corn Soya, the box is on the table. Milk's in the fridge." Gemma rolled her eyes in the direction of the Frigidaire squatting in the corner. I could see the dust balls lurking behind it. Someone needed to take a broom and a mop to this kitchen. I could hear OurGrandmother's voice in my head, tut-tutting the dirty dishes stacked in the sink.

I took the proffered cereal and covered it with the just turning milk from the bottle on the refrigerator's top shelf. Gemma saw my nose twitch, and grumbled about picky kids, but didn't seem to mind herself as she poured some into her coffee along with a huge spoonful of sugar. Maybe the sugar would cover up the funny taste, I thought. But it didn't.

After I ate what I could of the cereal, my bowl joined the remains of several other meals awaiting washing in the sink and I went down the hall to dress myself. I smoothed the covers (no sheets) on the twin bed mattress next to Scooter's crib and then brushed my teeth and hair in the little bathroom, returning to the kitchen in time to see Gemma release her son from the confines of his chair. "Now you go outside and play with your sister." She opened the back door and escorted both of us outside into a grey and gloomy late winter Oakland noontime. I had a pretty good feeling that the Corn Soya was supposed to last me until dinner. At least it was warm enough to play without my coat, but James seemed downright cold. He looked at me and started to cry. I put my arm around him and promised to take care of him.

I stand in OurFather's backyard on the spikey California grass and think that this is not grass for bare feet and I am glad that I have on my brown shoes that Mama always makes me wear—brown Buster Browns ("Hi, I'm Buster Brown I live in your shoe—that's my dog Ty, he lives in here, too!") with shoestring ties and heavy socks so I will not get another kidney infection. I say that the shoes do not keep me healthy, but Mama says that cold feet will make me sick. At any rate, the grass here feels sharp and pokes my hand. Scooter has no shoes, and he bounces from foot to foot, crying and pounding on the back door, but Gemma ignores him. I can see through the kitchen window that she is washing the dishes and I can hear that she is listening to the radio. Pepper Young's Family is on and she is chewing gum (Juicy Fruit in the yellow package with the shiny silver wrapper on each piece) and humming to herself as she washes the dishes.

A cloud rolls over us and spits raindrops onto my head and Scooter cries harder but Gemma ignores him. Finally, she is finished with dishes and looks out to her baby boy and her stepdaughter huddling on the back stoop. I try to keep Scooter dry as he cries on my shoulder. His nose is snotty and the gooey stuff smears on my face while he snuggles close for comfort. He is not like Robbie—he does not smell nice, but he is just a little boy and he appears to have no one to care for him.

At last, the back door opened, and Gemma let us in. She took James away to the bathroom, changed his diaper, and dressed him in clean pants and a little grey sweater. "Go brush your hair, Leah, and freshen up. Your father will be home soon and you don't want him to be angry, do you?" I did as she asked, in silence. I had not spoken a word to her all that day.

Presently, we heard a car coming up the driveway. The door opened and closed with a slam, and OurFather's face appeared in the little window on the back door. James froze in his tracks, his little face and big eyes signaling his apprehension at OurFather's homecoming. I was almost happy to see him, after the day I had had, but didn't think he would do anything about it. At least, dinner smelled pretty good, and my stomach growled in anticipation.

OurFather plopped his large black lunch pail down on the kitchen counter, along with an equally large silver thermos with a black cap/cup. It teetered for a moment before righting itself. He gave Gemma a kiss, and, almost as an afterthought, pecked me on the cheek. Scooter received a nod as he toddled into the kitchen. "What's for dinner?"

Gemma lifted the lid from a frying pan filled with grilled liver. My heart nearly stopped beating in my chest. "Not liver," my stomach screeched to my head, "anything but liver!"

I despise liver. I have been anemic for most of my life and the doctors order Mama to serve me liver at least twice a week. The liver is barely cooked and looks like bloody inner tubes. Even though she cooks bacon with it, the nearly raw liver sticks in my throat and makes me nauseous. "Please, God," I pray as we sit down to eat, "please help me to choke some of this liver down my throat." Somehow, I know that OurFather will make me clean my plate. I can only pray that he will let me fill it myself.

Dinner is not pleasant at OurFather and Gemma's table. She fills my plate and Scooter's plate and her own. She uses a generous hand with the liver for herself and Scooter. My plate is skimpy. I am secretly delighted, but OurFather notices and asks her why she has not served me a bigger portion. She reaches for my plate and I say no, no, that is enough. I am not hungry. OurFather gives me the same patented beetle brow look that Danny uses on me. Now I know where he learned it. I smile at him and pretend to eat my liver.

I can see in his eyes he is debating whether to force the issue, but he does not. He serves himself from the platter, taking the rest of the bacon rashers and most of the mashed potatoes. He eyeballs the green beans, boiled to a mush, and passes them by. It is his plate, and he is the king of his castle and he eats what he wants. The rest of us eat what is served.

As he tucks into his liver, he asks me if I had a nice day with my brother and my mother. I do not say anything as I am trying not to vomit up the liver. I try to swallow it without chewing and have not cut this piece quite small enough. I take a drink of water (not milk, like at home) and fool it down. OurFather has not forgotten his question and repeats it. I say that I have not talked to Mama or Danny today.

He stops, the mashed potatoes piled high on his fork halfway to his mouth, and glares at me. "I am talking about your brother James and your mother who is sitting across the table from you." His eyes dare me to defy him. I put down my fork and fold my hands in my lap. If he kills me quickly, I will not have to eat more liver. His hand snakes towards me and I flinch back, instinctively avoiding him. I have not seen him take his hand to Mama, but I have heard Danny tell of it and I do not think he will spare me. He stops his hand just short of my cheek, and, instead, ruffles my hair.

"Well, answer me, Cookie. How was your day?"

I can tell him the truth—that his new son sits all day in poopy diapers and his pajamas until four pm, and his wife sleeps until noon while the children go hungry—or I can say the minimum required to extricate myself without telling a lie.

I squinch my eyes up until my I-won't line appears between them, and I said:

"Scooter and I played outside all afternoon."

"—and your mother?"

I can accept Scooter as my brother. I have heard about adoption and I see he is too young to remember if his birth mama gave him away in some stranger's kitchen. But Gemma is not MY mama, and I will not give her the honor of naming her so. This woman has snatched my brother and me and has left me next to the garbage cans in an alley. I do not know **what** *to call her, but it will not be* **"mama.** *"*

"I didn't talk to Mama today," *I say in my meekest little girl voice with my eyes lowered and my hands clasped modestly in my lap.* "I didn't know you had a telephone."

OurFather's face goes bright red and his little moustache twitches beneath his thin, patrician nose. He always looks as if he smells something bad. "Gemma is your mother now, Leah, and if I choose not to give you back to Mayleen, she will be your mother forever."

My heart freezes into a tiny lump in my chest and almost stops beating. I hear myself breathing in little gasps, but I do not open my mouth and let that one word out. If I die tonight, I will go to Heaven and be with Jesus and Johnny—and I will not have to eat the rest of the liver on my plate. I do not know exactly what to call Gemma, but I do know it will never be MAMA!

OurFather rose to his feet, towering over me, and practically spat in my face. "Leave the table, Leah. Go to your room. You will not eat until you acknowledge Gemma as your mother."

"Aha," I thought as I folded my napkin and put it beside my mostly full plate, "I won't have to finish the liver," and I excused myself and went to the little room I shared with my new brother James.

In the end, he did return me to Aunt Marie and Uncle Bill's house in San Francisco. I spent most of my time in Oakland in that little bedroom eating bread and water and speaking only when asked a direct question. OurFather declared me the most defiant child he had ever met, but spared me the rod, he said, only because my mother would surely have him arrested if he left a mark. Personally, he could have beaten me to death, and it would have hurt less than his words. I never told my mother the things he said about her and my daddy Hal, or how he laughed when he compared her to Gemma.

Shortly after we returned home, his precious Gemma took James and left him, and I never saw my adopted brother or Gemma again.

The Bible tells us to Honor thy father and thy mother—it's one of the Ten Commandments from God. But to which father and mother does God refer? What's a little kid to think, when the father who did the begetting and the father who does the loving are not the same? I decided very early that love trumps biology; and as for mothers, the only one that really counts is the one who tends you all night through when you are sick, even when you throw up on her favorite sweater.

CHAPTER 18

In Which a Friend is Lost and the Die is Cast

In the months that followed our return from California, the Nelsons seemed to spend every spare minute with us, with Mimi determined to separate me from my bear! On one memorable visit, I caught her stuffing Winter Bear under her coat. "Someday I'm gonna have me that bear," she muttered as I confiscated her contraband and returned it to my room.

"She's a thief," I complained to Mama, "just a rotten little thief!"

"She's only a little girl, honey, and she doesn't have a toy as nice as your bear."

Mama always seemed to take her side. She even insisted that I let Mimi play with him as long as she liked when they visited. By Mama's rule, we shared our things with guests—no questions asked! If a toy were special or easily broken, she might let us put it up while visitors were about, but for some reason, Winter Bear didn't seem to fall into one of her categories. He was, after all, just a stuffed animal, she said, and for all I had kept his creamy white mohair fur clean and tidy, she didn't see why I would begrudge Mimi a chance to play with him during visits. All the "but Mama's" in the world wouldn't budge her. She thought I was being selfish and threatened to take Winter Bear away from me altogether.

Danny was no help. He was stuck with Little Fritz. Although Fritzie didn't break Danny's trucks and planes, he had actually taken Danny's favorite B-29. Mr. Nelson returned it to Daddy at the shipyard, who brought it back. Danny, much to his chagrin, had to apologize to Robbie for accusing him of making off with the plane.

"At least you caught her before she got out of the house," Danny complained when we were alone. "I'm still in trouble for blamin' Robbie!"

Shortly after I started second grade, Daddy broke his leg. When he came home from the hospital, he had a cast up above his knee and couldn't work in the shipyard for several weeks. Times were tough—soldiers and sailors were returning from the Korean conflict and needed jobs. Mr. Nelson had been laid off from the shipyard, and Daddy was afraid that he would follow suit if his leg didn't heal quickly! Eventually, Mr. Nelson obtained a position with the Milwaukee Railroad, maintaining the engines at the roundhouse in Harlowton, Montana. Mrs. Nelson and the children stayed with us while Big Fritz worked and looked for housing close to his job.

Life became a contest between Mimi and me with Winter Bear as the prize! Mimi was no longer exactly a guest, but since she was younger than I, Mama's rules still applied. "It's not fair," I opined to Mama one afternoon when we found ourselves alone in the kitchen. "She's always gonna be younger than me, and even if they live with us forever, she'll always be some kinda guest!"

"Don't whine, Leah, it's not attractive. God willing, Mr.

Nelson will find a house for them soon! I bet you'll miss having a girl around to play with when they're gone." I thought that highly unlikely but kept the opinion to myself.

Mimi had recently recovered from a sore throat, chills, and fever that kept her confined to the double bed we shared. Under duress from Mama, I let her keep Winter Bear as company. In the process, he acquired several unsightly spots that were proving difficult to remove. Even Mama couldn't eliminate them. More worrisome than the spots, however, was Mimi's proprietary attitude towards him! She now acted as if the bear belonged to her, as if my act of forced kindness during her illness gave her some sort of squatter's rights over my friend. We drew battle lines in our silent tug-o-war, with Winter Bear as the prize.

Halloween passed, and as the days shortened inexorably towards Thanksgiving, Mimi developed a low-grade fever and malaise that came and went, keeping her home from kindergarten and insuring more time with my bear. I was certain she was "fakin' it." Danny said that big kids like him (he was a lofty fifth-grader) did that kind of thing all the time to get out of tests at school. Mama just shook her head when I voiced my suspicions to her. "She's got some kind of a bug she just can't shake, honey. We're not sure what's wrong with her, but she's not 'fakin' it,' Danny, and I'd better not hear any more of that nonsense out of you!"

Thanksgiving came and went. The week before school let out for Christmas vacation, Mr. Nelson phoned with great news! He was on his way back to Washington with the key to a house in his pocket. The Nelsons (and not a moment too soon for me) had a home of their own, a small white clapboard two-bedroom on the far side of town, close enough so the kids could walk to school. Mimi perked right up, Little Fritz's face split with a smile, and Verna Lee, who had grown increasingly more silent as the weeks dragged on, had a spring back in her step.

Mr. Nelson showed up on Christmas Eve, "looking like something the cat dragged in," opined Mama. The old Willys Jeep he drove had broken down just this side of the Idaho border in a driving snowstorm, the worst of the year. He had been hard put to find parts to get it back on the road. He intended to pack up kids, household goods, and the family cat as soon as possible, waiting only long enough for Santa to fill the long row of stockings tacked to the fireplace mantle.

"If you have a few days to rest, Fritz," proposed Daddy, "I'll hitch a trailer to the Ford and help you with the move." He had an appointment on the day after Christmas to have his cast shortened below the knee, making it much easier for him to get around. Mr. Nelson sighed deeply and took Daddy up on his offer.

Christmas morning came and went. I was disappointed when Santa failed to fulfill my request. I had written my first (and last) letter to the old gnome weeks before, electing to skip my own presents if he would please bring Mimi a bear of her own. Instead, her stocking held a Raggedy Ann doll with her crazy quilt smile and curly red hair. Daddy seemed puzzled by my lack of enthusiasm for the bright blue bicycle I had been after for months, and Mama inquired as to my health. "I hope you're not coming down with Mimi's strep throat, honey," she murmured, feeling my forehead anxiously. Daddy just harrumphed and sucked on his pipe.

December 27th dawned clear and crisp, a perfect day for towing the fully packed trailer hitched behind our old Ford Elizabeth. Daddy took off for Montana just after breakfast with one of Mama's packed food baskets and a huge thermos of black coffee. He planned to make the drive as quickly as possible, hopefully arriving at the same time as the Nelsons, who were detained an additional day by Mimi's recurring fever. They could take turns and drive straight through, unlike Daddy, who would need to stop along the way.

That last night of the Nelson's long stay proved particularly difficult. Mimi lay snuggled between her parents in a makeshift bed on the playroom floor. From my bedroom, I could hear her sobs punctuated by pleas for Winter Bear. Raggedy Ann landed with a thump against my bedroom door. I lay in my own warm bed, my bear held close between my arms, gloating. Snatches of conversation between Mama and Mrs. Nelson filtered through the door crack. I heard mama say, "Leah's asleep—I hate to wake her up."

*"Mama's really on my side," I think with relief. A wave of charity sweeps through me. After all, this **is** Mimi's last night, and she is only six. I am a grownup eight (having celebrated my birthday the day before), and I, for once, am not sick this Christmas holiday. Taking my precious bear, I rise from bed and open the door.*

"Here ya go, Mimi—you can sleep with him tonight," I offer. "I will get him in the morning." Mimi brightens immediately and holds out her arms. A warm glow spreads through me as Mama smiles and nods her head in approval. As I return to my room, I pick up the cast aside Raggedy Ann and sit her against the wall, thinking that Mimi will soon transfer

her affections in that direction—as soon as she is well on the road to Montana. I sleep the sleep of the righteous the whole night through!

The next morning, Mama didn't wake me. I roused to the sound of good-byes drifting through my bedroom window. Mama, Danny, and Robbie stood on the back steps waving as the Nelson's Jeep and U-Haul headed up the long drive towards Werner Road. I erupted from the bed and grabbed my robe. From the corner of my eye, I spotted Mimi's doll, still propped demurely against the playroom wall. I snatched it up and bolted towards the back door, catapulting out into the driveway while waving Raggedy Ann by her bright red hair.

"Mama," I gasped, "Mimi forgot her doll!" Mama's face wore that worried look she reserved for perplexing problems. "Is something wrong?" I queried. She knelt down and grasped me by the arms.

"I don't know how to tell you this, Leah, but Mimi left the doll for you."

"Why would she do that—won't she need something to take to bed?"

"The truth is," Mama murmured, almost too low for me to hear, "that Mimi has Winter Bear to keep her company on the long ride to Montana." I jerked myself away from my mother, hot disbelief flooding through me.

"No, Mama—that can't be true," I exclaimed, "you wouldn't let that happen, would you?" My eyes searched Mama's face seeking some evidence of repudiation. All I saw was the hint of tears.

"It is, Leah—I had to let her take the bear! She's sick, honey, really sick, and I just couldn't take Winter Bear away from her." Then she uttered that phrase every little kid hates to hear. "You'll understand when you're older, honey—someday you'll understand. Besides, it's just temporary—Daddy'll bring him home for you. You can get by for a few days, can't you?" Her eyes searched my own for understanding, but there was none in my heart. I looked down at the hated Raggedy Ann clutched in my hands and pitched it as far as I could up the driveway in the direction my wonderful bear, my best friend forever, had disappeared in the arms of the enemy.

"No, Mama, I do not understand," I mutter. Down deep inside, I know that my kindhearted Daddy will never take Winter Bear away from some sick little kid. I will never see him again and my own mother has betrayed me.

Time passes, of course, and I eventually retrieved a rather bedraggled Raggedy Ann from the mud. Mama washed and ironed her dress and pinafore and cleaned her up as best she could. Some animal had chewed one side of her face, nibbling off half her smile and leaving her forever lopsided and scarred. I loved her, after a fashion—it wasn't her fault that she could never replace my wonderful bear companion. Ultimately, I forgave my mama, too, but never forgot that parents are fallible.

Over the years, Daddy and Mama kept in touch with the Nelsons. Big Fritz came out several times to hunt and fish with Daddy, occasionally bringing Little Fritz. At first, I eagerly queried them on word of Winter Bear, half hoping that Mimi would send him back. Eventually, Mama grew weary of the whole thing and forbade me speaking of the matter—the issue was closed, she said, and it was time to move on. I stopped asking, but as far as I was concerned, the subject was still, and would forever be, open!

CHAPTER 19
In Which I Begin to Learn About Family Dynamics

The year we moved to the farm, Mama petitioned the court to allow OurFather to return home. Danny and I saw him perhaps once a month. He was no longer married to Gemma, who, according to Mama, had failed to divorce a previous husband, so had entered into an unlawful alliance with OurFather. No one mentioned our adopted brother James, not even OurFather's Bremerton relatives. I later learned that only OurFather's mother knew of his existence, as OurFather sent checks every month to Gemma through Grammy. Well—*officially* they did not know. I heard my Great Auntie Gert remarking to her sister, Alma, that it was a pity that Mama didn't take him back to court as she and Hal could surely use the money OurFather was supposed to send her each month for our support. She was unimpressed with OurFather's response that he wasn't about to pay for a dead horse. If Hal were willing to pay for Danny and me, then let him do so! It galled her that he was paying for an "imaginary" adopted child but refused to pay for the two that bore his blood.

Now that the war was over and he was no longer happy with his California home, he wished to re-establish his position at the Bremerton Shipyard, bringing with him his new wife, our stepmother NINE-a. Her parents also lived in the Bremerton area and (supposedly) needed her help. He promised Mama to pay his court-ordered child support for Danny and me and to leave our family in peace. Danny and I overheard several discussions between Mama and Daddy concerning his return to town. Mama believed his entreaty, but Daddy had his doubts. Time would tell which of them had the right of it, but in the end, Daddy relented and backed Mama's efforts with the courts.

Consequently, OurFather and his new bride bought property in Navy Yard City, just up the hill from the little McCall Blvd house where we lived when he left Mama for Gemma. He brought his NINE-a to the farm and introduced her to Mama and Daddy, then had Danny and me brought out to parade before her. She smiled widely at us with her mouth, but her eyes didn't reflect any joy at meeting OurFather's offspring. She appeared far more interested in Robbie than in the two of us, and actually got down on the floor and played blocks with him. Mama offered coffee and cookies to NINE-a while Daddy took his once best friend down to the barn to show off our new Guernsey dairy cow. The two men reached detent, but no matter how hard Mama tried, NINE-a remained aloof. Daddy thought that she was jealous of Mama, but how could that be? She had moved on with Daddy, and OurFather was on his second wife since that nasty day when I was scarcely three months old and Gemma made her pronouncement.

NINE-a and OurFather built a garage/apartment on their Madrona Street property and began living there while they made plans for a permanent home overlooking the shipyard. Soon thereafter, Danny and I began spending one weekend a month visiting. Separately, of course, as they had no room for the both of us, and that would give NINE-a time to bond, whatever that meant. Apparently, she was not unhappy that OurFather could not give her children, as she could practice mommy skills at her own pace, then send the child home so she could recover. She also had several nieces, produced by her various sisters who lived in town, and she had a much better time nurturing them.

The first Christmas OurFather and NINE-a were back in town, they picked up Danny and me to spend Christmas Eve at our Great Aunt Mick and Uncle George's house not too far from our little farm. Aunt Mick and Uncle George had two boys of their own, OurFather's first cousins, who were a little younger than Danny and me. The Great Aunts all referred to them as Dear-Sammy and Dear-Jimmy. I thought it odd that their names both started with "Deer" until Danny pointed out to me (with that big brother boy-are-you-stupid look) that the aunties were calling them "dear."

Not one of them had EVER called me Dear-Leah. My own dear Grammy often called me her sweet Cookie, but never as part of my name.

Danny held his hand to conceal his mouth from the grownups and stuck out his tongue at Dear-Sammy, who was particularly obnoxious. He sat close to the enormous Christmas tree that swept the cathedral ceiling of the grand living room, examining the enormous pile of brightly papered gifts. Dear-Jimmy sat on the raised hearth beside a crackling fire, playing with the family dog, a small snarly animal with a pushed-in face. NINE-a called it a Pug. I stood, riveted to Danny's side, thinking about Mama and Daddy at home with Robbie, around our own small Christmas tree, hanging stockings in anticipation of Santa's arrival. OurFather had swept in unannounced and demanded that Mama dress us in "something appropriate" so that he would not be embarrassed to present us to the Great Aunts.

Daddy bristled, but Mama hushed him, murmuring that it was, after all, his first Christmas with the children, and that, in fact, he had never spent a Christmas Eve with me. As Mama pushed us off towards the bedroom, I heard Daddy invite NINE-a in for a cup of coffee while they waited. She, apparently, preferred to stay in the car. OurFather, however, settled himself at Mama's kitchen table and tucked into coffee with cream from our dairy cow and one of Mama's cinnamon rolls with raisins. Daddy filled his pipe and watched, as dinner was on the stove, filling the house with delicious smells of oven-fried chicken.

Danny squirmed while Mama gave his face a quick spit bath and buttoned his shirt up to the neck. "I'm not gonna get any of that chicken, am I—and Leah, neither. I'm hungry. Why can't we eat before we have to go, huh? And Leah and me don't even know anyone who's gonna be there." Danny seldom whined, but he was making a rare old fuss today.

"Quit moving around, young man. I want you to look good—and behave yourself, you hear? I'll save you some chicken, but your great Aunt Mick will have something for everyone to eat."

She finally let Danny go and turned to me. "Well, young lady, you look nice. Let me have a go at your hair." She slipped through my Dutch bob with the hairbrush, making me pull back my head as the bristles dug into my scalp. "Be a good girl, honey. Hold still while I put a clip in." She was always trying to do pretty things with my fine, blonde hair, but the clips and bows and ribbons just slipped out. She sighed, took me by the shoulders, and gave me a good going over with her eyes. "That will have to do," she said as she turned me around and motioned for the two of us to leave the room.

"Why do we have to go, Mama?"

"Your father wants to spend the evening with his children, with his family, and they are your family, too. Grandma B will be there, I'm sure, and you know Great Aunt Alma and Uncle Al. Great Aunt Mick is nice, and the boys are about your age. You should get to know your cousins."

"Well, I don't wanna know 'em," Danny snarled, curling his upper lip and wrinkling his nose, "and I bet they don't wanna know me 'n Cookie, either."

We had lived all our lives in the same town with Sam and Jim and had seen them only once when our Grandma B was taking care of them for her youngest sister Martha, known to the family as Mickey. Great Aunt Mick was a schoolteacher, and she and her husband, George, had waited a long time to have children. Although the boys were first cousins to OurFather, they were one and three years younger than I was, making them far too young to appeal to Danny.

Mama, finally approving of our general appearance and having briefed us on what the results of an unhappy Christmas Eve event with OurFather held for us, jack-marched Danny out to the kitchen, trailing me behind like a kite in the wind.

"It's about time," OurFather commented as he swiveled his

wrist to catch sight of his watch face. "Aunt Mick will have a fit if we hold up the festivities. Grab your coats and we're off." Without so much as a good-bye to Mama and Daddy, he yanked me by the hand and pushed Danny ahead of him out the kitchen door, through the mud porch and down the stairs to NINE-a and the waiting car. "I'll have them back about ten," he shouted as Mama stood waving to us from the back stoop.

He stuffed the both of us into the back seat of his car, which still smelled new. "Don't get your feet on the seat, and don't make a mess back there," OurFather ordered.

Danny snickered and whispered that he should give me a bag in case I got carsick. He had shared the back seat of our old Model A on more than one occasion when tummy trouble caused the family a problem. I pinched his arm and hissed that just going a few miles wasn't going to bother me. He grinned and whispered that maybe I should do it just because. Sometimes Danny had interesting ideas.

And so, I find myself standing next to Danny while Dear-Sammy and Dear-Jimmy parade their presents in front of us. Grandma B is not there—according to OurFather, she is spending the evening with Grampa B's family in Seattle. Great Uncle George passes around presents to everyone. I guess Santa comes early in this house or maybe does not come at all. There are no presents for Danny and me. I guess Santa will bring them to our house later tonight.

I hear Danny's stomach rumble—a sound matching mine. Great Aunt Mick does not serve us dinner, or maybe we are just late. OurFather laughs and drinks amber liquor out of a glass full of ice, a cigarette dangling from his lip. NINE-a has a drink, too. She has long nails painted red, and she holds the glass with one hand and a cigarette in the other. She smokes Pell Mells, at least that is what she calls them, although the spelling on the red package says Pall Mall. I notice this when she asks me to get her another cigarette from her package. Mama will be angry if I tell her that I was touching cigarettes.

Great Aunt Alma wrinkles up her nose at the cigarette smoke and the drink glasses. She says that it is Christmas Eve, and we should all be in church, not sitting around the house drinking booze and smoking our brains out. Aunt Mick and OurFather and Uncle George all laugh, but NINE-a looks a little ashamed.

Finally, the grownups put their drinks and smokes down when Aunt Mick announces that Dear-Sammy will play the piano for everyone. We all troop into the den at the back of the house, where a small, brown piano squats next to a glass door that looks out onto the huge backyard. We have a piano, too, although no one takes lessons. I like to pretend to play and can pick out little songs with one finger, songs like "Mary Had a Little Lamb" and "Rockabye Baby." Mama claps her hands and says I have the talent, although OurGrandmother snorts to herself about my playing.

Dear-Sammy sits at the bench, opens a piece of music, and plays a presentable song. All the adults clap and Great Aunt Alma hugs him as he sits on the bench. I clap, too. It is nice that he can play. OurFather is talking, too, and NINE-a smiles at me.

Danny poked me sharp in the ribs. "Cripes, Leah. He's talkin' about you. Listen to that!" Danny sounded indignant.

Then I hear what OurFather is saying, and I almost wet my panties. He is saying that I can play the piano. He is saying for me to get up on that shiny, slippery piano bench and play with my one finger in front of everyone. NINE-a is clapping, and OurFather is dragging me by the arm. I struggle loose from him and say that I do NOT play the piano. I have not had lessons on the piano. And then he picks me up and puts me on the bench. I begin to cry; the tears slipping silently from my eyes roll down my cheek and drop onto my dress, making little wet splotches. I hope they will not stain the cloth as Mama worked very hard to make this dress for me. I can feel my shoulders shaking and OurFather is spitting in my ear that I will play something on the piano or...and I do not hear the rest of what he is saying.

Somewhere far away, I hear grownups laughing. They are laughing at me as I sit on the piano bench and reach for the keys and try to play "Twinkle, Twinkle Little Star!"

Now I feel hands on my arms, and it is Danny, and he has put his arms around my shoulders and is helping me off the bench and he is wiping the tears from my face with the hem of his shirt. "Don't laugh at my sister," he growls.

In the distance, I hear Aunt Alma's voice taking OurFather to task for making me cry. Dear-Sammy and Dear-Jimmy and NINE-a have smirks on their faces, but Aunt Alma turns me around and holds me to her and lets me get myself under control. "Don't worry about it, little Cookie," she whispers. "No one will ever remember tonight."

That was not quite true. I never forgot that Christmas Eve. Years later, I sat at the very same piano and played a Debussy solo for Aunt Mick; it helped to take away the sting, but not the memory. I learned that some people are kind, and some are cruel, and it did not matter much whether they were family members or strangers. The hurt was the same, but I could make allowances for the strangers.

CHAPTER 20
In Which the Broken is Fixed

I entered kindergarten the fall before Johnny's death. Hatchet Annie and the summer's events lost out to new friendships and the wonders of learning. I no longer feared crossing Quaker Hill and had long since given up dreaming about hags in long black skirts who ate children. Walking to school through the cool, dappled woods with my older brother gave me new scope for imagination and ample outlet for my creative nature. Hatchet Annie might have ended up on my memory's cutting room floor had my mother not fallen and reinjured her back. She had never been quite the same since the accident a few years before had left her with permanent damage.

In late winter, after Christmas and my birthday had passed with my usual ailments, Mama became so debilitated that our family doctor sent her to Seattle to see a physician who specialized in fixing broken spines.

Mama was born during the 1918 influenza pandemic that swept the world, killing many people and damaging even more unborn children. Mama was one of those babies. OurGrandmother had had the "Spanish Flu" when she was pregnant, and Mama was born with her spine only partially surrounded by bone down by the tail end. She had a very mild form of what is now called spina bifida occulta, in which the neural tube does not completely close during fetal development.

Nobody knew that a problem existed, as Mama was born so tiny that her parents did not expect her to live. According to the family, Grandpa put her in a roasting pan lined with towels and kept her warm on the wood cookstove oven door. Her brothers called her "Hopeless" and her mother ignored her, apparently not wanting to form an attachment with a child destined for an early grave. Although Mama didn't walk until after her second birthday, she surprised them all and, although she was frail and fraught with problems with her legs, she "made it."

When it became apparent that Mama required a delicate and dangerous new surgery to repair her malformed and damaged vertebrae, Daddy made a special visit to OurGrandmother, asking her to come and help out, at least while Mama was hospitalized. He was hoping, he said, that she would volunteer to be there during Mama's recovery, since she was, after all, a nurse. OurGrandmother gave Daddy the sharp side of her tongue and sent him off in a hurry. Mama cried at this current rebuff, but Daddy held her tight and promised a solution.

OurGrandmother must have told OurFather before the sun set, as he was on the telephone to Mama first thing in the morning.

"Of course, the children must come and stay with me," he crooned. OurFather, now that Mama had had the court lift its contempt order against him, had wasted no time in contacting Mama by telephone. "If you are incapacitated for a long time or, God forbid, you shouldn't make it through the surgery, Danny and Leah belong with their *real* parent. My wife will make an excellent surrogate mother—you'll see, Mayleen. We must have a plan for the children's future, just in case..." His threat, although veiled, did not pass by Mama and Daddy.

Mama refused politely and called the courthouse. Judge Slayton issued an order preventing OurFather from making any attempt to remove Danny or me from our home. Only after being assured that we were safe, did Mama make final arrangements with the surgeons. Danny shuddered at the thought of being once again in the hands of our biological parent, and I still had the occasional bad dream of being swept away and left in an alley, although Gemma was now gone from OurFather's life, along with Scooter.

On the day Mama left for Swedish Hospital in Seattle, Daddy stayed home from work and helped her pack a small bag. Daddy drove Danny and me to school. "Just making sure you don't miss the bell," he chuckled as he walked us both up the stairs, opened the double doors for us, and marched us inside, much to Danny's embarrassment. "I know you want to stay home and see Mama off, but she is trying very hard to be brave for you kids, and it's hard for her to face this operation without remembering any teary-eyed good-byes." He aimed the last at me. I had to admit Daddy had it right. I cried all the way to the parking lot at school. Daddy took the big blue and white handkerchief from his back pocket and carefully dried my eyes, then helped me blow my nose. He gave me one of his bear hug squeezes and whispered that Mama would be okay.

He would make sure that she'd come home to us, better than ever. I think Danny had a tear himself, although he shrugged his damp eyes off to Daddy's pipe smoke.

After school, we walked together up through the woods bordering Parklane on the south, passing behind the little white picket fenced yard surrounding the one private home on the way. The trail led up a bush-covered hill and entered the woods from a narrow alleyway where the homeowner kept his trashcans and a pile of wood ready to be reduced to kindling as indicated by the stump beside it. A small hand axe embedded in the stump waited at the ready for someone to make the pieces of pine, full of pitch and all set to ignite easily, into smaller sizes to pop into a cookstove or fireplace. Daddy kept Mama's kindling pile at hand, placing the newly cut pieces in her wood basket in the mudroom.

I liked watching Mama light the shiny iron and enamel cookstove residing in our kitchen. By the next year, it would be replaced with an electric model, but for now, we relied on wood to cook our food. Mama could set a fire that burned either hot for the burners, steady for the oven, or just smothered to last overnight until she revived it for breakfast. Today, the sight of that little hatchet brought tears to my eyes.

Danny must have heard me sniffling, as he turned back and gave me his patented older brother condescending sneer. "Just shut up, Leah," he snarled. "No one needs you cryin' like a baby over a dumb axe, 'specially today." Any other time, I would have returned his snarl with one of my own, but now all I could think of was my mama in danger, far away in Seattle. I turned to face my big brother. Something in his eyes revealed a thin façade of impending manhood that prevented him from showing his own emotional turmoil. I reached out and took his hand. He tugged me close and put his arm around my shoulder. "She's gonna be okay, Leah," he whispered, echoing Daddy's promise. "Jesus wouldn't let us lose her." I thought as we walked side by side through the misting woods that Jesus might not take her away, but I wasn't so sure about God.

Aunt Dot met us at the door. Aunt Dot was married to Daddy's brother, Uncle John. She came to stay with us, bringing our cousin Chucky, who was a little younger than I was.

Mama is gone, and I am afraid that she will never come home again. I hear the grownups talking at night, Daddy and Aunt Dot and sometimes Auntie Nor. They say she may never walk again if the doctors cannot find enough bone to patch Mama's spine. I listen and cry into my pillow. Danny gets out of his bed and jabs me hard in the side and tells me to stop sniveling. Mama will be okay, he whispers in my ear. I do not think Danny is as sure as he sounds, but I let his fierceness convince me and find my way back into troubled sleep, where I dream of living with OurFather and Gemma's replacement. Robbie does not know that Mama may never come home. He just misses her and dogs Aunt Dot until she sends him out to play with Chucky.

Chucky has curly brown hair and dimples in his cheeks. He is the darling of Aunt Dot's heart and can do nothing wrong, even though he bites and kicks and pulls hair. Daddy takes me aside and makes me promise to help with the boys, as he calls Robbie and Chuck, so Aunt Dot can rest in the afternoons. It is okay when Daddy is here, but he goes over to Seattle on the ferry every weekend and stays at the hospital with Mama.

On the weekends when Daddy is gone, Uncle John comes over and helps Aunt Dot with us kids. I like this uncle. He is a schoolteacher, and he has an easy way of talking to me. When he smiles, his face has dimples, like Daddy's. He does not smoke a pipe, but he does wear Old Spice aftershave. Aunt Dot's tummy is so big that I am afraid she will burst. Daddy says she has lots of time before the baby comes, but I am not so sure. She lets me sit close to her and I can feel little hands and feet moving about inside her. "Let me tell you a secret, Cookie," she says to me. "There are two babies. When they are born, Chucky will have to be a big brother to two little sisters or brothers." I smile up at her and say I will keep her secret. (Cousins Fred and Frank were born early, just two weeks after Mama came home from the hospital.)

School drags by, although I love Miss Benson's classroom. My best friend and I sit next to each other at our brown desks with the wrought iron sides and a hole for an inkwell on the top. Other kids have carved their initials on the surface, making it bumpy. I try not to let my mind wander. Miss Benson asks me about Mama, and I tell her I do not know when she will come home (if she will come home). Miss Benson cups my face with her hand and smiles into my eyes and says she will pray for my mama.

Since I can already read the Alice and Jerry book, Miss Benson has me help some of the other kids with learning. She says it will take my mind off of Mama. I try to keep my mind on school, but it is hard.

Daddy came home from work on the third Friday following Mama's surgery bursting with smiles.

"Hey, kids," he blurted out as soon as the back door closed behind him, "do you all want to go to Seattle tomorrow and see your mother?" Danny grinned so big I thought his face would split, and Robbie screamed with delight.

"Cookie—why no happy face?" Daddy came over and gave me a special squeeze. I could smell his Prince Albert tobacco mixed with Old Spice aftershave. It comforted me, and I put my head on his shoulder.

"Is Mama really gonna be okay, Daddy?" I whispered.

He snuggled close and whispered back, "Yes, honey. The doctors think she will be fine."

I sighed and sagged into Daddy's arms.

In the morning, we rose earlier than usual, did our chores, and ate a quick breakfast—at least Daddy and Danny ate. I had a sip of Coke syrup and some water since riding in the car for any distance made me nauseous, and as a "just in case" the ferry ride to Seattle was rough. I had never been sick on the ferry before, but Aunt Dot said why should we take any chances. Daddy had Elizabeth ready at the back door. We piled in, Daddy, Danny and me. At the last minute, the grownups deemed Robbie too young for visiting in the hospital, so he stayed behind, wiping his nose with the back of his hand and hanging on to Aunt Dot's skirt.

We made the 8:00 am ferry, hiked up to the passenger deck, and settled down for the hour-long ride across the Sound to Seattle. The water was a little rough with whitecaps punctuating the grey-green waves tossed about by the wind. Clouds hung low and grey, occasional clear spots letting through pale yellow late winter sun. Gulls hitched rides on the railing surrounding the deck at both ends of the ferry and running in a narrow strip along the sides. Daddy sat us down at window seats. The slippery green benches faced each other. Ordering us to be on our best behavior, he left us alone for a few moments while he went to the stern, where a small kitchen dispensed coffee and soft drinks. He reappeared with a cup of brew and seated himself next to Danny, who was fogging up the window with his breath and drawing pictures of gulls.

I spent my time appearing to gaze at our progression through Rich Passage and into Puget Sound. Actually, I was trying to picture Mama in a strange bed, surrounded by nurses like the one in Dr. Haller's office at home.

His nurse wears all white—straight-skirted dresses down to her ankles, long sleeves, starched-stiff collar and cuffs, white shoes with squeaky rubber soles, long white stockings, and a funny hat perched atop her head. She always carries a thermometer in her pocket, ready to pop it into my mouth, pushing it sharply up under my tongue. Her fingers are ice cold as she takes my pulse, pressing hard on my wrist to count each beat. She has grey hair poking out under the cap, and a moustache and chin whiskers, stiff as broom straws. She never smiles but hums something under her breath that smells of coffee and mints.

I do not like the smell of Dr. Haller's office or his nurse with the hurting hands, but I do like Dr. Haller. He takes care of my family and helps to make me better when I am sick. If all of the doctors at this Swedish Hospital (like the little meatballs Mama makes with gravy) are like Dr. Haller, then my mama is in good hands. Except for the nurses. I close my eyes and see Dr. Haller's nurse taking Mama's temperature, sticking the thermometer sharp under her tongue and wagging her finger at Mama. "Don't take it out, dearie, or it won't tell us the truth."

Now Daddy is shaking me and saying Cookie, we are almost at the dock. Are you asleep? And we go back down the stairs to Elizabeth, who is waiting patiently for us on the car deck. We take our turn behind the other cars driving up the ramp between ferry and dock. Blue smoke from exhaust pipes fills the ferry with the smell of burnt gasoline. Now we are free of the ferry and its smoke. Now we start up the steep hill that separates us from Mama's room in the hospital. It is scary, driving up that hill. Daddy uses a few of the words Mama tut-tuts, but I will not tell her. He puffs on his pipe and blows his own blue smoke out the window as we teeter at a stoplight and Elizabeth threatens to roll backwards all the way to the bottom of the hill. Then the light changes and we inch forward until the back wheels level out and we are climbing the next hump.

Eventually, we arrived at Swedish Hospital—not at all like our own little clinic at home. We found Mama on the top floor in a room with a view out over the city to the waterfront, although Mama's bed was against the wall on the far side of the room. An empty bed occupied the space by the window. Mama's bed had a little table at the end sitting on long legs. A crank handle on the side allowed the nurses to raise and lower the table to fit the height of the bed. The bed itself had two cranks at the foot—one that raised the head of the bed, and one that raised the foot. Another crank on the side raised the whole bed to make it easier for the nurses and doctors to take care of Mama. It looked quite wonderful to me, although the surface where Mama was lying was level with the top of my head. Danny gave me a poke and whispered that he could give me a wild ride on that bed—and could quite likely get it to toss me out the window. Daddy gave him a fanny swat and told him to hush, then picked me up and held me high enough to see Mama.

She lies there, so pale she almost fades into the sheet (no pillow), that covers her up to mid-chest. Her arms lie atop the white woven cotton blanket, hands clasped so tightly her knuckles appear blue. Then she sees me and smiles, and her whole face lights up! Danny climbs up on the chair next to the bed and mugs at her. She laughs, gently, so as not to shake the bed. Daddy pulls Danny back with one arm, keeping him from touching Mama with his outstretched hand. "Whydja do that?" he mumbles, and Mama says that jiggling the bed hurts a little. Danny gets tears in his eyes and he carefully lowers his head and kisses her forehead. "When are you comin' home?" I ask. "We all miss you." And Mama winks at me and says "Soon, Cookie, very soon." Then Daddy puts me down and shoos Danny and me to the other side of the bed. He kisses Mama and whispers that he misses her, too.

As I climbed up into the straight-backed chair next to Mama's bed, a nurse bustled in carrying a tray with a little white paper cup filled with pills. She plopped it down on the table at the foot of the bed and poured a glass of water from the pitcher sitting there, inserting a straw into the glass. She looked a little like Dr. Haller's nurse, but her whole face smiled, and her uniform was different. She had a blue and white striped dress down to midway between her knees and her ankles, partially covered by a white pinafore, and her boat-shaped hat had a blue stripe on the brim. "Here's your pills, honey," she smiled down as she raised Mama's head just enough to pop the pills into her mouth, then held the straw so that Mama could sip enough water to swallow them down.

"That should make you feel better so you can enjoy your company." She turned to Daddy, "and don't you all stay so long that you tire her out!"

Daddy winked at her and assured her that we wouldn't be staying long. "Have a ferry to catch, and these kids'll need some food soon." Mama smiled wanly at the thought of us leaving, sighed, and said that we had just arrived. The nurse reminded Daddy that we could all eat in the cafeteria, but he shook his head.

"We needed special permission for Danny and Cookie to come see their mama today, so we won't be staying long. Thanks, though."

Danny looked at me and frowned. "Then I got to tell Mama all about what's goin' on at home!" Daddy smiled and allowed that he had better get started. The nurse laughed and, taking her little silver tray, left the room.

We spent the better part of an hour filling Mama in on all the happenings on the farm. I started to tell her about Aunt Dot's special secret, but Daddy stopped me in time. "That's between you and your aunt," he said, "not for public consumption." Mama looked at Daddy with a quizzical smile. "Later, honey. That's not for you to think about now. Just so you don't worry, it's nothing bad. Dot's gonna be fine until you get home." Mama relaxed again and turned back to Danny.

"Are you helping your auntie with the work? She has a lot on her hands." Danny answered that he was, but his crooked grin gave him away. "Cookie, I know I can count on you. Try to keep your brothers in line, will you?"

I didn't answer. Mama knew she was asking the impossible but hoped that Danny was getting the message.

Then the nurse was back, this time with another. "Time to turn you, missy," she admonished, turning to Daddy "and time for your company to leave." Daddy leaned over and kissed Mama and Danny stood on his tiptoes to do the same. Daddy picked me up out of the chair, holding me close enough to whisper in Mama's ear how much I loved her and give her a good-bye kiss. Then we were at the door, turning to wave in time to see the nurses, one on either side, adjusting Mama in the bed.

"Can't she move herself?" I inquired of Daddy as we rode down in the creaky old elevator. "She's not to do it herself, honey. That's why the nurses turn her. We don't want the bone in her spine to be dislodged." Danny asked what that meant, and Daddy explained that the surgeons had taken bone from Mama's own hip and ground it up, then packed it around her damaged spinal column to grow new bone. Then the elevator reached the ground floor and the door squeaked open. We rode back to the ferry terminal in silence, each alone with thoughts of Mama.

The following weekend, Mama came home.

CHAPTER 21

In Which I Learn the Dangers of Cooking

I can see Mama now, pale face framed by her dark hair, lying perfectly still on the tall, rented hospital bed. She came home from Seattle's Swedish Hospital by ambulance more than four weeks after her operation, to finish recovering. At first, Daddy helped her with everything. He fed her, brushed her hair, washed her hands and face. He even read the newspapers to her. We were forbidden to see her except for brief visits before bedtime. Daddy's face grew new lines, and for the first time, I noticed little grey hairs appearing in his glossy, black hair.

Robbie and I lay flat on our stomachs on the bare playroom floor sharing the box of broken and worn crayons between us as we fill in our respective pages of the Red Ryder coloring book Santa left me the previous Christmas. Danny sits beside the oil heater in Mama's rocker, humming along with the scratchy recording of "Cruising Down the River" playing on our old wind-up Victrola record player and amusing himself with some of the new crop of kittens produced by one of a pair of twin calico cats foisted upon us, according to Daddy, by a spiteful neighbor. Mama calls them Spic and Span after the

205

cleaning product, as they are constantly licking and grooming themselves and each other.

Spic produced litters of kittens at regular three-month intervals while her sister, whether from lack of sex appeal or some internal plumbing problem, proved barren. Span toiled faithfully, caring for each of her sister's litters, while Spic callously walked away until her breasts were full and dripping, then returned to feed her offspring, before once again relinquishing their care to her sister. The arrangement worked well for the pair but seemed unfair to me. Mama said that life was often unfair, and I should get used to it. Daddy called Spic a barnyard slut when Mama wasn't around but refused to explain the term.

"Too much lickin' and not enough mousin'," mumbled Daddy as he evicted yet another rodent from the trash burner in the kitchen range. "Thank God the second one's infertile!"

Robbie looked up from his coloring and watched as Danny put the kittens down on the floor and urged them towards where the two of us lay on the floor.

"Stick those damned cats out on the porch," directed Daddy with a bit of a bite in his voice. He was preparing stew for dinner as Mama napped.

"Cookie, get in here and help me peel these potatoes." I rose from the floor and left Robbie applying an apple green crayon to the mane and tail of Red Ryder's horse.

"Don't color them green, Rob, that's hair!"

"Looks like grass, to me," snarled Robbie defiantly.

"Are you coming?" exclaims Daddy with more than a little exasperation in his voice. I leave Robbie to his artistic license and join Daddy at the kitchen sink. He hands me the metal

*peeler and points to a colander of potatoes, carrots, and
rutabagas, then carries a container of cubed meat, drenched
with seasoned flour, to the stove where Crisco sits heating in
Mama's old pressure cooker. I hear the spatter of hot fat as
Daddy deposits the meat. A cloud of steam surrounds his head,
and the smell of browning beef permeates the kitchen. Daddy
deftly spears and rearranges the cubes as they brown, then
adds tomato sauce, water, and onion chunks. He reduces the
heat and returns to the sink to chop the now peeled vegetables.*

Daddy looked tired. After working all day in the Bremerton
Shipyard, he stood cooking dinner for his hospital bed-bound
wife and three hungry children. He sighed as he added the
vegetables to his stew and placed the heavy metal lid on the
pressure cooker. After regulating the heat and waiting until
steam rose from the petcock, he adjusted the little weight that
hopped and spun as pressure rose and fell in the cooker.

"Danny, time for chores—Leah, you look after Robbie and
listen for the telephone. Don't wake your mama and keep
away from that pressure cooker." Daddy's directions were
crisp, succinct, and not to be ignored.

I listened as Daddy and Danny tromped in unison through
the kitchen door. Apparently, Danny let it slam, an action that
earned him a whack from Daddy clearly audible in the
playroom and punctuated by Danny's howl. The mudroom
door shut with a muffled thump and silence crept through the
house—a silence interrupted only by Mama's gentle snore and
the chatter of the petcock on Daddy's pressure cooker stew.
Robbie reached for another crayon and hummed softly to
himself.

We had colored in silence for several minutes when

delicious smells began drifting from the kitchen to the playroom accompanied by a soft, monotonous split-splat. Gentle stirring sounds from Mama's room told me she was waking up from her afternoon nap. I shifted my position on the rug to monitor Mama's movements more closely, in the process disturbing Robbie's crayon pile. He had the broken and peeled crayons, while I had the box with its four rows of brilliant colors, each still sharp and unbroken.

I had discovered the wonderful box of 48 that included such special colors as copper and silver and gold at the bottom of my Christmas stocking and hoarded them carefully. We seldom had anything other than hard candy and an apple, and maybe an orange at the toe of Daddy's long, wool hunting stockings that Danny, Robbie, and I hung on the mantel in hopes that Santa would find us worthy. The crayons were a prize I did not yet feel like sharing.

Suddenly, Robbie grabs the box and dumps the contents onto the hardwood floor. He snatches the gold crayon (my precious gold that has never been used—the gold I am saving to make a special card for Mama) and scrubs it vigorously across his page of coloring book.

"Robbie, give that back," I hiss fiercely. Robbie shakes his head and continues scribbling. I grab the hand holding my purloined crayon in an attempt to wrest it from my brother's grasp, but he yanks back furiously, squealing exactly like the little piglets squeal when someone tries to remove them from their favorite teat.

In Mama's room, I heard increased sounds of stirring.

"Come on, Rob—give it to me, and be quiet about it—you're gonna wake up Mama." Robbie grunted and held on so tightly that the crayon broke in half. Without thinking, I smacked my little brother hard on the offending hand.

Increasing hissing sounds from the kitchen distracts me long enough for Robbie to retrieve both pieces and scoot himself into the corner formed by the playroom wall and our mother's bedroom door. He sits there, banging his head against the wall with his silly try-to-stop-me Robbie look, and concentrates on peeling the paper off the distal end of my broken gold crayon. I want to smack him again but know it will do no good and certainly will earn me a trip to the woodshed from Daddy.

Just as I decided another good smack was worth the risk of an equally good spanking, a horrendous noise erupted from the kitchen. Robbie's eyes grew as large as saucers and he let out one hellacious scream of utter terror, abruptly shutting down into silence. From Mama's room, an equally horrified scream erupted. I looked toward the kitchen just in time to see the heavy metal lid explode from the pressure cooker. It hit the ceiling along with bits of tomato, meat, carrots, potato, turnip and gravy, then ricocheted off and through the living room door, landed with a clatter, and caromed into Daddy's easy chair where it came to a halt, still trembling with energy.

From her bedroom, Mama could just see into the kitchen—in particular, the ceiling beyond the stove. As she lay flat on her back, unable to turn anything but her head, she had heard the explosion coupled with Robbie's scream, but did not see the lid fly off and out of sight.

Silence filled the house with its own palpable presence. Robbie and I looked at each other in shock, unwilling to put voice to what had happened.

"Hal, what was that? Hal!" Mama's voice quivered. "Someone—for the love of God—please tell me that that STUFF on the kitchen ceiling isn't one of my children?" Mama sounded desperate. The pleading in her voice released us from our deer-in-the-headlights trance and together Robbie and I rushed through Mama's bedroom door. She lay there, grey-faced, eyes telegraphing her terror. Recognition and relief brought color to her cheeks. Robbie crawled into the big chair next to her bed and carefully put his arms around her neck.

"Stew pot," I squeaked as I ducked into the kitchen just as Daddy and Danny swept through the kitchen door.

"Holy jumped-up Christ!" Daddy sputtered. "What happened here?" I cannot, in all conscience, repeat the tirade that poured in three languages from my male parent's mouth.

Mama often said that if swearing were an Olympic sport, Daddy was assured a gold medal. I didn't understand what she meant for many years but finally decided that Mama had been wrong. Daddy would never have qualified for the Olympics—his profanity rose to the heights of the professional!

Daddy paused in his tirade long enough to track down the pressure cooker lid and stop by Mama's room to make sure we were all right.

We ended up with eggs and biscuits for dinner, all of us crowded into Mama's room with plates on our knees and a picnic atmosphere. All's well that ends well, as my grandpa often said, and no one was hurt. Daddy did a half-hearted cleanup in the kitchen, pledging to finish the job on Saturday. After Danny, Robbie, and I were in bed and supposedly fast asleep, I heard my parents discuss how badly the day could have ended if Robbie or I had been in the kitchen when the cooker blew.

"How could I forgive myself if one of the kids were hurt—or expect you to forgive me," Daddy confessed to Mama. I heard her hush him, then the voices became murmurs and I drifted off to sleep assured that my parents loved each other. Unlike Spic and Span, where one fed and the other nurtured, Mama and Daddy, Danny, Robbie, and I were a family.

On second thought, perhaps the cats did work as a team—providing as best they could as their particular talents enabled them. Daddy may not have been the world's greatest cook, but we had food on the table—and occasionally on the ceiling! Someday soon, Mama would walk again, and life would return to normal.

CHAPTER 22
In Which I Meet Anne Marsh

While Daddy was at work, Miss Ruth (hired, reluctantly, by OurGrandmother) came to clean house and care for Mama and Robbie while Danny and I were at school. On weekends, we all helped around the house (although Daniel thought housework beneath his dignity) and did outside chores as well. That's how I happened out of the henhouse with eggs early one Saturday morning and came face-to-face with Hatchet Annie. She carried an armful of Scotch broom and a napkin-covered lard pail that emitted delicious smells!

"Hello." Her voice was gentle and a bit whispery. I startled and might have run, but she smelled so spicy and buttery and warm that I forgot to be frightened.

"I hear that thy mother is sick. Now be a good girl and trot those eggs to the house and thee can show me where thy coffee is kept. Then it's fresh cinnamon rolls and good talk." I followed her up the path.

She wore a long black dress that hung straight from a gathered yoke and brushed the grass with a whooshing sound as she walked. Black, I remember, because it matched her stockings which showed when she climbed the porch steps.

Her shoes were sturdy and well worn. I could see where she'd had them half-soled. She wore her white to grey hair gathered atop her head in a bun secured with hairpins. Little wisps at her hairline curled damply under a scarf tied at her chin. She paused on the covered porch and motioned for me to precede her into the house.

"Thy mother has a lovely kitchen." She set down her parcels, removed her shawl, folded it neatly, and placed it on the wooden rocker by the oil heat stove. I remember my feeling of pride at the kitchen's neatness, glad I had taken time to clear away supper dishes the previous night. Sometimes, we didn't keep up with inside chores too well on the weekends.

"Now, where is thy coffee pot?"

"Who's out there with you, Cookie?" Mother sounded apprehensive.

"'Tis only myself, dearie. Do not fear for thy girl," Annie replied. "I have brought thee something good to eat."

She had sturdy, capable hands, worn with time and work, that arranged the broom, made coffee, cut rolls, and poured frothy, warm morning milk with care. As she bustled about in Mama's kitchen, she hummed a hymn I remembered from church.

> "This is the day the Lord has made;
> He calls the hours His own;
> let heav'n rejoice, let earth be glad,
> and praise surround the throne."

"Now, where is thy mother's tray?" I pointed to where Daddy kept it atop the refrigerator. Annie stood on her tiptoes to retrieve it. With quiet competency, she loaded goodies on the tray and garnished it with a sprig of blooms in a jelly jar. I followed her into Mama's room.

After she settled my mother with her tray, Annie pulled up a chair. "Young lady," she nodded towards me, "I would thank thee to fetch me a cup of coffee from the kitchen. I will sit here beside thy mother and we shall chat." Mama nodded in assent and smiled at me.

From the kitchen, I could hear their low conversation punctuated with bursts of laughter. My mama really liked this woman. How could I ever have been afraid of her? When I remembered last summer, I felt like an idiot. Surely, she must know about the horrible stories I had made up about her. How could I ever look her in the eye—she would probably see that little black book of lies hidden inside my soul!

I poured the coffee with shaking hands, but before I could pick up the cup, Annie called from the bedroom. "Pour thyself a glass of milk, child, and bring it along as well." When I rejoined the ladies, Annie had pulled up another chair.

"Is that for me?"

"It sure is, honey." Mama was enjoying herself. "Here, have a cinnamon roll."

I held back, unsure of Annie's motives.

Annie motioned for me to approach. "Thy name is Leah? A lovely name. Leah, there has been a misunderstanding between thee and me. If my manner has in any way offended thee, here is the apology. Please sit down and break bread with me."

Many years passed before I realized how adroitly she had allowed me to save face. I climbed onto the chair and accepted a cinnamon roll. Then we three ladies "sat a spell" that

Saturday morning, sipping our beverages and getting better acquainted.

Her name really was Annie—Anne Marsh, a member in good standing, Society of Friends, and the Quaker for whom the hill was named. She and her husband discovered the Pacific Northwest during World War I. They had come seeking a place of refuge. As Quakers who objected to war on religious grounds, they had been driven from their previous home. In the logging towns of the Olympic and Kitsap Peninsulas, nobody asked questions as long as you did your job and kept your nose clean. Here, they found acceptance, quietly establishing their little home on the sunny slope of a small grassy hill and raising their children. The children, grown and with families of their own, lived in Seattle and Portland. They seldom visited. Mr. Marsh passed away before World War II, so Annie had lived alone for many years.

"I can see thy family needs the woman's touch when thy housekeeper is not here," announced Annie as she helped clean up our coffee cups and dishes in the kitchen. Mama was sleeping quietly in her room, tired out from the morning's festivities. "When she wakes, tell thy mother Anne will be down on the morrow. Saturdays and Sundays shall be mine to see after thee."

When everything was tidy and in its proper place, Anne Marsh wrapped herself in her shawl and set out for home. I walked beside her as far as where our driveway met the upper road, then stood and waved until she slipped out of sight.

As spring wore into early summer, Daddy began whistling again. He had missed fishing with his cronies and Annie freed him from household and children, and we all looked forward to weekends. Annie mended and cleaned and baked, made clothes for my doll and cooked Daddy's favorite Sunday dinner, contributing the little things we all missed so much with Mama confined to bed.

She took great pains not to interfere with our housekeeper Ruth's weekly duties. "That would not be a kindness," Annie confided to me, "and would add to her burden. If something falls short of your expectations, little one, give the problem to God and let Him handle it."

When Daniel tried to pick a fight with me, she took him aside; "Let everyone, especially thy sister, count thee as a friend. Then no man's hand will be set against thee in times of trial. Most of all, always listen with your heart." Daniel shot her a skeptical look, but I thought she gave him good advice. She certainly gave me food for thought.

As our mother began to heal, she was allowed to sit propped in a chair for brief periods. Annie lifted her from the bed as easily as she lifted little Robbie to give Mama a goodnight kiss. She fussed over Mama, bringing her treats and special items she called "titbits."

"Thy face is so peaked! Let me fetch thee a glass of milk." Annie would bring Mama some coffee cake with the milk, or fresh bread thick with home-churned butter. My mother would laugh and remind Annie that she didn't want to outgrow her clothes. "You'll get me so fat that nothing will fit!"

"Piffle, sweetness! We c'n let things out and make do or make new. Besides, thy little face has filled out and there are roses back in thy cheeks. Clothes will be no problem." She slipped a huge spoonful of homemade berry preserve onto Mama's hot breakfast muffin before she could protest.

"You'll spoil me."

"Thee does me a favor to allow me the opportunity. Thee and thy brood have grown dear to my heart." She patted Mama's hand.

At first, I resisted Annie's overtures. For too long, I had thought of her as Hatchet Annie, tormenter of small children, taking care not to remember that I had invented the whole sordid tale. Eventually, her gentle ways and loving kindness toward my mother won my heart. Annie had become my friend—treating me more as an equal than a small child. She cheerfully showed me how to set bread to rise, how to hem sheets and, after helping to plant our truck garden, how to use a hoe.

Much to my surprise, I actually enjoyed gardening, especially after school let out. Annie often joined me on Saturday mornings. We'd spend the early hours gently freeing up the soil around seedlings and young plants, warding off predator weeds that scrabbled for a foothold amongst our neat vegetable rows. We'd talk and laugh, but often enough we communicated most in our silences. Being with Annie in the garden required no words.

"How do you know if you got one of those listening hearts?" I asked Annie one Saturday morning as we knelt in parallel rows thinning carrots. I had given the matter a lot of thought after she mentioned it to Danny.

"Thee doesn't 'get' one, girl," she answered with simplicity, "thee is born with one. Some think a listening heart is a burden. Others know its blessing. God has given each recipient a choice in the matter—thee can choose to learn how to use it, or thee can choose to ignore it. Think on this thing—

what might God want thee to do with thy heart? We will talk more of this another time."

My soul grew up that summer. I no longer needed to compete with my brothers. They were who they were—boys in a man's world, and I was only a small girl. Perhaps someday ways would change, and I might play some small part in that change. For now, I had today. One can simply count on today. I formulated my life's philosophy hoeing in silence with Annie. Never go to sleep with unsaid words hanging between yourself and the people you love. Apologize for angry words; say "I love you," make your peace. Do nothing to bring shame upon yourself or your family. Only then can you go to God with a clear conscience. No one but God knows if tomorrow will come. Most of all, remember to listen with your heart.

When I close my eyes, I smell that garden—the earth rich, black, breathing life into seeds and plants. It feels smooth and cool in my hands, and very much alive. I developed an appreciation for the complexities and relationships between all living things—animals, plants—and air and water, sunshine, rain and snow. I need these things to live, and they need me, as well. All of God's creatures have their niche on the wheel of life. I struggled to find mine.

As our garden grew, my mother's health improved. Her legs became stronger, almost able to bear her weight. She spent more time sitting up now, beginning to reclaim her role as wife and mother. One Saturday in mid-July, Mama and I sat shelling peas for supper while Annie prepared a fryer rabbit.

"I'm thinking of letting Ruth go on Monday," Mama commented. "What do you think, Anne? Our girl's a lot of help with Robbie, and since I'm out of bed so much, keeping Ruth on seems an extravagance."

Annie turned from her rabbit; "Well, girl, 'twould surely save some money, and I could pop in on thee once or twice a day."

"Oh, you wouldn't have to do that! Hal can get me out of bed before he leaves for work. If I'm tired, Danny and Leah can help me onto the sofa for a rest. We'll manage without bothering you. You've done enough, don't you think?"

"I have done no more'n no less'n thee's done for me. Thee and thy family have greatly pleasured my life. It can be no small thing to bring such joy to an old woman, so I shall come to thee in the afternoons and lift thee off to bed!"

Mother closed her eyes for a moment. "Yes, Anne. I suppose that's best—but it's just not in my nature to be so dependent on people. I'm used to doing for others."

"And God had other plans for thee. Take advantage of it, girl, take full advantage." Annie returned to her rabbit, expertly cutting the carcass into serving size pieces and dredging them with flour. She soon had them browning in our big cast-iron Dutch oven.

While Mama and I finished shelling peas, Annie made a pot of green tea, pouring two thick, white mugs, and they sat at the kitchen table sipping hot tea and talking, their heads together, like two schoolgirls. I peeled and quartered potatoes, happy to be included as one of the "ladies" on this ordinary Saturday afternoon.

Slowly, my relationship with Mama had changed; during her illness, I became more her confidante than her daughter, skewing the balance between us forever. Not to say that this was a bad thing, but it was different. We were friends, on a more or less equal footing, except when Daddy or other grownups were around, or she chose to reassert her parental authority for some specific reason. Then we played the game of mother and child. As much as any of us can pinpoint the time when our childhood ends, that was mine; and though Annie still came in after lunch, I was Mama's mainstay, her hands and feet inside the house, her eyes and ears outside, while she grew strong and confident again.

"What a relief!" exclaimed Mama. She and Annie sat on cool grass beneath a weeping willow tree in the side yard. Annie had prepared fresh lemonade and brought sweet butter cookies, still warm from the oven.

"I'd actually forgotten how wonderful it is to sit under a tree and feel the shade on my face!" She took a sip of lemonade. "That's heavenly!" Mama sighed and snuggled into the pile of pillows Annie had brought from her room.

"Have a cookie." Annie moved the plate in her direction. She took one and munched absently. "Thee looks far away. Is something worrying thee?" Annie helped herself to more lemonade.

Mama shrugged. "I don't know. Oh, Anne, I guess everyone's been taking care of me for so long it's hard to rejoin the real world. I fretted so for being dependent on everyone— now part of me doesn't want to let go of that darned hospital bed!"

Annie chuckled. "I warned thee."

"I have such mixed emotions. Maybe the problem is just that—emotions. I should be appreciating all the things I missed for so long." She sighed. "I guess I've changed."

"Thee has passed through a very difficult time. Thy body

is almost healed—now thee needs a healing of the heart." Annie put her arms around my mama's shoulders and gave them a little squeeze. "Give thyself time, girl, give thyself time. God delivers in his own pace. When you walk will be time enough."

Two weeks later, Mama walked, and when Annie came on Saturday, she stepped out to meet her. From my viewpoint in the tomatoes, I saw Annie stop, hauled up short in her tracks. My mother walked toward her, smiling, arms outstretched. As they met, Annie's eyes welled with tears.

"Oh, my dear friend, it is so very good to see thee on thy own two feet!" Annie took my mother in her arms and rocked her gently—two women, bound in a sisterhood older than memory, whispering together in the dusty late summer afternoon. I froze this moment in time—fixed forever in my memory lest I forget that common bond that ties all women together. These two had shared a journey of personal crisis, and though time and distance might one day separate them, that journey had reached safe harbor.

I see dimly now that which will someday become clear—that women travel apart from men, excluded from the camaraderie of male-to-male bonding. We walk the same trail but are forever either one step to the rear or one step to the side. To men falls the hunt—working together towards common goals, brandishing sticks, and throwing rocks at intruders—protecting the tribe. Women bear young in sorrow and hold the sacred responsibility of nurturing the next generation. We meet briefly at night, then go our separate ways—together, yet always apart. Daddy and my brothers circle the wagons while Mama and I and all the Anne Marshes of the world fight fiercely for our young. Each brings strengths to relationships, and faults, as well.

The time for circled wagons ended with my mother's first hesitant step. The men were now free to resume the hunt with clear consciences. It is not a question of equality. We are all equal, male and female. God made us so, and human law cannot change that; but He also made us separate from one another, each unique, each wonderful, each flawed. It doesn't matter if we ignore one another—if our fears betray us, if our minds play tricks on us—in the end, we, male and female, engage in a great cosmic dance that at one moment brings us together, and with the next beat throws us apart. In the end, only one thing counts. We all need to listen with our hearts.

CHAPTER 23
In Which I Gain a Friend and Learn a Skill

Gradually, our household returned to normal. Annie came less and less often, until finally when school started, she stopped coming altogether. Now I waved to her when we met in the woods or on the road.

One blustery October day as I walked home from school, I met Annie near the creek. She motioned me close and invited me to her house on Saturday. Mama was pleased at my excitement and agreed to the visit.

"I'm glad you're over your silly notions about Anne," she said with pleasure. "She's pretty fond of you, you know! Why don't we make some applesauce cake for you to take? I'll help you Friday evening."

On Friday after Danny and I had the dinner dishes washed and dried, Mama helped me with my cake. We used fresh eggs and milk from our own hens and cows, and applesauce we had canned the summer before her back surgery. I had helped her peel, core, and slice the apples. Mama filled the deep well cooker inserted into the left rear range burner hole with apple slices, sugar, and a little water. I tended the cooking apples with care, stirring them as they came to a slow boil to prevent them from burning.

After testing the apples for tenderness, we sieved them through a food mill and ladled the still-hot applesauce into sterile Mason jars. Mama capped and ringed the jars, then packed them carefully into her huge pressure cooker to process. Our applesauce, rosy and still slightly tart, the way Daddy liked it, sat side by side with jars of canned pears, peaches, apricots, and cherries.

We needed the applesauce, eggs, and milk for my great-grandmother's recipe which also called for cinnamon, raisins, nutmeg, and butter. Since Mama didn't have the required sour milk, she showed me how to use vinegar to sour, or clabber it.

"I thought cake had flour and baking powder, Mama," I commented as I read from the old, yellowed recipe card. I could see where ancient batter had been wiped off from time to time.

Mama thought for a moment. "This recipe is very old, Cookie. Back then, every woman knew that you put in enough flour to make the batter as stiff as you needed it. You added baking powder or soda depending on how much flour you used and whether your milk was sour or sweet. I'll help you measure them." She dipped flour from a canister on the kitchen counter, carefully leveling each measured portion with a table knife. I sifted together flour and baking soda into a soft, white heap on a square of waxed paper.

As I stirred the batter, alternately adding wet ingredients and dry, Mother buttered and floured the cake pans. She showed me how to adjust the oven temperature, making sure the shelf sat exactly in the middle of the oven. Then we divided the batter equally into two pans and put them in to bake. I resisted the temptation to peek since Mama said peeking could change the oven temperature and make the cake fall.

While the mechanical kitchen timer ticked off the minutes, I cleaned up the cooking mess, then sat at the kitchen table alternating my stare between oven door and timer. Soon, a wonderful spicy aroma permeated the kitchen. Danny popped in from the playroom, demanding a piece of whatever smelled good. Mama fended him off. Eventually, the timer rang. I held my breath as Mama opened the oven door. Both pans of batter had domed above the sides and baked an even, toasty brown. Mama showed me how to check for doneness with a toothpick in one layer and a touch to the other.

At last, she pronounced them perfect! I carefully extracted the layers, one at a time, using thick potholders quilted together by my Grammy B. Mama showed me how to decant each layer from its pan by placing the cooling rack on top and flipping both pan and rack at the same time. I held my breath as Mama lifted each pan off its still steaming layer, praying that nothing would stick to sides or bottom. At last, they both sat—perfect circles—each atop its own rack.

"After the layers cool, we'll turn them out and frost them." Ma reached for more butter, a little top milk, and powdered confectioner's sugar. "Let's flavor this frosting with vanilla," she suggested. I agreed.

At last, the cake stood—tall and proud, and mounded with creamy sweetness. Danny stood by the sink, coaxing out the last vestiges of sweetness from the mixing bowl with his index finger.

"This stuff's pretty good," he sniggered, "but don't let that go to your head, Leah. The cake's prob'ly dry and needs this frosting so's we can gag it down."

"The cake's not for you, Danny. I'm taking it to a special tea party tomorrow. You don't get any."

"Oh, yeah," sneered Danny, "tea with the old hatchet lady. Well, I hope you choke!"

"Daniel Charles!" Mother came into the kitchen in time to hear Danny's last remarks. She snatched his ear and pulled him close to her down-turned face. "That was a very unfortunate remark. I was prepared to ask your sister for half that lovely cake on your behalf. Now, she will certainly take all of it tomorrow! And you, young man, put down that frosting bowl and clean up for bed!"

Mama and I cleared the frosting things in silence. I savored the apparent success of my first cake and hoped it tasted as good as it smelled. Finally, Mama sent me off to bed to dream of tea parties and moist applesauce cake.

Saturday morning dawned gloomy and wet. Dark clouds hovered low overhead, spitting cold autumn rain in almost solid sheets. Mother frowned, shaking her head at sending me up Quaker Hill in such nasty weather.

"Oh, Mama," I begged, "please let me go. If it's okay for me to go outside to feed the chickens and collect eggs, why isn't it okay for me to go see Annie?"

"Let's wait an hour or so, Cookie. Maybe the rain will let up a little."

When the sky showed no hint of change by noon, I could see that my mother would not relent. No amount of pleading would change her mind once she had set it.

I considered getting Daddy to intercede and might have pressed my luck had Fate not intervened—a tapping at the back door attracted my attention. Through its tiny glass pane, I could see Annie, dripping wet, smiling from ear to ear. I flew to open the door.

"My, what a goodly storm! I knew thy mother'd keep thee home, little one." She popped her slicker onto one of the back porch hooks and slipped off her boots, leaving them standing alone in their own puddle. Mama motioned her into the kitchen and pulled out a chair from the table.

"Have a hot cup of coffee. It might be a little strong—we've had the pot on since breakfast! I never expected to see you trudge through weather like this." Mother poured another cup for herself and stood with her back braced against the kitchen counter, sipping and blowing at the hot brew. "What brings you out?"

"Thy daughter and I have a tea party planned. I figured I'd just come along and fetch her, seein' how the weather's so poor."

"You shouldn't have bothered," demurred Mama. "Leah could have come some other time."

"A promise is a promise, girl." Annie gave me a wink. "I have promised thy young 'un a visit. If thee will allow, I will walk her up the hill to my cabin, then bring her down before dark. Weather should not be permitted to spoil our plan. After all, 'tis only a little rain and wind."

Mama turned to me. "Do you still want to go, Cookie? It's really nasty out, and you can go next week if you like." My eyes pleaded with her as my voice asserted my desire to go with Annie. "Well, if you dress up warm, and wear your puddle ducks, I guess you can go." Mother smiled broadly.

I ran for my rain gear and the little red boots—those

puddle ducks, as Mama called them. They were almost impossible for little hands to slide onto shoes, but on this Saturday, the Gods smiled upon me. I was ready in a wink.

Annie took my small hand in hers. "Thee'll have thy girl back before dark, be you sure."

"Oh, Anne, you don't need to come back. Hal will be glad to walk up and get her home."

I interjected that I was quite able to walk home by myself, but both of them hushed me. It was obvious that an escort was required.

Mother bundled up the applesauce cake and handed it to Annie. "Cookie made this for your teatime. I hope you enjoy it!"

"T'smells powerful good, girl. You 'n I shall have a wonderful tea for ourselves." I beamed all the way to Annie's house.

Annie lived alone with her cats and chickens, a brown goat, and a beautiful sloe-eyed Jersey cow (undoubtedly the source of that long ago mysteriously full milk can). She had no electricity, no telephone, and made do with a two-hole outhouse located downwind from her tightly chinked cabin. A deliciously cold well outside her door yielded icy water that tasted much better out of a tin dipper than from a glass.

In her tiny kitchen, Annie's wood cookstove baked its delightful woodsy smell into bread and cookies. Its hot water reservoir provided an ample supply for bathing, clothes washing, and general cleaning up. The little cabin stayed warm and cozy as long as a cheerful fire burned in the fireplace. Kerosene lanterns cast warm beams illuminating even the farthest corner of this simple, single-room dwelling.

"Well, what does thee think?"

"Oh, Annie, it's wonderful," I cried.

This masterpiece of simplicity provided me with a snapshot of the past. I was not too young to know the meaning of homeliness in its truest sense; Annie's home had a humble quality I had never seen before.

Her four-poster bed, made by her husband's loving hands, sat at the exact center of the west wall, directly opposite the fireplace. This bed was still the heart of Annie's house, as it had been before her family grew up and left and her husband died. Annie had heaped it with lovely homemade quilts—not for decoration, but utility. They covered a huge feather bed and two overstuffed pillows, providing warmth no matter how cold the night. One special quilt stood out—a pattern of intertwined circles. Annie called it her wedding quilt. "Someday I will tell thee of this quilt," she promised.

The rest of her sparse furnishings matched the bed, homemade with more love than skill, and polished to a lovely patina through years of diligent care. A long trestle table surrounded by arrow back chairs made comfortable with homemade braided cushions on seats and backs divided her sleeping area from the kitchen-sitting room. Before the hearth sat comfortable-looking rockers, one large enough for the average to large adult, the other scaled more towards a small adult or child. Both chairs sported braided cushions as well. I was enchanted!

"Now, have thee a chair at my table. Won't take but a moment for tea." Annie dipped water from the stove reservoir into a plain crockery teapot. "This is my own blend. Thee shall have it with milk and sugar, same as my children did. A little secret between us—thy mother need not know about the tea." She smiled and winked at me, a co-conspirator. I nodded and smiled back. I had never had tea before—I hoped I liked it!

Annie carefully unwrapped the applesauce cake forgotten in my excitement. "Did thee make this cake for me?" I nodded, watching her eyes smile approval as she cut two huge chunks and placed them on thick, white pottery plates. She brought them to the table, including forks and spoons and large, blue and white checked napkins to match her tablecloth. "Thee did a lovely job of it, girl. A lovely piece of work, indeed. I myself would be proud to take this cake to Meeting."

As she talked, Annie added a creamer and sugar bowl to the table and brought over two huge mugs. With care, she filled mine half-full of rich top milk from the creamer, added two heaping scoops of sugar, then snatched the teapot from the warmer and added steaming amber liquid. The cream rose in lazy circles through hot tea, swirling and blending. She gave the mug a stir with her spoon.

"Have thy tea while it is hot, my dear. It will warm thy heart." She took a mouthful of cake, exclaiming all the while on its moistness and flavor. I sipped my warm, delicious, creamy brew and nibbled at applesauce cake, hoping for this wonderful afternoon to last forever. Soon enough, my father tapped at Annie's door and fetched me home to supper.

I went often to Quaker Hill after that, in spite of snow and rain, sun and wind. The little cabin became my refuge against my brothers' torment. (They had recently joined forces, as brothers often do, and I was not included.) It did no good to complain to my parents; they seemed preoccupied and at odds with one another. More than once, I interrupted some disunity between them, although Mama pretended otherwise at my inquiry. "Just a little disagreement between Daddy and me," she'd demure, "nothing to worry yourself over." I didn't quite believe her words, as they didn't match what my eyes had seen, but I let it alone, hoping that Mama and Daddy would resolve the issues that kept a strain between them. Climbing up to the little cabin and spending an afternoon with Annie allowed me a space of my own. I always came home with a smile on my face.

"Has thee yet made thy sampler?" Annie asked one Saturday. She sat rocking in her chair beside the fireplace, mending stockings. I knelt at her feet, poking about the embers with a broom straw, repeatedly catching it on fire, then withdrawing it and extinguishing the flame.

"What's a sampler?"

"If thee needs to ask, thee needs to make one." Annie stuck her needle into the toe of her stocking, carefully placing the point within a fold, then rolled up her darning and set it aside. She bent over and rummaged about deep in the basket beside her chair, finally pulling out a packet of material. "Samplers make good work for idle fingers. Here, girl."

She carefully opened the packet and smoothed out the fabric, revealing a linen rectangle imprinted with alphabet and numbers from one to ten. Flower outlines sprawled along the borders.

"Gosh, Annie, I don't know how to sew!" I gently followed a flower outline with the tip of my finger. "Are you gonna show me how?"

"If thee would like me to, I will be pleased to show thee." Annie handed me the sampler and rose from her chair. "First, thee will need a thimble. My daughter used this one when she worked her first sampler. Give me thy hand and let us see if it fits thee. There!"

The thimble sat firmly on the middle finger of my right hand. Annie selected a needle from her pincushion and showed me how to thread it.

"After thee masters a few simple stitches, thee can start on the sampler. We will use this scrap to begin." I spent the rest of the afternoon carefully stitching beside Annie as she worked on her mending.

I made excellent progress with my stitching in the visits that followed. Soon, Annie allowed me to pick out colored embroidery floss and begin work on the actual sampler. I found great pleasure in sitting beside Annie at the fireplace on a rainy afternoon, stitching and chatting.

One Saturday afternoon, Annie sat sorting colored fabric, swatches and scraps of worn-out clothing into like-colored piles, preparing materials for a new quilt. As she worked, she instructed me in quilt fabrication, explaining some common quilt patterns and their meanings. When it came time to select a pattern for this quilt, Annie chose the double wedding ring pattern—two interconnected rings symbolizing marriage—the same as the wonderful old quilt on her bed.

"I am working this quilt for my granddaughter in Seattle," she explained. "She will marry in the new year. Though I will not be at her wedding, I shall send her a quilt, nonetheless! All the children of my heart should have their own wedding quilt. Since she cannot make her own, I will make it for her."

Annie seldom talked about her children and their families. When the subject came up (as it did with the quilt) her voice caught and her eyes filled with sadness. I wanted to ask her why she wouldn't be at her granddaughter's wedding, but I suspected the subject would cause her pain and listened with my heart instead.

Annie had taught me much about listening. "When thee listens to what a person says, thee must hear with both thy mind and thy heart," she counseled. "Things of the mind everyone can understand. One may safely comment on these; but things of the heart, they touch the soul. We cannot see them with our eyes—or hear them with our ears. These things that pass unspoken but are deeply felt—upon them we make no comment. They travel straight as God's arrows, from one heart to another—but only if thee listens carefully. Upon these things, a silent tongue is golden."

It is during these times I share my secrets with Annie. I tell her that daddy is not my blood father, but the father of my heart. Beside the fire, I tell her of my blood father's betrayal of my mother and his theft of Danny. I tell her of the hours and days I wait for my brother to come home and how my mama's bravery returns him. I tell her of Johnny and his cerebral palsy and how he dies with my name in his mouth. And Annie listens with her heart, her silence assuring me that what I tell her will remain there, unspoken, forever.

On this particular day, we worked together in silence until I left for home.

By Christmas, I had finished my sampler. Aside from a few minor stitching errors on the first few alphabet letters, Annie pronounced the work acceptable. Mama would be proud of my work—and surprised. That was the best part. She usually knew what Danny and I made for presents at school. This would be a special Christmas!

At Annie's encouragement, I let Daddy in on the secret and asked him to help me make a frame for the sampler. He grumbled a bit, but we spent the Saturday afternoon before Christmas out of sight in his workshop while he selected scraps of wood from one of his finished projects. Daddy loved to work with his hands, producing charming bookcases and sturdy little tables. One Christmas, he made me a built-to-scale kitchen hutch and sideboard fashioned after an Amish piece he had seen in a magazine. Mama filled it with kid-size pots and pans and little china dishes decorated with the blue willow pattern. I had that kitchen cupboard, as he called it, until it finally fell apart during one of our many moves.

Daddy helps me plane and sand the selected wood, cut the pieces to fit in his miter box, then fasten the strips together with wiggly little metal joiners. We polish the joined pieces to bring out the soft glowing heart of the wood. Finally, Daddy pronounces it finished and pulls out his pipe. I sit there, watching the blue Prince Albert smoke coil softly around his head as he carefully fits my sampler into the frame.

"This is a nice piece of work, Little Beaver. Your mama will be pleased." He held up the framed sampler admiringly.

"Thank you, Daddy—the frame is wonderful, isn't it?"

"I was speaking about the sampler."

Daddy sucks thoughtfully on his pipe stem, then pulls out his matches and relights the tobacco. I snuggle up close to him and place my chin on his shoulder. I love my daddy. I love his black, wavy hair, slicked back over his ears with care. I love the smell of his aftershave and the feel of his cheeks, silky from shaving. I even love his afternoon stubble when he lets me run my fingers over the sharp little sticky-up bits, ever amazed that they can erupt so rapidly from the morning's smoothness. Lately, though, his blue eyes, usually sparkling and happy, seem distant, as if his thoughts are somewhere else. I do not know what possesses me, but I hear myself speaking softly into his ear.

"Is everything okay with you and Mama?"

Daddy jumped to his feet, nearly dumping me on the workroom floor. His head snapped around, his eyes steely slits beneath glowering brows.

"Have you been listening in on the phone, Leah?"

"No, Daddy—why would I do that?" I stammered, shocked at both his accusation and his actions. His face softened.

"Sorry, baby." He took my arm and pulled me close to his chest. "I didn't mean to scare you. Of course, everything's okay with us. Don't you worry—everything's okay. He smiled and kissed my forehead. "And let's not mention this little conversation to your mama, you understand? Now, we better finish cleaning up. Mama's gonna wonder what we've been doing all afternoon!"

Although I tried to follow Daddy's admonition not to worry, I did—every night—and I paid a lot more attention to the telephone than I ever had before! Although we had one telephone on a very long cord that reached every room in the house, privacy was nearly impossible. Notwithstanding family members, we had eleven other households on our telephone line, any or all of whom could listen in. This came in handy during times of emergency—helping to spread the word to everyone—but it was almost impossible to keep personal business within the family. Daddy secretly rigged an extension jack down in the barn into which he sometimes plugged an old, beat-up phone he found at the dump. Danny stumbled onto the setup one Sunday morning when we came home early from church and he interrupted Daddy deep in conversation. Daddy pledged him to silence, but Danny had already filled me in. I guessed that he sometimes sneaked the phone from Daddy's special hidey-hole as he suddenly seemed to know a great deal about what was going on in the neighborhood.

We did not have the type of Christmas that children expect today. My parents were of modest means, and this year, before the advent of health insurance, had been particularly difficult. We didn't starve—home-canned fruits and vegetables, fresh and frozen meats and chickens, plus wild game provided by Daddy assured food on our table. We lacked the frills—store-bought treats such as bananas, oranges, nuts, and candy—and knew our Christmas Eve stockings would be slim this year. Daddy had warned us that Santa had budget problems and we were prepared.

I, however, was definitely looking forward to my birthday which immediately followed Christmas. Mama had promised me a party this year. Invitations went out and were accepted by six of my classmates for games and ice cream on December 26th.

Christmas morning arrives cool and crisp with a possibility of snow. We greet this news with delight as Santa has left us a beautiful sled. My brothers and I open the perfunctory socks and new underwear. Daddy oohs and aahs over his papier-mâché ashtray from Danny and his painted-tin-with-stenciled-flower pencil holder from me. Mama appreciates her papier-mâché spoon rest from my brother and painted-tin (same stenciled flower) utensil holder from me. I notice that Mama and Daddy do not exchange presents and wonder if it is because of finances or a product of the growing tension between them.

Before we took our stockings down from the mantle-piece, Daddy noticed one package partially hidden beneath the tree. "What's this? Look, honey," he held the package out towards Mama, "a gift for you!"

"Oh, Hal, I thought we weren't exchanging gifts this year!"

"It's not from me." Daddy read the little tag attached to the wrap. "Take it. It's from Cookie!"

Daddy placed the gaily-colored package into Mama's hands. Annie and I had used the Sunday comics as wrapping paper and tied it with braided yarn. I had made the tag myself, decorating it with small fir cones, and was actually quite pleased with the result.

"Cookie," my package rested on Mother's lap. "What can this possibly be?"

"Open it, Mama, open it!" My brothers crowded close, poking and shoving at one another to gain a few inches. Daniel elbowed me in the back. "You tryin' to get on Mama's good side, huh? Well, don't think you'll get away with it. She loves me the best, ya know!" For some reason, my brother thought we were in competition for our mother's affections.

Mama examined the tag, commenting on how neatly I had printed her name. She carefully untied the braided yarn, coiled it around her finger, and slipped the resulting wad into her apron pocket. My brothers jostled and cajoled her to hurry up.

"Now look, boys." She sounded exasperated. "This is my

present and I intend to enjoy it!" Daniel glared at me so fiercely his dark eyebrows appeared to meet over his nose. I ignored him. Carefully, Mama pulled back the paper and unwrapped the sampler, revealing a cardboard backing. "Whatever can this be?" She gave me a quizzical look.

"Turn it over, Mama." Robbie was impatient. "Something's on the other side."

Mama, her face quite serious, slowly turned her present over. "Oh, Leah! A sampler. This is really wonderful." She turned to face me. "Did you do this all by yourself?"

I nodded, suddenly tongue-tied.

"All those afternoons up at Anne's house. This is what you were doing?" I nodded again. "I have never seen such a lovely sampler. Thank you, sweetheart. I will keep it forever!" She pulled me close and kissed my forehead.

Danny sidled up behind me and pinched my back. I knew I'd have a big, purple bruise, but chose to ignore the pain.

"You are very welcome, Mama. Daddy helped me make the frame. Merry Christmas!"

Mama looked up at Daddy. When she turned her face, she appeared to have tears in her eyes. "Oh, Mama, are you crying?" I leaned over and put my arms around my mother. "I didn't mean to make you sad!"

"I'm not sad, baby. You have given me a wonderful present and these are happy tears." I didn't quite believe her, though— I was listening with my heart again.

"Let's change the subject," interjected Daddy. "Santa's left something in your stockings!" He unhooked Danny's stocking from the mantle and handed it to him. "Here, kids, take a look."

The stockings we hung every year actually belonged to Daddy. They were wool knee-length stockings worn in his hunting boots (larger than anything a little kid had), and perfect for Santa's booty. Mine held filberts, walnuts and hazelnuts, and hard ribbon candy (my favorite). The toe contained a special and unexpected treat—a beautifully ripe navel orange, all for myself. Danny and Robbie had similar treasures that were already disappearing with gusto. My stocking vanished into Mother's protective custody—she would make sure that my brothers couldn't snitch my goodies.

By mid-morning, snow began to fall—single flakes, at first, teasing us as we cleaned up wrapping paper and quarreled over Christmas candy. Soon, solitary flakes became clumps that fell, thick and white, covering first the driveway and paths, then pastures, trees, and bushes. We gathered so close to the French doors that our combined breath steamed up the glass panes.

When our shoving and jostling for position threatened to lead to blows, Mother separated us, sending my brothers to the playroom under threat of the woodshed if they didn't play quietly. She hauled me into the kitchen and stood me at the sink to peel potatoes.

"I hope this snow doesn't keep your aunt and uncle from getting here." Mama sounded a bit wistful. I knew she was looking forward to having Christmas with family, although I wasn't keen on the prospect of two male cousins come to join my brothers against me. I settled into potato peeling, then helped Mama baste the turkey.

Our turkey had come as a huge surprise, donated by my daddy's employer as a Christmas bonus, and it was the most beautiful turkey I had ever seen. The only drawback to this serendipity came when Daddy brought it home—not properly dressed out and ready to stuff, but still alive and strutting as only a Tom can strut! We children lobbied to keep him as a pet but were outvoted. We never felt it quite fair that adult votes counted so much more than children's votes. Mama delegated death duties to Daddy, who obliged while I wailed and cried as if he were executing a family member. Now Tom, properly stuffed and trussed, roasted quietly in our oven. In spite of my protests, I knew when dinnertime came 'round I'd be the first to demand a drumstick!

Just as an early dusk began to fill in the spaces between snowflakes, Danny spotted our uncle's car in the driveway. "They're here, they're here," he shouted in delight. Mama smiled and her shoulders relaxed. I knew she felt relieved that they had arrived safely. Soon, we sat down to a sumptuous feast made tastier by love and family. While Christmas was over, tomorrow was my birthday, and Mama had planned a wonderful party for me.

CHAPTER 24
In Which I Lose a Birthday Party to Danny

At 4:00 am on my birthday, I awoke unable to breathe. I suffered from croup as a child, and although this was neither the first, nor far from the last, bout I would endure, I never learned to suppress the feeling of panic that rendered me speechless. Unable to scream—even to talk—I would run to my parents' room for help. Mama knew how to calm my panic and help clear my throat. She finally led me back to bed in our tiny spare room, set a vaporizer beside me, and coaxed me back to sleep.

I woke again to full daylight. From the bedroom window, I could see my brothers taking turns on our new Christmas sled. A tear slipped down my cheek. I curled my tongue from the corner of my mouth and stopped its salty descent.

"Oh, good, you're awake." Mama poked her head through the doorway then stepped inside. She carried a tray. "Here's something for your breakfast, so hop back into bed, honey."

"Not coddled eggs, Mama, please no eggs!" I whispered. I hated coddled eggs with their runny yolks and slimy whites. I preferred my eggs fried into solid rubbery blobs, yolks properly stabbed flat and cooked hard as boards.

"No eggs. I have some nice milk toast, soft and buttery, just as you like it. This should slip down without hurting your throat."

Mama thinks that every sickness in the world can be cured by milk toast, coddled eggs, or chicken soup. Of the three, I like chicken soup the best, but it is too much to expect soup for breakfast—even if it is my birthday. I poke around unenthusiastically in the bowl of cooling milk and congealing toast.

"What about my party, Mama? Can I still have my party?" My voice faded and rasped.

Mama ignores my question. "Try to eat a little, Cookie. You need some food in your stomach."

I take a few spoonsful of mangled toast and milk, mush it around in my mouth, and wince as I swallowed. "Please don't make me eat anymore, Mommy," I plead. "It's gonna make me gag!"

I had a well-developed gag reflex. Mama often accused me of vomiting on purpose. She was wrong, of course, but I wasn't above using the threat to avoid eating. Today she believed my warning and quickly removed the tray.

"Your face is white as a sheet!" she exclaimed. "Here, use this if you need to." She covered my lap and chest with a bath towel.

"About your party, Cookie, I'm afraid you won't be able to go. Oh, your friends are still coming—it's too late to call everybody and cancel—but we'll have the party without you. You can watch from your bedroom. I'm sorry, honey. I know what a disappointment this is, but you don't want to infect your friends, do you?" I shook my head. "And there's always next year!" I nodded sadly, knowing she was right.

Deep inside, I could feel tears threatening to fill what little gap in my throat had been cleared by the vaporizer. My head drooped and my shoulders shook with the effort of warding them off. Crying would only trigger another coughing attack—remaining calm meant being able to breathe.

Mama sat down beside me, pulled the covers up around my shoulders, and kissed my forehead. "Rest now, sleep if you can. You'll feel better when you wake up." I closed my eyes, turning so Mama couldn't see the tears creeping down my cheeks. If she were listening with her heart, I knew she could see that mine was broken!

When I opened my eyes, the room seemed dark. Someone had pulled the shades. I could hear laughter from the playroom, the sound of cars in the driveway, children and parents coming and going. I jerked upright, terrified that I had slept through my own birthday party!

My door opened and Mama came across the room and sat on the edge of my bed. "I'm glad you're awake. Your friends are all here and anxious to say hello. Take this, honey. It'll help you feel better." Mother proffered a spoonful of aspirin crushed with berry jam. I knew it was no use complaining about the taste, so I swallowed the concoction as quickly as possible and washed it down with water. Saliva filled my mouth and I could feel nausea rising in waves. It took all my concentration to keep the aspirin down.

She produced a warm, wet washcloth and wiped my hands and face, then smoothed my hair with her hands, plumped the pillows, and kissed my forehead. "You're hot this afternoon," she commented. Then, she opened the door. My friends milled around in the playroom, laughing and anxious to start the party.

"Here she is, kids. Now, not one inch across that threshold! Just say hello and let's get started."

From my bed, I could see a pin the tail on the donkey game on the wall between the two playroom windows. My birthday pie sat in the middle of the card table, set up in the center of the room. It rested on Mama's best luncheon cloth—a chocolate meringue pie as I had ordered, surrounded by gaily wrapped packages.

I didn't really like cake. "It's too sweet, Mama," I'd say and scrape off all the icing. I preferred pie, so Mama made me birthday pies. This one had eight candles nestled neatly amid peaks of perfectly browned meringue. I knew I would probably not get a piece and felt so ill I didn't care.

My birthday party got underway. Friends laughed and shouted at one another as each took a turn at blindfold and donkey tail. During musical chairs, the party grew rowdy. Mama moved the card table to one side and half-closed my door. I lay still, breathing in moist vaporizer air, and nodded off. Once, Danny risked our mother's wrath by popping in on me. She caught him up short by his shirt collar as he headed for my bed.

"Where do you think you're going, young man," she queried as she snatched him back into the playroom. I could hear him whining some answer to Mama. She must have accepted his explanation because she laughed.

Mama poked her head back through the door. "You're awake, good! It's time to open your presents and have pie! Do you feel up to it? I motioned for her to come closer. "What is it, Cookie?" She knelt beside me, hand on my forehead.

"Can you open them for me, Mama?" My voice came out in a croak. "I just want to stay here and watch."

Over her shoulder, I could see Danny poaching for information at the door. He obviously wanted to creep closer, but fear of another tongue-lashing—or worse, a good smack, kept him out. He leaned as far forward as he dared, straining to hear and leering at me like some out of season jack-o-lantern.

"Maybe you should ask Daniel to open them. I know he'd like to do something nice for you." Mama must have seen the look of disbelief on my face. "Your brother loves you, you know!" At the door, Danny nodded his head in agreement with her. That was a surprise. I thought I had a pretty good handle on just how my brother felt about me—love was not the first word that came to mind!

I hesitated. Mama cocked her head and gave me "that look." "Honey, don't you want to give your brother an opportunity to do something for you?" Actually, I didn't. He would exact a toll on me for this "opportunity," quite aside from the intrinsic pleasure he'd enjoy while opening my presents.

"Okay, Mama, if you think so." I didn't feel well enough to argue. "Let Danny open them for me." I sat up in bed and shot a piercing glare towards my brother. He ducked back quickly before Mother could see he'd been eavesdropping.

I knew why my mama asked me to choose my brother, although she didn't say so. Daniel was the eldest child—he naturally felt such an honor should fall to him, although he'd make me feel that it had been a chore. Mama had been through so much in the last six months, including whatever problem existed with Daddy that she had not shared with me, I just wanted to see her smile. Sometimes listening with one's heart was not easy!

I tried to act enthusiastic as Daniel opened each gift, thanking my friends. I truly appreciated the small toys and trinkets they brought me. I noticed that my brother had reserved a game for himself. I would quite likely never see it again but hoped he'd let me play occasionally. As everyone ate pie and ice cream and shared their Christmas stories, Mama brought the gifts into my room. I doubt she noticed the missing game. I didn't mention it.

"I've brought you your gift from Daddy and me, honey." She held out a small, brightly wrapped box. "You can open it now or save it for later if you want."

"Thank you," I murmured, and motioned for her to place the box on my little dresser. "Maybe I'll save it for tomorrow. I'm kinda tired, right now."

Mama sat the little box down and returned to my side. She plumped my pillow, smoothed my crumpled sheets and settled me in, then checked the water level in the vaporizer. "Why don't you close your eyes again. I'll bring you something to eat, later."

I slept through my friends' departure, not waking until she came in to close the shades against the evening's freezing wind and turn on my bedside lamp. "I see you've joined us again." My mother's smile included all of her, not just the mouth. She took the thermometer from her apron pocket and leaned over me, saying "Open wide, baby, now hold this under your tongue. Close your mouth, Cookie." (She always added that last part.)

The thermometer stabbed the underside of my tongue. It tasted of rubbing alcohol, as always. Repositioning it earned me a slap on the hand.

"Leave that alone, now. I'll be back shortly." She turned at the door and faced me. "Now, no cheating! I know it's uncomfortable, but do not breathe through your mouth—and Cookie, don't squirm! It's only a few minutes!"

I removed the thermometer. "But Mama, I have to go to the bathroom!"

"You can wait three more minutes, young lady. Now," she motioned with her hand, "back in your mouth!"

Mama returned with a basin of warm water, soap, towels, and washcloth. After she removed and read the thermometer and returned it to her pocket, she brought fresh pajamas from my drawer. "You'll feel better after a cleanup. Then we'll see about supper, sleepyhead!"

Mama rubbed my chest and back with Mentholatum and pulled one of my daddy's tee shirts over my head. We played out this ritual each time croup gripped my chest and throat. Whether through actual therapeutics or suggestion, I always felt better as mentholated gel infused my upper body, its warmth held close by Daddy's shirt. At the very least, vapors rising from my throat eased my nasal congestion. Mother added clean flannel pajamas and cozy socks. Then she escorted me to the bathroom and captured me for more aspirin on the return trip.

When I was safely back in bed, Daddy came in to see how I was doing. He sat beside me, smelling of tobacco smoke and subtle barn odors—cows, fresh milk, feed grain, and hay. He always told me jokes or stories from work that Mama didn't think were suitable. Periodically, she glanced in to monitor what he was saying, occasionally commenting with sighs or flashing him knowing looks.

Eventually, she brought in a bed tray. "Help her sit up, will you, Hal? And drape that towel over her." Daddy did as instructed, then stepped aside after giving me a whiskery kiss. Mama plopped the tray astraddle my legs. "Please try to eat a little, honey. I brought your favorites."

The tray held a small bowl of tomato soup, half a toasted cheese sandwich, and a small glass of milk. I sighed, knowing how much my throat hurt since my tonsils were almost always infected when I had croup. I managed a few sips of soup, two bites of sandwich, and half the milk. This satisfied Mother, who whisked away the tray with a smile.

"Wouldn't you like to open your present now?" she asked. "Daddy and I would like to share something with you on your birthday." I nodded. Daddy brought the package to me and I slowly opened it. "At least you got to open one of your presents for yourself. We hope you like it."

Inside the box lies a doll—a rubber baby no more than five inches long! She wears a pink crocheted bonnet and dress, and a tiny pink flannel diaper fastened with a little brass pin. White crocheted booties keep her feet warm. I am delighted! I have seen a little baby like this at the doctor's office. The receptionist volunteered to Mama that a friend of hers made them for sale.

"Do you really like her, Cookie? I saw you looking at her a while ago. Daddy called the lady before Christmas and she had just this one left."

"I'm gonna call her 'Itsy Bitsy,'" I whispered.

"Like the spider in the song?"

"Yeah." The sound came out more like a croak than a word. "Like the spider and"—I paused for breath—"and because she's so small." Mama smiled at Daddy, a warm smile that filled my heart with hope. He grinned back and made an okay sign with his right hand.

I thanked my parents, snuggled Itsy Bitsy close to me, and fell asleep. My birthday had turned out okay after all.

CHAPTER 25
In Which Annie Teaches Me to Make Change

When I woke, my brothers were eating breakfast. The smell of eggs and bacon turned my stomach.

I can hear Mama at the telephone. She has pulled it to the end of its long cord and stands just outside my door. From her end of the conversation, I know she's talking to our doctor. "Okay, we'll be at the clinic as soon as we can," I hear her say, then the receiver clicks in its cradle and Daddy says something, low and muffled.

Mama responded in her soft, even tones. "We'll be all right. We can drop you off at the shipyard and then get along to the clinic. I'll pick you up after work."

Daddy said that he thought he could get a ride home with a neighbor. "In fact," I heard him pick up the phone, "I'll bet he hasn't left yet." Daddy whistled as he waited for the operator. "8037J1, please." Daddy was silent for a few seconds, then someone must have answered on the other end. "Joe, this is Hal. Glad you haven't left yet."

As Daddy made arrangements with his friend, Mama bustled into the room with a breakfast tray—this time, coddled eggs on toast. "Get up and eat this, Cookie. Then put on your thick robe. We have an appointment in town."

"Mama, I don't wanna go—I feel fine today. Really, I do!" I croaked like a frog, the sound coming from deep in my blocked throat, words barely able to squeeze between my swollen tonsils. She fixed me with a disapproving look.

"You sure don't sound like it to me. Now quit whining and hurry. The roads are bad, and we haven't much time." When she reached the door, she turned and pointed to the tray. "And eat those eggs!"

I opened my mouth to protest, thought better of it, and got dressed. The eggs were stone cold by this time, so I fished out their toast beds, pushing the eggs around on the plate. The toast hurt going down, but my attempt satisfied Mama after she coerced me into two gagging bites of congealed egg white.

Since Mama didn't believe in letting cold air anywhere near her sick babies, she bundled me up like a mummy. I nearly suffocated, but my muffled protests fell upon deaf ears. In the car, she gave me a warning eyebrow raise and turned on the heater. "Don't faunch around," she ordered. "You'll make yourself worse."

I tried to sit still, but going to the doctor ranked right up at the top of any little kid's horror lists, along with trips to the dentist, the principal's office, and the woodshed (not necessarily in that order). Sweat trickled off the back of my head, making my skin tickle as it headed for my shoulder blades. I was so confined by coats and bedding that no amount of squirming relieved my discomfort. When Mama began making unhappy noises, I abandoned my efforts and drifted into a half-sleep.

A blast of cold air jolted me awake. Mama had opened the

passenger door and was maneuvering me onto her shoulder. "I can walk, Mama," I croaked. "You shouldn't be carryin' a big kid like me—not with your bad back!" Mama ignored me and hustled quickly into the clinic through knee-deep snow, taking care not to slip on the ice.

I actually liked my doctor—a smiling man with children of his own. He had delivered me. "Well, what's up with the towhead today?" Doctor Haller came through the door pulling on his white coat. "Tonsils and chest again?" His hand ruffled my platinum blonde Dutch bob. Mama murmured assent as I dutifully opened my mouth for the tongue depressor.

"Well, I should say," he commented. "That is a truly remarkable sight! Your tonsils, Cookie, are a lovely crimson with white and yellow streaks, and large as sausages! How do you manage it?" He grinned down at me, knowing I couldn't answer. "What shall we do this time?"

Usually, he swabbed my throat with a nasty tasting solution and sent me home with orders for liquids and aspirin and steam for my chest—all the things my mother had been doing for me. Today, he reached inside his coat pocket and, with a flourish, withdrew a large green glass bottle.

"Ta-da! Today, we have magic!" He presented the bottle to Mother as if it were made of gold and encrusted with precious jewels. "Behold, sulfa!"

"Oh, good Lord," she gasped. "How did you get your hands on that?"

I had been hearing them talk about this stuff for a couple of years now and had mentally put sulfa in the same category as dragons and unicorns—unobtainable or imaginary.

"Do you think it will work?"

"This should knock her infection for a loop. Might just save her kidneys, too!"

They didn't think I knew about the kidneys. I also suffered from terrible bladder infections that often kept me in bed. A bout with tonsillitis or croup usually preceded a bladder infection that repeatedly attacked my kidneys. Doctor Haller feared these infections would eventually damage my kidneys beyond repair. They had talked over my head for years, he and Mama, not realizing that I was now old enough to read between the lines.

"How does she take this?" She opened the bottle and shook out some of its contents into her palm.

I stared down at muddy yellowish pills the diameter of a nickel and twice as thick. "Give her two to start. Just crush 'em up with jelly or something. Then give her one every four hours around the clock. Let's have her back in here on Friday and see how she's doing."

I cannot take my eyes off those huge pills! Mama drops them back into the bottle and caps it tightly. As she reaches for the doctor's hand, I get a whiff of sulfa from hers. My stomach lurches.

"Ya know, Doctor, some other little kid could probably use those sulfur things more'n me," I croaked.

"Oh, no, you don't." Dr. Haller grinned at my mama. "We've waited a long time for these little magic bullets—and you're taking every one!"

By the time Mama had me properly bundled and muffled and in the car, a fitful snow was blowing. She turned the heater up on high and started the windshield wipers.

"I'm sure glad we don't have to stop at the pharmacy." She

looked a little worried. "This snow is starting to come down hard. Hang on, honey. The streets are slick."

I brightened, hoping that Fate and snow would intercede between the sulfa and me, but my mama was an excellent driver and we made it safely home.

As she hustled me off to bed, Mama began her usual return home inquisition. She had left Danny in charge—an unenviable position for him, as this time his second-in-command was not present to assume responsibility for any errors in his judgment. He was free to take both accolades and blame, but today his answers proved satisfactory. A quick survey failed to unearth any obvious breakage in household or younger sibling. I watched Daniel closely, as cursory inspections had, on occasion, failed to unearth some pretty interesting misfortunes. His face remained unworried.

Mama buttoned my flannel pajamas up round my neck and settled me under the covers. "As soon as I feed your brothers, I'll bring you something to eat and your sulfa." She smiled, cupping my chin with her hand. "I just know this medicine will make you feel better fast."

She was back before I knew it. I feigned sleep, struggling to control my breathing. My eyelids betrayed me, however, as Mama could see them flicker with the effort to keep them closed.

"Cookie—sit up. Sit up, young lady, I know you're awake!" She prodded my arm with her finger. I slowly opened my eyes, hoping that she would decide to wait on the pill. No such luck. Her left hand held a large tablespoon.

"Oh, Mama," I demurred as I slowly sat up and arranged myself against my pillows; "How do you know that pill won't kill me? That's an awful big pill for a little kid."

"Don't be a baby. Open your mouth and let's get this over with." Confidently, she pushed the spoon, its bowl filled to the brim with a bilious mixture of berry jam and powdery bright yellow particles, towards my mouth. I jerked my head backwards, jaws clenched tight, like a trout on the fly!

"No you don't, sister!" She snatched my arm and hauled me up short. "Just open up. Now!" She punctuated her commands with the spoon.

It is not just the sight of the spoon that bothers me—its contents have a moldy, nostril-curling odor that make my gorge rise. I know with icy certainty this stuff will make me vomit. Nonetheless, my mouth flies open at Mother's command. Before I can close it, she aims and with lightning speed deposits the vile mixture at the back of my tongue. Without hesitation, my body rejects both sulfa and jam, hurling them into mid-bedroom.

Mother's eyes became little slits to match her mouth. "You did that on purpose." She reached down and scraped the rejected stuff back into the spoon. "This cost a fortune, and— You. Will. Take. It," she enunciated through clenched teeth.

A struggle ensued in which blows were struck on both sides. I lost a little hair—Mama lost control of spoon and medicine. Both ended up on the floor, this time irretrievably. In the ensuing silence, we glared at each other. "I did not throw up on purpose," I declared with passion, although this emerged as more of a croak.

"You did!" My mother was adamant. Her hair fell over her forehead in brown, tousled strands. "I know when you do something on purpose. Now, I am going out to the kitchen and crushing up another pill. And **You. Will. Take. It.**"

I knew that no amount of explanation on my part would convince her of the truth—the stuff simply smelled and tasted so hideous that I was incapable of retaining it. We were in for a long and stormy (on more than one front) afternoon.

In truth, Mama was shocked by both my vehemence and my strength. She retreated to the kitchen to rethink her position. When she returned, her spoon held a mound of brownish material that completely disguised the sulfa. This time she had mixed it with marshmallow and cocoa and stirred it in thoroughly.

"Honey, Doctor Haller says this will disguise the taste. Please, try again, will you?" Her change in attitude plus the concoction's lack of obvious particles and smell lulled me into a false sense of security. I opened my mouth, dutifully.

This mixture actually makes it to the stomach before my brain gets wind of smell and taste and orders my built-in ejection system to cycle. It pauses barely long enough for Mama to think she has won (a smile growing), then whooshes past her ear, bringing with it my breakfast toast and eggs.

Mama snorted. Her face worked as she fought for control—her hands fluttered, and she made a couple of attempts to speak. I cringed, waiting for retribution. The vomiting had been entirely involuntary. I could no more control it than I could fly! After a few moments, I opened my eyes. Mama had slipped quietly out the door.

She reappeared almost immediately, carrying washcloth, towels, and clean sheets. Silently, she stripped the soiled bedding and remade my bed. Mama helped me wash up and change into fresh pajamas, then settled me back into bed and sat down beside me.

"Cookie, we have a problem here. You need to understand how important this new medicine is. You have to take it. It's going to help you get well." She took my hands with hers, turned them palms up and kissed them. "I want to believe that you aren't deliberately throwing up—but—"

I interrupted. "It's the smell, Mama. It smells terrible—and the taste is just awful! I couldn't help myself, please believe me! You have to believe me. You do believe me, don't you?" I began to cry, quietly, trying to control the ropy cough I could feel building in my chest. Mama just looked at me with her sad eyes, not speaking.

After a few seconds, I continued. "I could try swallowing it with water."

"I do believe you, honey. I suppose I do know you wouldn't throw up on purpose. And maybe you could swallow a small pill, but how could you get those enormous things down your poor, swollen throat? I don't want you to choke!"

Just then, Annie popped her head through the door. "Perhaps I can help thee! Danny let me in—I hope thee doesn't mind!" She smiled as she bustled in. "I just came down to see if our girl is feeling better."

"Of course, I don't mind, Anne—and if there's any way you can help get this pill down her, please do!" Mama shook one out into Annie's hand. We all stared at it as if our combined effort could reduce its size.

"Thee has tried crushing it, of course."

"Yes," Mother sighed. "Twice. She says the taste makes her vomit. I'll admit, I took a taste myself, and I don't know if I could fool it down. Actually, it smells nasty as well."

"Put the thing down on the tray, please. Yes, like that." Annie pulled a small knife from her apron pocket and quickly cut the ugly yellowish lump into four equally sized pieces. "There!" She turned to me, "thee can surely handle four small ones, can thee not?"

The sulfa crumbled a little at its cut edges. I eyed each piece with displeasure. "I can smell it, Annie—I can still smell it." My voice quivered.

"Well, thee must take the medicine. Quickly, plug thy nose and swallow each piece with lots of water. Thy cannot smell or taste it that way."

Giving me no time to think, Annie held my nose and popped a piece into my mouth. I took a slug of water and worried it down, following quickly with the other pieces before I lost my nerve. The fourth piece lodged at the back of my throat. Fighting the urge to gag, I gargled it loose with water and got it down. We all smiled.

"I'm so proud of you!" Mama beamed down at me. "Anne, thanks for the help. I didn't think she'd ever do it."

"God always helps us find a way to accomplish that which must be done. I did not permit her to think otherwise. And you, little girl, take thy pills for thy mother." She paused for a moment, then, with a twinkle, she continued; "After all, we turned a profit on that pill."

"What do you mean, Annie?"

"Well, t'were the size of a nickel—and we changed it into four quarters. I call that a clear profit of ninety-five cents!" Mama laughed for the first time in days.

Sulfa really did the trick. I felt so much better by morning that Mama let me sit by the fireplace as long as I stayed quiet and warm. Daniel and Robbie were outside with the sled. I could hear them whooping with delight as they took turns riding down the slippery driveway. I read for a while, then Mama and I listened to "Young Dr. Malone" and "Pepper Young's Family" on the radio. During "Ma Perkins," the boys ran in, breathless and smelling of snow, ready for hot cocoa and sandwiches.

Shortly after lunch, Annie arrived carrying a covered sewing basket. We shut ourselves in the spare room when Mama decreed I'd been "up quite enough, thank you!" Annie helped me start piecing a log cabin quilt as a surprise for Mama while she worked on her wedding present quilt.

We sewed and talked until Annie noticed me yawning. "Thee needs thy rest, little one." She stacked my quilt patches neatly in the sewing basket beneath her own. "Now thy mother will not see thy surprise! I will go now and bring thy sewing back some other day. Rest well, Leah, and God be with thee."

Annie tiptoed out and closed the door softly behind her. I lay quietly beneath my warm blankets daydreaming about sledding with my brothers and drifted slowly off to sleep.

CHAPTER 26
In Which I Learn the Cost of My Heart

I often look back on this Christmas vacation as a watershed, a benchmark against which to measure the days of my life before and those which came after—separating yesterday's reality from tomorrow's promise. My parents had entered some kind of truce for the holidays, and like little kids everywhere, I was sure everything was now alright. In reality, everything changed after New Year's Eve.

My parents were going to a party—something they hadn't done for a long time. Mama buzzed with excitement as she anticipated dancing, food, and adult conversation. She often felt isolated, relying, for the most part, on her children and Annie for company. Our neighbors dangled along the poorly paved country road like widely spaced beads on a necklace. Walking was out of the question during winter, and Mama had spent most of this last year confined to her bed.

The morning of the party, Mama washed her hair and set it in curlers, then trimmed and filed her nails. She had soft brown shoulder-length hair usually worn swept back from her forehead and rolled around a rat. For the party tonight, she planned on a sophisticated French twist held in place with coppery hairpins. She chattered away at me, asking my opinion on what she should wear, which jewelry accented her dress, and what nail enamel best complemented her coloring. I hadn't seen her so animated in months.

"Oh, Cookie!" she sparkled. "I feel like a little kid!" She was sitting in the bathtub, up to her chin in warm water and frothy bubbles. I sat quietly atop the closed toilet lid, legs folded Indian style, feeling honored to be party to my mother's joy. "A new year is ahead of us," she spoke with enthusiasm, "and this one's going to be the best yet. I really feel that Daddy and I can work out our problems."

This was the first she had said about problems between the two of them. I had guessed as much both from her actions and from things she had **not** said in the last few months, but until now, my suspicions were unconfirmed. I readjusted myself on the toilet seat and remained quiet.

"This party is just what the doctor ordered, and I intend to have a wonderful time tonight!" She pulled the plug and sat for a moment watching the level of suds drop.

"Would you hand me a towel, please?" I unwound my legs and hopped down, grabbed a towel from the wooden drying rack next to the sink, and handed it to her. "Thanks, honey. Say, would you go get that pink nail polish we picked out? I think we left it on my dresser."

If Mama had asked me earlier, or perhaps waited five more minutes to send me, I would not have overheard the phone call. I suppose it made no difference to the final outcome, but it might have saved me a lot of grief. When I popped open the bedroom door, I found Daddy with the receiver to his ear. His back was to me and he appeared to be listening intently.

Instinctively, I stood quite still, unwilling to attract his attention. Finally, Daddy spoke.

"Yeah, that sounds fine to me. We'll be at the party early. No, no. Don't stay home! That would raise all kinds of questions." He listened again for a few moments. "Don't worry. No one will notice us slip out. She'll be having so much fun she'll never know." Another pause, then; "Okay. Yeah. I do, too." Then with irritation, "Yeah, I said I love you, too!"

I heard the receiver click on its cradle. Daddy looked up and caught my reflection in Mama's dresser mirror. "Cookie." He made my name a statement, not a question. "How long have you been standing there?" His voice had a bite to it.

"I just came in, Daddy. Mama needs her nail polish."

"Here it is." He grabbed the bottle from the dresser and tossed it to me. "No need to bother your mother about any phone calls, got it?" Daddy pinned me to the wall with his eyes.

"No, Daddy. I didn't hear anything, anyway."

"Well, that's good. Now scram—I have to dress for this party."

When I returned to the bathroom, Mama was wearing her slip. She had the door propped open to let out the steam before she removed the rollers from her hair. She hummed as she toweled condensation from the mirror. I went in and set the small bottle of nail enamel on the toilet tank lid.

"What took you so long? I almost sent out a search party!" Mama turned around, laughing. She stopped when she saw my face. "What's the matter, honey? You look odd."

"Nothing, Mama. I'm sorry I was gone so long. Daddy was getting dressed and I had to wait."

Telling my mother about the telephone call would serve

no purpose. I was still puzzling out just what I had heard, and what it meant. Actually, there was nothing I could tell her—at least for now.

I watched as she combed and fixed her hair, polished her nails, and pulled on her hose. She had a new pair, wonderfully silky looking with dark seams and clocks at the heels. She took great care rolling each stocking separately, inserting her carefully pedicured foot and smoothing the stocking up her leg, fastening it to garters at her thigh. When she had finished, she ran her hands appreciatively down her legs, straightening the seams at the back.

"There!" she exclaimed with satisfaction. "There's nothing like a new pair of hose to make a girl feel rich!" She stepped into her dress and asked me to zip her up. I stood on the toilet lid so I could reach all the way to her neck, taking time to fasten the little hook and eye that held the neckline together above the zipper.

She stepped away and whirled around.

"Wow, you sure look beautiful!" I exclaimed. "Are you gonna wear perfume?"

My mother wore the most wonderful scent— "Evening in Paris," it was called, and it sat in a place of honor on her dresser in the bedroom. Evening in Paris came in a small midnight blue tubelike bottle with a blue tassel on the top. Mama would carefully open the glass stopper, gently tilt the opening against her forefinger, then gingerly apply the liquid to her throat, behind her ears, and in the crack of her bosom. "Pulse points," she called them, "where you can feel your heartbeat. It warms the perfume and makes it smell better," was her explanation. When she was finished with herself, she always used the last remaining traces on me. I can still remember that scent and how special I felt when she touched it to my face and smiled.

"Well, how do I look?" she asked as she slipped into her shoes—black patent open-toed evening pumps with tiny ankle straps fastened with shiny silver buckles. "Finally! I can wear high heels again. I feel like a queen!"

"You look like one, too, Mama. Just like a beautiful queen."

She stands there in her black cocktail dress, hair coiled neatly atop her head. She wears her rhinestone choker and sparkling rhinestone earrings with dangling teardrop-shaped stones. I have cleaned her jewelry for her, carefully polishing the stones with an old toothbrush and a paste of water and cream of tartar as she has taught me. Her complexion glows with health, aided by the barest touch of mascara, eyebrow pencil, and pale pink lip color to match her nails.

"Hubba hubba hubba." *Daddy appears around the corner with Mama's coat. He whistles his special "wolf whistle" and says she looks wonderful. He winks at me while he helps Mama with her coat.* "I'm taking the most beautiful lady in the world to the party tonight, huh, Cookie?"

I nod, not really wanting to speak. They both look so happy—Daddy, handsome in his dark blue suit with pinstripes and a matching tie, Mama smiling widely, her cloth winter coat obscuring her elegance, rather like brown paper and string covering a wonderful gift. I love these two people, my parents. I take a mind picture this night—the kind of photo that never fades but remains until time strips the last memories from your soul. Right now, they give every indication of being happy. Why, then, do I feel such sadness?

"Be good, you two, and see Robbie safely off to bed as soon as we're gone." Mama kissed Daniel, who wiped it away with the back of his hand.

"Oh, Mom, I'm too old for that mush."

"Well maybe you are," laughed Mama, "but I'm not!" She kissed him again. "Leah, mind what your brother tells you. He's in charge." She kissed me, too, ignoring my brother's Cheshire Cat grin. I guess she didn't realize how Danny lorded it over me when he 'babysat.' "You may both stay up to hear the New Year in. Make sure you turn off the radio before you go to bed."

Daddy winked at me as he escorted our mother through the open door, bowing low, his arm across his waist. "Madam, your carriage awaits without!"

"Without who?" my brothers and I shouted in unison.

"Without your mother, of course!"

We all laughed at our silly family joke.

Daddy assisted Mama into Elizabeth's passenger seat, helping her tuck her coat around her legs to keep out the cold, crisp end of December air. He swept around to the driver's side, mounted the running board, and waved elegantly to the three of us kids standing on the back stoop. Then, with a flourish, he seated himself and closed the door. Elizabeth started with a cough and a jerk and slowly putted off.

Danny started acting snotty before Mama and Daddy got to the end of our driveway. I could still hear Elizabeth the Puddle Jumper huffing in protest when he ordered me to put Robbie to bed.

"Mama left you in charge—you do it!" I shouted as I flounced up the back steps and into the mudroom. I knew this tactic had little chance of working, but it was always worth the try. Danny ran ahead and gave me a shove as he passed. I paused at the archway between living room and kitchen, waiting for Robbie. Catching me off guard, Danny thumped me with Mama's special sofa pillow. I staggered back against the kitchen counter, painfully cracking the back of my head and clipping my tongue between my teeth.

"Hey, stop that!" Tears smarted my eyes as I explored my tongue for signs of blood. "That's the pillow Unca Jerry brought from Manila. Mama's gonna kill you if anything happens to it."

"You'd better hope nothing happens to you!" Daniel brandished the pillow over his head. "Pillow fight," he shouted.

He dove into me again, whacking my back and legs without mercy. Dust puffed from Mother's pillow each time it connected with my body. Soon Robbie joined in, flailing about with his small bed pillow. They chased me into the living room and successfully wrestled me to the floor.

"Say uncle!" Daniel's order was punctuated with several telling head blows. "I said, say uncle and we'll stop."

I clenched my teeth and shook my refusal, although moving my head made me dizzy. Robbie saved me from more pummeling by dropping his pillow and beginning to cry.

"What'cha doin' that for?" Danny turned to Robbie with a puzzled look. He sounded exasperated but got in a few more cheap shots before I struggled beyond his reach. "Robbie, us boys gotta stick together. Look, she's gettin' away!"

Robbie sobbed louder.

"Well, for cryin' out loud. Did'ja get hurt or somethin'?"

Robbie snuffled and shook his head.

"Well, then why're ya cryin'? Nobody's hurtin' you."

Robbie stopped crying and wiped his eyes. "SHE'LL get me. Leah'll get HER to get me."

"What're you talkin' about? Who's gonna get you?"

"That hatchet lady, that's who. Cookie, please don't tell. I won't hit you anymore." Robbie resumed his crying.

"Ah, she was just makin' that stuff up to scare you. Tell him, Sis!"

I kept my mouth shut. Robbie had so far failed to connect his beloved "Lady Anne," as he called her, to the far more sinister Hatchet Annie of more than a year before. Danny whacked me a few more times, hoping to force a confession for Robbie, who wailed louder with each blow as if it were he being pummeled, not me! Finally, Danny gave up in disgust. He tossed the pillow back onto the sofa and stomped off. Mama's special pillow missed the couch, but not Danny's stomping foot. Danny looked at me in horror as we stared at each other.

The death of this pillow is an omen. I can feel it in my heart and somehow, I know that deep in his, Danny also knows the truth. Robbie stares with open mouth, then plops his thumb into it and makes a sobbing noise. Does he feel the cold rising from its death as Danny and I do? Danny and I collect up the feathers in silence, putting them, along with the fabric cover with its map of the Victory in the Pacific into a brown paper bag, and place it beside our mama's favorite chair.

We quieted Robbie with a cup of cocoa made by Daniel with much panache and a great deal of mess, thoughtfully left for me to clean up. Robbie went off to bed, probably to dream of ugly old crones with hatchets and pillows exploding into the air. Although I could do nothing about the death of our family, I promised myself that someday he would know the truth about Hatchet Annie. Actually, I never took the chance, when offered, and Robbie passed away not hearing an apology from me.

Daniel and I straightened the living room and sat down in front of the radio to wait for midnight. We fell asleep on the floor wrapped in blankets, heads snuggled together, not saying a word about Mama's special pillow. I didn't hold a grudge against my brothers for my treatment at their hands. In the long run, anger would hurt me worse than any blow. I loved them both, with all their flaws, and I hoped they cared a little about me. We would all need each other in the days to come.

CHAPTER 27
In Which I Witness the Beginning of the End

I woke up New Year's Day in my own bed. The boys slept soundly. Danny lay on his back, snoring gently; Robbie slept face down with no pillow, mouth open, drool staining his sheet. I tiptoed past their sleeping forms, stopping short when Robbie grunted and rolled to his side. He sighed and settled. I waited a few anxious moments, then escaped quietly into the playroom.

Mama and Daddy's bedroom door stood slightly ajar. I could hear my mother's soft murmuring sleep sounds and daddy's louder ones. I nudged the door shut as I passed, careful not to disturb them.

Outdoors, I recognize clanging milk buckets and soft voices. Daddy must have hired someone to come in and milk our cow this morning. I wonder about feeding chickens and collecting eggs, but before I reach any decision about getting dressed, the back porch door opens and Pete, our fourteen-year-old neighbor, places a basket of eggs next to a row of boots. He sees my face at the kitchen door and smiles, giving me a quick salute, and pops back out. The screen slams behind him.

Pete, the love of my young heart, was handsome, friendly, and the proud owner of a beautiful black mare named Velvet. I'm not sure which of them I loved more—Pete or his horse. Faithful Velvet carried him everywhere, rain or shine (or snow). I ran to the French doors in hopes of seeing them go by, but they must have cut across the field.

A few snowflakes drift insolently down on fields already knee-deep in white crystals. I marvel at the odds of having snow for both Christmas and New Year's. I worry that Annie might not have enough wood for her fireplace. She has not been around for a few days—I hope her new year will be wonderful. I think about my recent bout with croup and the sulfa I am still taking every day. I feel fine and hope that Mama will let me off the hook and save the rest of the bottle for the next time I get sick. Maybe I can suggest that to her when she wakes up. I think about my birthday party and the game that Danny has purloined. Maybe he will get careless and I can get it back.

I don't know how long I sat at the window lost in thought before the rise and fall of angry voices from my parents' bedroom attracted my attention.

I hear the tears in Mama's softly undulating tones. My father's gruff response overrides Mama's pleadings. Although the words are muffled, their tones are unmistakable. I slide quietly from the overstuffed chair as I consider moving close enough to make out words but freeze as the door slams open, and Daddy, clad in his tee-shirt and jockey shorts, storms out.

"Not one word about her, do you hear me? I don't want to hear her named mentioned!" He shot the words like bullets, short, spitting, and solid. Behind him, through the doorway, I could see Mama. She sat in the center of the bed, knees against her chest, face buried in her hands, huddled in a heap of crumpled bedclothes. She jerked as each word hit her. Daddy whipped around, nailed me to the chair with his eyes, then stomped through the kitchen arch carrying his blue jeans and flannel shirt. I waited until I heard the bathroom door shut before quietly approaching their bedroom.

Mama's shoulders trembled with effort to hold back her tears as I snuggled in next to her. I wanted to touch her shoulders, but some instinct held me back. Instead, I spoke softly. "What's the matter, Mama? Why are you crying? Did you and Daddy have a fight?"

Last night's interrupted telephone call flashes across my mind. I see Daddy's face; I hear how warmly he speaks to the mystery lady on the other end of the line. He is saying that he loves her. Does this mean he does not love my mother?

Mama lifted her face towards me and removed her hands. Her eyes, rimmed by red, swollen lids, were black pits punctuating her pale skin. "Nothing's the matter, Cookie. Just a misunderstanding between your Daddy and me." She smiled at me but couldn't hide her misery—it lingered behind her dark eyes and gave lie to her upturned mouth.

"Are you sure, Mama? What did Daddy mean about a woman?"

Mother's hands shot out and snatched my arms in vice-like grips. She jerked me upright and pulled me nose-to-nose, those dark eyes burning into mine. "What do you know about her?" she demanded.

"I don't know about any woman, Mama. It was whatever Daddy said. Please believe me!" I yanked my arms free and fell flat on my back across the bed. Mama sank into her huddle and covered her face again.

"I do believe you, honey. I'm just tired. Could you please leave me alone for a little while? I'm okay, really I am." She sighed deeply.

Before I slid off the bed I reached out and patted Mama's hand. "You know, you can talk to me about anything, Mama— I'm your best friend. Anything you say to me is a secret."

"I know, Cookie. Maybe later we'll talk. Right now, I need to think."

I kissed my mother on her cheek and silently left the room.

Daddy had made a pot of coffee and cooked breakfast. He sat at the kitchen table sipping from his cup. My brothers sat on either side of him presenting a phalanx of male solidarity. Daddy glowered at me but motioned to my chair. I sat down, feeling isolated.

Danny and Robbie were attacking plates stacked high with pancakes and syrup. A few bedraggled pancakes rested dejectedly on a platter in the table center.

"We saved ya some. You'd better hurry and get 'um, though, 'cause I'm almost done and we're all still hungry!" Daniel made a proprietary grab towards the platter.

"That's okay with me," I answered.

Daddy motioned to my chair. "Sit down and eat. And you boys, let her have those pancakes." Daniel snatched his hand back and shot me a look that said he'd get even. I forked the smallest cake onto my plate and looked for the jam. Daddy shoved the syrup at me and grunted. It didn't seem prudent to make a fuss this morning, so I poured a little dab of syrup onto my cake and let my brothers squabble over the rest.

Mama slipped by me on the way to the bathroom. She

paused at the door and stared at the back of Daddy's head. Her face carried such open pain it hurt me to see her. She opened her mouth as if to speak, thought better of it, then entered the bathroom and closed the door quietly behind her.

Daddy squirmed in his chair, his mouth twisting in disgust. He muttered something profane under his breath and shook his head, then pushed himself roughly away from the table and stormed out onto the back porch. The door slammed shut behind him, leaving its little window vibrating wildly. We stared, openmouthed, half expecting the glass to shatter. Mama bolted from the bathroom, wild-eyed.

"What's happened? Is everyone okay?" Her eyes scanned the scene, surveying for damage. Apparently, she was satisfied with our safety, as she withdrew again to the bathroom.

"What the heck's goin' on around here this morning?" Danny frowned, his eyebrows appearing to meet between his eyes. "Everybody's grouchy. Come on, Rob. Let's get outta here and get dressed. Maybe Mama'll let us take the sled out." They pushed their chairs back from the table and scampered from the kitchen, leaving dirty dishes on the table. I sighed, knowing I'd been assigned KP duty by default, and began clearing the breakfast mess. I could hear them laughing in the bedroom as they dressed.

Presently, Mama shuffled back into the kitchen. "Is **HE** still outside?" She looked intently about the room as if expecting Daddy to pop out from under the table. I nodded as I pulled a clean cup from the cupboard.

"Want some coffee, Mama? I can get you a cup."

"I'd like that, baby. Thank you." She sat down at her regular spot and began arranging condiments on the center mat—salt, pepper, sugar bowl, and syrup. "Did you eat your breakfast?" She eyed my plate, still full of pancake. "Oh, I see Daddy forgot the jam. I'm sorry, Cookie. I know you don't like syrup."

"It's okay," I said as I slid my mother's coffee towards her. "I don't think he's in a very good mood. What's goin' on?"

Mama bristled. "Well, I'm not in a very good mood myself. He's really done it this time." I sat down prepared to listen intently and cradled my chin in my hands, elbows inelegantly propped on the table. Mama hesitated; "This isn't a good place to talk, actually. And I sure shouldn't be talking to you!"

I remained very still, certain she was thinking out loud. If I were quiet (and lucky), her need to tell someone would outweigh her desire to protect me from the truth. I waited.

Mama absently sipped her coffee. She stared at the wall phone, weighing the pros and cons of calling her sister or mother, then appeared to remember our twelve-party phone line and thought better of it. "If I call Aunt Noreen, the whole neighborhood will listen in. If I don't talk, I'll explode!" Mama slapped her hands on the oilcloth tabletop and jumped up. "Come with me, Leah. I have to tell someone, and I trust you to keep a secret." We ended up in my parents' bedroom with the door locked.

Mama sat in the middle of the unmade bed with her legs pulled tight against her chest, held in place by her arms. She rested her chin on her knees and smiled wistfully. She looks like a little kid, I thought, like a hurt little kid.

"What happened at the party, Mama? Why are you and Daddy mad at each other?"

"I was so excited about that damned party—sorry Cookie,

I shouldn't swear—but now I wish we'd never gone! That woman..." Her voice trailed off. Tears welling up in her eyes began in her throat, choking off the words. I waited quietly for her to continue. "And your daddy—how could he do this to me—to us!"

I didn't know exactly what he had done, but Mama left me no doubt that his actions had harmed both her in particular and our family in general. She buried her face in her hands, surrendering herself completely to her tears. Muffled sobs shook her body as she rocked back and forth on the bed. Instinctively, my hand touched her shoulder to give comfort. Mama froze, strangling her sobs. I snatched back my hand, mentally cataloging my error, but puzzled by my mother's reaction. Maybe someday I would understand complex adult emotions. Now I was just learning.

"I don't understand. What did the lady and daddy do?"

"It's complicated, Cookie. They didn't do anything but dance with each other. And it wasn't the dancing, exactly. It was how they danced. I can't explain it to you, honey. Someday you'll understand." She began rocking again, gently, her own arms offering the comfort she had rejected from me.

I did understand—my daddy loved this other lady!

I climbed up beside her on the bed and laid my head on her shoulder. "Don't worry, Mama. I won't let anybody hurt you—not even Daddy! What can I do to help?" Remembering Daddy's phone call on New Year's Eve, only last night, although it seemed so long ago, made me feel guilty—I should have told Mama about it. I had promised Daddy not to tell, and now it was too late.

She patted my knee. "Brave little girl. I know you mean

that. Right now, you can help me best by just lending me an ear and keeping what we talk about to yourself. Do you promise?"

I nodded, making a solemn vow to myself. I would never betray her confidence—not even to Daddy.

CHAPTER 28
In Which Mama Becomes a Heroine

We woke on the first day back at school after the Christmas recess to most unusual weather conditions. The clouds hung grey and ominous over the eastern half of the sky, gathering together in huge brooding clumps. Although the snow of Christmas week had partially melted, a good amount still covered the pastures and most of the back-country roads. Daddy had laboriously shoveled our own long drive up its little hill to the old road, but he had his doubts that Elizabeth would make it. Consequently, he asked a ride of Frank Moen. Although Frank and his family lived even further up the road than we did, his property, hidden as it was by tall trees, was both level and protected somewhat from the Christmas snowfall. He had been out to town and was happy to have Daddy for company.

Mama and Daddy appeared to have patched things up since the infamous party on New Year's Eve. Mama accepted Daddy's apology, she explained to me, and I had my fingers crossed. Mama found what was left of her favorite pillow and heard Danny's tale of its tragic end with some skepticism but allowed that accidents did happen. The pillow sat repaired, if somewhat limp with fewer feathers, beside her chair—and I hoped it stayed there!

"I don't think the kids should go to school today," Mama said over breakfast oatmeal. Mama liked to serve oatmeal on particularly nasty days. She said it stuck to the ribs and helped keep us warm. I didn't agree, but the one time I said as much to Mama, she gave me "that look" and shook her head. Danny and I stared at each other in amazement—not about the oatmeal, but Mama's comment about school. Mama was a stickler on that subject, especially for me, as I had already missed far too many days with tonsils and kidney infections.

Daddy gave Mama a squeeze as he passed behind her and picked up the telephone. "Let me give Frank a call, honey. I bet he'll drop all the kids off at school on our way into work."

Consequently, twenty minutes later, Danny and I squeezed ourselves into the back seat of Mr. Moen's Packard, elbow to elbow with his two youngest, Kevin and Sarah. Kevin was in kindergarten, a year older than Robbie, and Sarah shared fifth grade with Danny. Pete, the love of my life, attended high school—apparently, he had another ride.

The sky was a solid and menacing ceiling when we reached the school, almost low enough to touch, and tinged with a fierce almost yellow color. The wind had picked up, blowing hard enough to ruffle the heavy Christmas snow still blanketing the schoolyard. Now and then, a transient flake shot past my nose as Danny and I trudged up the steps to the school door. At the landing, I turned and waved to Daddy and Mr. Moen. They were waiting to make sure we got through the door safely. Mr. Anders, the principal, held the door open, fighting the wind that threatened to slam it flat against our backsides. We all made it inside without incident, although the wind had chilled us to the bone.

I separated from the others at the door and scurried to my classroom on the east end of school. The large ceiling-to-almost-floor windows looked out on the side playground where hopscotch diagrams and dodge ball circles were painted bright yellow against the blacktop. Today, they lay covered with crusty snow emblazoned with dog tracks and crisscrossed by a thousand seagull prints. That ominous sky now fell even lower, the clouds so heavy with impending snow they nearly brushed the tops of the monkey bars and swings. Now the wind blew fierce against the windows and the transient flakes became a gush of icy particles plinking at the glass like haphazard fingers on Mama's piano. The room seemed over-bright against the menacing darkness outside.

Mrs. Eldon lowered the shades and busied herself distributing test papers accompanied by groans from her thirty-odd students.

"Silence, children," she pronounced sternly, "this should get us all back in the classroom mood after our long vacation." She retired to her desk and pulled a kitchen timer from its home in the side drawer, turning the dial to ten minutes. "You may begin now." We pulled out our pencils and began, albeit with little good humor.

When the timer ran its course and signaled, Mrs. Eldon stood and instructed us to hand our papers down the line to the front desk in each row. I sat behind my best friend, Abby Bailey, who had the front seat. She passed our row's papers to the left, as directed. The stack moved from row to row, ending up neatly stacked on Tommy Goddard's desk, waiting for Mrs.

Eldon to collect them.

Our teacher walked to the windows and pulled back one of the long, manila-colored shades just enough to allow her a peek outside. Tommy, who sat next to the windows in the front row, tried to get a look, but she let it drop with a slap that startled him. He shot back into his seat, knocking the neat stack of test papers to the floor. Mrs. Eldon directed "that look" at him and stooped to pick up the scattered tests. As she rose, she directed Tommy to the back of the room with her pointer finger. He peeked at the class as he sloped dejectedly back to the stool in the far corner, where Mrs. Eldon seated those who had incurred her wrath.

Someone towards the back of the class snickered, but without turning my head, I couldn't pinpoint which of the boys dared to do so. Mrs. Eldon, on the other hand, had an unobstructed view. The "someone" was in trouble, but before she could take action the classroom door opened and Mama, tailed by Robbie and Danny and Sarah Moen, walked in with Mr. Anders, the principal.

"Sorry to interrupt, but we have a serious problem here, Violette." That must be Mrs. Eldon's first name, I thought. Violette Eldon—I had never thought of her as *having* a first name, let alone one so benign. She was nothing like the sweet little Johnny-jump-ups that Mama called wild violets!

I smiled at Mama, who motioned for me to get up and come to her. Before I rose, I glanced at Mrs. Eldon, asking silent permission to do as Mama requested. She frowned but nodded her head.

"Leah's mother has come off the hill because of the weather," explained Mr. Anders. "The school district has decided to cease today's session and send the children home. Those who live on the hill will have a ride home with her. Abby, please get your things and follow Leah."

By the time we gathered our coats and boots from the cloakroom and joined Mama in the hall, Abby's sister Annie, and Sylvia and Bernie Zader, who lived close to the Bailey's house, arrived. We followed Mama to the main school door, stuffing ourselves into overcoats and boots and gloves, laughing at the privilege of being let out of school so early in the day. When we arrived at the main exit, we gasped in amazement at the scene outside. No winter wonderland, this. The wind howled in rage, picking up snow from the ground, adding it to the hard, frozen flakes driven sideways before us, obliterating the cement sidewalk and the three levels of stairs leading to where Mama had parked Elizabeth at the curb.

"Hurry, kids! We have to get back up the hill before the car can't make it." She took Robbie's hand, dragging him behind her like a ship's rudder, packing the snow under her feet and guiding the rest of us around the hidden stairs and onto the slope where grass, trimmed neatly by the grounds staff, once stood. We floundered in the powdery stuff that rose nearly to my hips but eventually made it to the car.

Mama wiped piled snow from the windscreen, forced open the doors, and squeezed us inside. Abby, Sarah, and I sat in front beside Mama, Robbie riding on my lap. Danny, Annie, Sylvia, and Bernie scrabbled for seat space in the back, eventually cramming themselves in. It was a good thing that Sarah's little brother Keith was home today. Mama managed the doors shut, then struggled to the driver's side. She had to scrape snow from the road before she could open the door, but finally crawled inside, breathing hard, and cold as ice. She pulled off her gloves and tried to warm her blue fingers, first using her breath and then sticking them under her coat, arms crossed, hands stuffed into her armpits.

Presently, she withdrew her hands and replaced her mittens. I could hear her whispering a little prayer under her breath. Her lips twitched as she turned the ignition key and pushed on the starter button on the floor next to the brake pedal. The engine coughed, spluttered, and Mama gave the choke a tug, coddling it with a little burst of fuel—not enough to flood it, I hoped. I could hear Mama muttering, low but fervently as she tried a second and a third time. On her fourth attempt, the engine revved and caught hold. Mama literally heaved a sigh of relief and gingerly released the hand brake. Using the long floor shifter and her left foot on the clutch, she shifted into first and applied a little gas. Reluctantly, the little Model A lurched forward. We were on our way!

We left the school around ten-thirty that morning, arriving home well after one. It had taken us almost two and a half hours to travel the three miles. Several times, Danny and Bernie were forced outside in the biting cold and whipping wind to remove snow from the road so Mama could force the car a few more feet. Once, we slid sideways into an irrigation ditch. Mama put her head down on the steering wheel. I could tell she cried in frustration, as her shoulders shook with the effort to conceal her tears.

We were actually quite close to Sylvia and Bernie's little house that sat on the west side of the road opposite the lower edge of the Broomers' farm. If we looked west and south from where we clung to the edge of the ditch (and if the sideways snow had permitted) we could just see the roof of our barn. Not far as the crow flies, but an impossible distance in our present circumstances. Mama cleared her throat and spoke.

"Well, kids, we are in a bit of a pickle here. I know we're really close to your place," she turned as best she could in the crowded front seat and looked at Sylvia and Bernie, "but I can't risk letting you walk alone from here, and I can't leave the other kids alone in the car, either. If we all try to walk it, someone might get lost." She thought for a moment more.

Bernie, who was in the sixth grade and by far the biggest of us all, piped up. "I know my Daddy's home, and if I can get there, he can come back and help us get your car back on the road. I want to try and make it."

Mama considered this offer, but declined it as too dangerous, "although I don't know what other choice we have," she muttered, almost to herself.

"Doesn't Daddy have that long rope in the trunk?" Danny offered. "You know, Mama, the one he put in there in case he had to pull something out of the way? It's pretty long—maybe long enough to reach almost to Bernie's house."

"Danny, you're a genius!"

"Did'ja hear that, Leah?" Danny hissed with glee as he flicked me hard in the back of the neck. "Mama thinks I'm the genius in the family, now!" Although I flinched at his sharp fingers, I was happy that Mama had rewarded Danny for his quick thinking. It wasn't easy to be big brother to a too-smart little sister, even though I had never wanted the label slapped on my person by OurGrandmother.

Behind the back seat existed what passed for a trunk on this little old Model A Ford. One had to pull the seat portion away from the back cushions to reach the small cavity behind. This held tools to patch and change tires and fix engine problems, a jack, a flashlight, and not one, but several lengths of rope. As cramped as the space was in Elizabeth's back area, Danny and Bernie managed to gain access, notwithstanding a few squished fingers and trampled feet. Danny withdrew the ropes with glee and he and Bernie set to work tying one to another until they had a hodgepodge of length that looked to Mama to be almost enough to reach Bernie and Sylvia's house.

For a few moments, the wind dropped, allowing us a relatively unobstructed view up the road. "I can see my mailbox," Sylvia cried. "Look, Bernie, Daddy's car is in the drive!" We could all see it, half-buried in a snowdrift.

"Okay!" Mama tried to force the driver's door open, with no luck. "Cookie, try your door." With a great deal of difficulty, the heavy door finally opened enough for Mama to crawl across and squeeze herself out. "Quickly, boys, bring that rope!"

Danny and Bernie scrambled out of the back seat, rope draped over their shoulders. Mama tied one end around Bernie's waist and the other to the back door handle. Just as Mama let go and Bernie started up the road in knee-deep snow, the wind began to howl again, and Mama almost pulled him back. Danny put up a fuss when she wouldn't let him go along "for the fun."

As Bernie disappeared into the blowing snow, Mama reeled out the rope and began to pray under her breath. Presently, the rope stopped playing out and Mama slumped back hard on the car door. "Oh, God, Cookie—I hope he got to the door!" She pulled hard on the rope, but it remained taut.

We had waited for what seemed hours when the rope slackened again in Mama's hand. She nearly dropped it from the shock, but as she began reeling it back in, a smile lit up her face. Out of the oblivion that covered everything a few feet from where we waited, Bernie and his father appeared, covered with snow and puffing white steam—two ghostly snow-people—bearing shovels and a thermos of hot chocolate.

"We'll get you out of this ditch in no time," Bernie's dad said as he passed the thermos to Mama. She took off the lid-cup and removed the cork. Hot, fragrant steam rose into the frigid air, spreading out like a sweet, chocolaty fog. The aroma of cocoa filled the car, making my mouth water. Mama took a cautious sip, then drained the cup. She filled it again and passed it to Sarah, who took a sip and passed the cup along to Abby. We all had a taste before the empty cup made its way back to Mama, who filled it and gave it to Danny in the back seat. He drained it. Mama snatched the cup back and gave him one of her "wait until we get home" looks. She emptied the rest of the cocoa into the cup and motioned for Annie to take it. After everyone had had a sip, she replaced the cork and screwed the soiled cup onto the thermos.

"Now, boys—let's put our backs to it and get this beast back on the road," challenged Mr. Zader. Between the boys' efforts at shoveling, Mr. Zader pushing, Mama at the wheel rocking the car back and forth, it finally popped free of the ditch and stood, engine throbbing, back in the fast-filling ruts on the road. Mama thanked Mr. Zader, who took off with Bernie and Sylvia. There was a lull in the snow, and we sat and waited until they reached the row of mailboxes adjacent to their driveway. Then, Mama put the old Model-A in gear and we began to inch slowly towards the Baileys' house.

No one appeared to be at home as we passed the drive, so Mama kept on going. She didn't want to risk stopping and getting stuck again if Mr. Bailey wasn't there to help us get on the way again. "I'll walk you home, girls," Mama offered, "but I won't drop you off at a locked house."

By the time we gradually inched our way to the turn on Egan, Mama's ruts from earlier and those from Daddy and Mr. Moen's outbound trip to work were totally filled. She nosed into the turn with caution, keeping a steady foot on the gas pedal, the transmission in low gear. The sturdy little car gradually made the arc, slipping only once, as Mama's skill at the wheel kept us in the very middle of the road. We plowed slowly to our drive, where Mama turned again and made her way down the long drive to the back door.

When the car slid silently to a stop, Mama slumped over the wheel, her arms encircling her head, her cheek resting on the horn cover. She drew a deep breath and exhale slowly through her mouth, then sat up. I saw a tear, whether from fear, fatigue or relief, slowly slide down her cheek. Her tongue darted out and licked it as it slid past her lips. She looked up at me and winked.

"Well, kids, it remains to be seen if we can get these doors open and slog our way to the porch. Shall we give it a try?" Danny and Sarah both pushed with all their strength on the driver's side back door while Mama tackled the front. Together, their efforts slowly plowed the snow into two white walls as the wind furiously attempted to blow the doors shut. Mama got out and put all her slight strength into jamming the front door into the snow pile to hold it open, then she turned her efforts to helping Danny and Sarah do the same with the back. We all climbed out, then struggled round the car behind Mama, who acted as a plow, breaking a path for us to the back door.

The mud porch was dark and cold as a meat locker when our numb troop tumbled in. The wind struck the door open with a vicious gust that forced the knob through the lath and plaster wall, where it stuck. It took both Mama and Danny to free it and push the door reluctantly closed. Mama reached for the deadbolt and shot it home to seal the deal.

"Now, at least we're safe." Mama sat down hard on a pile of feed sacks she kept for wiping dirt and muck off our footwear when we came from the barn. After a moment, she rose and ushered us all into the kitchen, coats, hoods, scarves, boots and all.

The kitchen was dark and cold. Danny switched on the lights, but nothing happened.

"Darn it!" Mama's breath made a little cloud that jutted forward into the darkened kitchen. She pulled open our cluttered "everything" drawer and selected a large candle and a box of matches. "Will you get that candle holder from the living room, Cookie?"

I made my way through the murky light from the French doors in our dining room, groping into the dark corner where I knew the candle holders sat on a small table beside the sofa. I grabbed a couple and scooted back to Mama, avoiding the furniture and making a detour around the fireplace tools that sat on the hearth.

Our fireplace was massive—big enough for all three of us kids to stand in shoulder to shoulder and fully upright. It took huge logs that Daddy could bank to burn slowly all through the night, if necessary. Fans and ductwork distributed the heat to every room in the house. When the furnace hidden in the dugout area beneath the house didn't operate, whether from lack of fuel or lack of electricity, this fireplace kept us warm and snug as long as Daddy had a stack of wood to burn. That was usually not a problem, as we had all the woods below the back pasture to help supply it. Danny and Daddy had worked many hours during the previous fall, clearing fallen logs and chopping them up for just this purpose. We would not freeze, even though the rooms might be dark as bat caves!

Mama had the candles lit in a jiffy and set one on the kitchen table and another on the counter next to the sink. They gave the room a warm if dimly lit glow. She built a small fire in the center of the fireplace, banked it well, and placed the screen in front, admonishing all of us not to touch it, even if the fire went out.

The hands on the kitchen clock above the stove had stopped at 10:35. Mama checked her wristwatch and noted that it was now after 1:00 in the afternoon. Outside, the wind picked up, howling like a hundred banshees as it whipped the powdery snow against the side of the house. We all went quiet, Robbie's eyes huge as an owl's in his little, white face.

Mama reached for the telephone hanging on the wall beside the door leading to the back porch mudroom. Fortunately, those of us on the party line could still talk back and forth, even when the electricity and telephones were out, if we picked up at the same time. The neighbors sparsely scattered along our two country roads had used this method to keep in touch during previous outages by designating certain times of the day to pick up and listen. Now, she prayed under her breath that someone—anyone—was on the line. She was in luck, as the pleasantly voiced operator asked "number, please," when she lifted the heavy, black receiver. Our number was 8029J3, which meant we were on the left side of the ten-party line and our ring was two longs and a short. I never figured out how the phone company lady could tell from the numbers and letters just who was who and how many rings to ring, but as long as it worked, I didn't care.

Mama sighed deeply, then asked Annie for her number and relayed it to the operator. After the requisite rings on the other end, a man's voice answered. Mama briefed Mr. Bailey on the present situation, and after a brisk conversation, she agreed to walk the girls home. She shook her head as she replaced the receiver. I could tell she was angry with Mr. Bailey, but she didn't let that show in her voice.

"As soon as that wind dies down a little, I'll take you two home," Mama indicated to Abby and Annie. "You can wait here until I get back, Sarah, and help Danny keep things under control." As we waited, she busied herself making peanut butter and homemade blackberry jam sandwiches. They disappeared down greedy throats, washed along with fresh milk from our old dairy cow, Jenny. I had the milk but passed on the sandwiches. I could never abide anything sweet with my peanut butter, and Mama had forgotten that today. It was okay with me—I wasn't hungry, anyhow.

By 1:30 pm, the wind had diminished a bit, although the sky hung almost low enough to touch, a weird silver-grey color, pregnant with snow. "We can't wait any longer," Mama commented as she bundled the girls as warmly as she could.

She debated whether to take the long route up our driveway, down the road to the corner, then follow it down past the Broomers' farm all the way to the Bailey's little shack, or to cut across the pasture behind Broomers' barn. This was by far the shorter route but open to the wind all the way.

On closer inspection, she noted that the wind had stripped most of the snow off the grass, piling it up wherever it came against a barrier. Our car was nearly covered, as was the entire west wall of the porch, snow piled almost to the eaves. Mama selected a long piece of baling twine and tied it to her waist, then to Abby and Annie, who brought up the rear. They started off towards Broomers' pasture fence, looking for all the world like three beads on a string, forging through the knee-high snow, Mama stamping it down for Abby and Annie. When they reached the fence, Mama separated the barbed wire for Annie and then Abby to crawl through, then carefully threaded herself between the strands. As they began the long trek towards the far road, the clouds erupted as if punctured by the tall fir trees along the fence line, the snow drifting softly at first, then began their sidewise flight, driven by the rising wind.

We stood on the back steps, Danny, Sarah and I, and watched as the three of them disappeared, then Danny pulled us all inside and shut the door. All we could do now was to wait. After a while, the wind died down again and it stopped snowing.

We had no way of knowing how much time passed before we heard the mudroom door open and the sound of stomping feet. Danny flew to the back door and opened it as Mama, red-faced and puffing, almost fell into the kitchen. "Did you get

Annie and Abby home?" inquired Danny. Mama nodded her head, her teeth chattering so hard she didn't even try to get the words out. He half dragged her across the floor and into the living room, depositing her in front of the still-burning fireplace.

After a few minutes, she unwound the scarf from around her head and face and unbuttoned her overcoat. Her hands, inside her mittens, were blue and she held them, first between her armpits, and then to the glowing fireplace screen. Her whole body shivered uncontrollably. As I held her close, Danny wrapped her in the afghan OurGrandmother had crocheted.

"Thanks, kids," she murmured, "I'm frozen to the bone."

She glanced at her wristwatch. "Oh, my God! It's almost 3:00. Sarah, I have to get you home before it's totally dark outside. Quick, get your coat on!"

Danny protested as Mama dropped the afghan and headed for the door. "You can't go now, Mama," he almost shouted, "you just got back and you're still cold. Can't she wait until Daddy gets home?"

"No, Danny, she can't. Her mom doesn't know where she is and there's always the possibility that Daddy and Mr. Moen won't be able to make it up the hill in all this snow." She snatched the telephone off its cradle, listened, then made a face. "Well, it's dead for now."

There was only one route to Sarah's house. Straight up the drive, left on the upper road, then right on the little dirt road that led to the Moen's log house sheltered beneath towering fir trees. With luck, the snow and wind would have left the road fairly free of snow, and Mama and Sarah would have an easier trip.

At half-past three, Mama and Sarah stepped out into the wind and snow and into the now nearly filled path from Mama's return trip from the Bailey's. The drive was completely covered, protected from the wind as it was from the tall, thick trees lining its western length. We watched through the French doors in the dining room until they disappeared on the upper road. The wind picked up ominously and whipped the front yard snow in furious flurries down towards the eastern pasture. Robbie put the palms of his little hands on one of the glass squares and began to cry silently, tears making furrows of clean down his grubby face.

I wanted to cry, myself, but Danny put his arms around me as I pulled Robbie into mine. "It's gonna be okay," Danny whispered into my hair, "Mama's gonna be okay," but he didn't sound like he believed it. The three of us stood at the windows until cold drove us to the fireplace.

It was nearly full dark when Mama stumbled back down the drive and into the mudroom. The candles had burned themselves out and Danny had, against the rules, lit another and put it on the kitchen table. Between the two of us, we had managed the heavy iron gate that squatted in front of the fireplace and inserted another log to keep the fire going. Mama might be angry, and Danny and I quite probably had earned a trip to the woodshed from Daddy, but we didn't care. Robbie was cold and hungry and we both knew he was afraid of the dark.

We mobbed Mama as she entered the kitchen, nearly knocking her over. She had shed her snow-covered outerwear in the mudroom and quickly dove for the afghan folded neatly on the fireplace hearth. Her lips were nearly blue with cold, and the tip of her nose stood out in stark white against her red, wind-whipped face.

"Oooh, that feels so good! Danny, did you and Cookie put more logs in there?" She motioned towards the fire. "You shouldn't have, but I am so glad you did! We have to keep the fire going—the temperature is dropping like a rock out there. It's three degrees on the thermometer by the back door!"

Now it was five o'clock, and Daddy should be home. The darkness surrounded our little house. Outside, the wind still howled, and snow still pelleted the windows. In the barn, our old Jenny needed milking—chickens, rabbits, pigs, and steers, huddled in their barns and hutches and sheds and sties, were hungry and thirsty.

"We'll give Daddy until 6:00 and if he isn't home by then, we'll have to make it to the barn," Mama said as she stoked the trash burner on our old kitchen stove and put a kettle on to boil. She had tried to start the oil stove that squatted in the corner between the doors to the playroom and the living room, but it wouldn't light. An electric pump helped raise the fuel from the big drums stored inside the cellar below the kitchen.

When the water was ready, Mama made hot chocolate for all of us, then put a pot of soup on to heat. We sat huddled around the kitchen table in our sweaters sipping cocoa and slurping noodle soup and waiting for Mama's watch to click around to 6:00 pm.

Just as Danny and Mama readied themselves for the trip to the barn, Daddy burst through the door, covered in snow and looking for all the world like a big snowman. "Whooo, that was tough! Frank and I had to leave the car at the bottom of the big hill and walk from there. What a trip!" Danny looked at Mama. She had made the trip across Broomers' farm and back, and all the way to the Moens', keeping everybody's kids safe and sound. That made her a hero in my book, and Daddy agreed after he heard all the details.

"My God, Mayleen," he exclaimed as he gave Mama a big hug. "That would have been a tough job for me—and to think I complained about walking from the car!" He kissed her, then ruffled Robbie's hair. "I want to hear all the details after we take care of the stock."

It took another hour for Daddy and Danny to milk and feed and water. Danny made it up from the barn with two baskets of eggs and Daddy carried the milk pail up, although the wind whipped almost half out when a particularly strong gust hit him.

After Daddy ate, we all snuggled in front of the now roaring fire. Daddy built it up so that the bedrooms had a little heat in them, sucked in by convection through the pipes since the fans lacked electricity. Daddy told stories in Czech, translating as he went. He did this so we would learn some of his original language, then Mama sang and we joined in until it was time for bed.

I lie in bed and think that maybe the storm will help to heal the breach that is slowly widening between Mama and Daddy since New Year's Day. Maybe being snowed in—just the five of us—will give the two people I love the most in all the world time to remember how much they love each other, and how much we love them. Maybe God has sent this storm to give us all time. I smile and listen to the hiss of snow and wind on the windowpanes and remember to say my prayers.

In the morning, the Moens moved in.

CHAPTER 29
In Which We Learn the Perils of being Snowbound

"A blizzard! Who would think we'd have a blizzard in western Washington!" Mama remarked ruefully as she dealt the cards—three to Frank Moen, three to his wife, Mona, three to my daddy. She dealt her own and began another round, the cards snapping crisply on the table.

The four adults sat at a card table placed as close as possible to our huge circulating fireplace. Mama wore long pants tucked into two pairs of heavy socks and one of Daddy's wool hunting shirts over a thick, cable-knit sweater. Her tiny frame almost disappeared in the burden of supporting such a clothing load. Mrs. Moen, considerably larger than Mama, snuggled in a nearly full-length fur coat with a huge stand-up collar to protect her ears and neck from the icy drafts circling viciously through the house. Daddy and Mr. Moen seemed warm enough in sweaters and jeans.

"Mom, the toilet won't flush, and I'm cold!" complained my big brother, Danny, as he backed himself up to the fireplace to warm his fanny. Down the hall, I could hear the other boys, my baby brother Robbie and Keith Moen, shouting and laughing, even though the cold away from the fireplace required heavy sweaters and mittens!

"Daddy'll go see what's wrong with the toilet, Danny. Come on over here and cuddle with me—I'll get you warm!"

Danny shook his head, made a face, and dashed back up the hall towards the noise in the playroom where he settled down to play Monopoly with Sarah, who was in his class at school. I accepted Mama's invitation, though, and curled up in her lap, wrapped close in her warm, loving arms. She gave me a squeeze and sighed.

I was okay with the Moens coming to stay with us while the electricity was out, saddened only that Pete, my heartthrob, had chosen to stay behind in the cold and dark to care for the dogs and cats and his wonderful black mare, Midnight. The eldest Moen, Bud, had recently joined the Air Force and was off to parts unknown. Mama, on the other hand, did not seem pleased. I thought it had something to do with Daddy and Mrs. Moen.

"What a sweet little thing your Leah is—just like her precious mommy," cooed Mrs. Moen, a smile on her carefully made-up face. She sighed as she pulled the silky mink fur protectively around her, tucking it in tightly about her legs. "I declare I will surely die of cold—that fiah is down to just those tiny ol' embers!"

Mrs. Moen talked funny. She came from "The South," as she called it, in the state of Georgia. Her voice was raspy and low and her words ran together like melting lard. Something about it set my teeth on edge and made Mama shudder.

Mrs. Moen always looks like she has stepped out of a magazine advertisement. When she speaks, her right hand emphasizes each word with waves and dips of long, painted nails. Her left hand is reserved for its ever-present cigarette. Sometimes, when I am not paying attention, she wraps her arms around me and squeezes. Blue smoke from her dangling cigarette tickles my nose and makes me cough.

Mama smells of Ivory soap and bath powder and Evening in Paris perfume from the tiny dark blue bottle she keeps on her bedroom dresser. Mrs. Moen smells like cigarette smoke and patchouli. "You are sweet as sugah," she croons in my ear, "I could just Eat. You. Up!" She punctuates each word with a squeeze. Occasionally, her nails leave little half-moon dents in my arms. Her first name is Mona, according to Mama, but in my little kid head, I see it as MOAN-a.

"Thank you, Moan-a. She is my little angel." Mommy's mouth grinned back at Mrs. Moen, but her eyes didn't crinkle at the corners like they did when her whole face smiled. "Honey," she turned to my father and gestured toward the fireplace, "Moan-a's right—we could use a few more logs."

"At your service, ladies—I shall return!" Daddy rose from his place at the card table, bowed low to Mrs. Moen, and saluted Mama. Turning neatly on his heels, he headed for the kitchen. I heard the door to the mudroom slam before a whoosh of frigid air sent goosebumps up my arms.

Mrs. Moen threw eyeball daggers at her husband, who sat silently rearranging his playing cards. Frank Moen was the antithesis of his wife—tall and slender, and very, very quiet. He had a full head of dark hair brushed with silver at the temples that gave him a distinguished air, but he always seemed to look at the ground. Occasionally, he'd mumble something barely audible, his eyes furtively seeking Moan-a's approval.

Usually, she dismissed him with a wave of those primped and painted nails.

Daddy pushed open the door, staggered through the kitchen, and deposited a huge stack of snow-dusted wood into the large wooden box on the hearth.

"Here it comes," Mama whispered in my ear, "here it comes." Moan-a leaped from her chair and clutched Daddy's arm, squeezing it with rapt admiration.

"Oh, Hal, you are so strong! Look at all that wood!" She leaned confidingly towards Mama and declared, "Why can't my Frankie be as gallant as your Hal—going out in all that wind and snow just so little old me won't get cold? You are a truly fortunate woman, Mistress Mayleen!"

Mama's body tensed. I could feel her coiling up like a cat preparing to spring on an unsuspecting bird, only Mrs. Moen wasn't some little robin—she was a full-fledged raptor with its prey in sight! She eyeballed my Daddy as if he were a fat, juicy rabbit!

I had never seen a grownup behave as this guest in our home was behaving. Rather than have Mama realize that I was privy to such goings-on, I slipped from her lap and crept into my special little corner near the fireplace. It had been my practice on more than one occasion to sit here quietly while I observed the idiosyncrasies of the adults in my life. My brothers were far more interested in pillow fights and playing with their Red Ryder BB guns. I sat back now and waited for the scene to unfold.

Moan-a continued to squeeze my father's bicep.

Daddy's face erupted into a wide grin as he disengaged her clutching fingers from his upper arm. He gave Mama a fleeting look and winked.

"No problem, Moan-a. You looked chilly." He tossed a chunk of wood on the fire. Snow hissed and sputtered before it yielded the wood to greedy flame tongues. "This will warm you up!"

Mama's eyes rolled. Across the table, Frank Moen smiled wanly at her as if to say, "I married her and that's my problem—yours, too, because we're neighbors, and you've got a good-looking husband." I had seen many such looks pass between my mother and Mr. Moen during the last four days.

According to the ladies on our ten-party telephone line, Mrs. Moen had had her eye on Daddy ever since her family had purchased the old house at the end of County Road 44 and became our closest neighbors. The house needed a great deal of repair, much of which was not completed, when we were hit with the coldest January in recent history!

The blizzard had howled in Tuesday morning, its winds blowing the already deep powder into drifts that reached the eaves along the west side of our house. Daddy challenged the frigid wind for hours to keep our roof free of snow. Trees fell over power lines and poles toppled, leaving our rural neighborhood in darkness.

We relied on electricity for more than light—individual wells requiring electric pumps to fill holding tanks supplied our local water. Fortunately, we had a standby diesel pump. Our huge fireplace could, in a pinch, circulate enough heat to subsidize our oil heater, even without electricity for its fan.

Unfortunately, proximity and the blackout had conspired to place the Moens squarely in our household. When the family arrived wet and freezing on our porch, compassion overcame Mama's usual common sense and she invited them to stay until power was restored—an invitation that was becoming exceedingly difficult to live with! Affairs had started out politely enough, but after four days, tempers frazzled and Moan-a had unsheathed her claws.

"Hal, the boys say the toilet won't flush. Will you check up on it, please?"

"Sure, honey," hummed Daddy. He left the room, his broad back and curly black hair still speckled with white flakes.

"Oh, Mayleen, you shouldn't send him off to that cold bathroom while he's still half-frozen from get'n wood! At least let him sit heah by the fiah and warm his toes!" Moan-a made a little face and smiled after Daddy.

Mr. Moen gathered the cards, shuffled, and began dealing three hands. "Come on, Moan-a. Leave off Hal for a minute. We can play three-handed until he comes back."

"Mama! Mama!" A plaintive wail rose from down the hall. Keith Moen, a hulking seven-year-old, puffed into the room with Robbie in hot pursuit. Robbie was half a year from his sixth birthday and weighed about forty pounds soaking wet. Keith dove for his Mama's lap, shrieking.

"He hit me! He hit me on the head."

Robbie stopped short of Mrs. Moen's reach and brandished a balsa wood hockey stick.

"And I'll hit you again if you don't give me back my car."

"Ooh, Robbie. How dare you hit my baby! Your mama ought to lay you across her knee and blistah your behind, sir!"

A look of distaste briefly flashed over Mama's face. I could see her jaw clenched with the effort of not speaking her mind.

Mama believed in treating guests as just that—guests!

Big slug, I thought. Twice Robbie's size and blubbering like a baby. I had no compunctions about saying what I felt but held my tongue lest Mama realize I was still in the corner. I had plans, however; a little retribution of my own when next Keith and I crossed paths outside our parents' view!

"Robbie," Mama admonished, "We don't hit our friends."

"He's not my friend!" hissed Robbie.

"Well, he's your guest, and you should let him play with your things if he wants to. Learn to share."

"He's **NOT** my friend and he broke all the wheels off my fire truck and then he **STOLE** it 'cuz I won't let him play with anything else and if he doesn't give it back, I'll **HIT HIM AGAIN**!" In his haste to have his say before Mama cut him off, Robbie's words sprayed out generously flecked with spittle.

"You little brat!" hissed Moan-a abandoning her southern drawl. "You give me that stick or I'll snatch you bald-headed!"

My mama turned that interesting tomato color she reserved for times of impassioned emotion. Mr. Moen's eyes bulged as if he couldn't believe what his wife had said to Robbie. Mama started to rise from her chair—she had "that look" in her eye—but Mr. Moen touched her arm and nodded his head as if to say, "Let me handle this." She sat back down as he turned towards his wife.

"Moan-a, get that big kid off your lap." Mr. Moen spoke quietly but firmly. "He's the one who ought to be spanked, breaking other kid's toys!"

"Frank Moen, you are a brute, sir! You know how fragile and sickly Keith is! How dare you suggest I should strike our son!"

"Whether or not he's 'sickly,' he's as big as you are, Moan-a. Besides, in case you've forgotten, we're guests in this house." He leaned close to Keith's ear and whispered something. Keith's head jerked back, his eyes flew open, and his mouth made a big O. I was personally amazed at Mr. Moen's interference in this matter; judging from the look on Mrs. Moen's face, he was in for the rough side of her tongue.

Daddy appeared at the door and quickly surveyed the situation. He confiscated the offending hockey stick and issued one of his edicts, the kind we children obeyed instantly. "Robbie, you and Keith get back in the playroom, and I don't want to hear either of you fighting again—**IS THAT CLEAR**?" Keith stopped his snuffling and got off his mother's lap. At least the big brat knew an order when he heard one! As he waddled past, Daddy deftly removed Robbie's de-wheeled fire engine from Keith's grasp.

"There," simpered Moan-a admiringly, "is a man after myah own heart. Gives an order and it's obeyed. Why can't you be more like that, Frankie?" Her eyes followed Daddy adoringly. Mama bit her lips. I couldn't see Mr. Moen's face, but his shoulders made a sharp little jerking motion.

Daddy gave Mama's shoulders a little squeeze and ruffled her hair. She brushed his hand away as if annoyed, but her face softened at his touch.

"What's wrong with the toilet, honey?"

"The pipes froze. Frank and I will have to go down to the cellar and thaw 'em out."

"Well, dinner needs getting. If you fellows will fetch me a couple 'a buckets of snow, I'll get started. Okay?" Mama rose from her chair at the card table.

"I'll get those buckets, Mayleen." Mr. Moen rose from his chair. "And Moan-a, help Mayleen with dinner for a change. I mean it." Mrs. Moen seemed fairly unimpressed with this additional show of strength from her spouse, but before she could respond, he grabbed his coat and hastily darted out of the room. Daddy pecked Mama on the cheek and followed him.

Moan-a made a face at her husband's disappearing back and snickered. "There, you see what I have to put up with? Now you know how lucky you are to have someone like Hal lookin' aftah you."

"I see, all right," muttered Mama on her way to the kitchen.

I tag along behind. "What's the matter, Mama? What's wrong?" I whisper.

"Nothing, honey, nothing at all," she answers with a dismissing little headshake. But there is something wrong—I can tell.

Things between Mama and Mrs. Moen had started out with civility on Tuesday, but now seemed headed towards a replay of the shootout at the O.K. Corral!

"Why don't you just tell 'em all to go home," I whisper. She smiles one of her honey warm smiles at me.

"I can't, sweetheart, not just yet. It wouldn't be right. Someday you'll understand why." Grownups always say that—and maybe it's true. One thing I do understand is that my Mama is a lady, and Mrs. Moen is not!

Mama opened the door that led from the kitchen to the mudroom, where Daddy and Mr. Moen were busy filling blowtorches with fuel. Two milk pails heaped with clean snow sat close to the kitchen door. Daddy stopped what he was doing and hauled the buckets into the kitchen.

"We're gonna take care of those pipes right now," he muttered as the kitchen door slammed behind him.

Mama scooped clean snow from one of the pails into the huge granite coffee pot usually reserved for camping trips and put it on the trash burner part of our old kitchen range. She lit another lamp and placed it on the drainboard.

Outside, the wind still howls and hisses, forcing its way through invisible cracks in the walls of the strong old house, although snow has finally stopped falling. Inside, the lamps spread a warm, flickering glow, softening all the sharp corners and casting shadows everywhere. I wonder if the snow and wind will ever end, so the Moens can return home, leaving Mommy and Daddy and us kids in peace.

Moan-a wandered in from the living room, drew a chair close to the trash burner, and lit another cigarette. I tucked myself at the farthest corner of the kitchen table, half hidden in the lamp shadows. Mama brought me a paring knife and a sack of potatoes.

Mrs. Moen chuckled from her roost next to the stove. "You are so efficient in the kitchen, Mayleen. Why, watchin' you just tyahs me out. You get so much done! I take hours to plan a meal—and cookin' just exhausts me."

The words sounded like a compliment to my mama's skill, but I could feel a deeper exchange taking place between them. She continued; "Must be this unbearable Washington weathah. My motha' warned me not to marry a Yankee; I should have stayed home and married Elton Jorry. He lived in a big mansion down the road and raised blooded horses."

As she sliced carrots, Mama surveyed the dwindling store

of food. Feeding all those extra mouths had put a huge dent in our pantry. "I sure wish we had some horsemeat right now," she muttered under her breath.

I tried unsuccessfully to stifle a snort. Mama hadn't mentioned horsemeat for a long time. After the War ended, sometimes the only meat we could afford was horsemeat from the "Pony Market" in Charleston. That was our little secret, Mama's and mine. Daddy and the boys didn't know it, but a lot of those meatloaves and pot roasts had once whinnied and neighed over oats and hay!

"What was that? Did you say somethin', sweetie?" Moan-a queried.

"I said, possibly you should have, at that. Blooded horses sound so—interesting." Mama rolled her eyes at me and winked. Moan-a lit another cigarette from the stub of her last.

"There's no need gettin' your hair up, Mayleen, just because I was brought up by gentle people and taught the finah things of life."

Oh, this was getting interesting!

Mama slapped the carrots and knife down hard and turned around. Fortunately, the water began to boil and she had time to compose herself as she prepared coffee.

I wonder if Mrs. Moen would notice the flavor of rat poison in hers. Daddy keeps the stuff over the bathroom sink at the top of the medicine cabinet, far from prying little hands. Moan-a is the only one who uses sugar in her coffee. Maybe I can put some in the sugar bowl...

Danny interrupted my machinations.

"Mom?" Danny, an odd expression on his face, stood in the archway between the kitchen and the living room. Mama had returned to her carrots and remarked without stopping.

"Daniel"—chop!—"your daddy told the boys"—chop!—"to stay in the playroom"—chop, chop!—"until dinner." She reached for another carrot. "I think you should do the same." The chopping resumed.

"But smoke's coming up around all the baseboards, and we can hardly breathe in there!"

"Scaredy-cat," Moan-a interjected. "Frankie and your daddy are in the cellah thawin' the pipes. It is just steam, that's all." She dismissed my brother with a wave of her cigarette hand, sending blue smoke coiling softly toward the ceiling shadows. Danny didn't move.

"Wait a minute, Danny—smoke? Are you sure?" Mama's head snapped around and she laid down her knife.

"Yeah, Mom. Come and see for yourself."

I follow Mama down the hall. She stops short at the sight of something curling out from under the bathroom door. Mama yanks the door open. Smoke oozes from around the toilet base, climbs up the wall, and collects in a muddy pool in the far corner of the yellow ceiling.

"See, Mom, I told'ja..."

"Hush, Danny. Let me think." We could hear Daddy and Mr. Moen down below, laughing. Mama stomped hard on the bathroom floor three or four times. Thump, thump, thump! From below, one of the men repeated Mama's frantic tattoo. She knelt with her head close to the floor and shouted.

"Hal, there's smoke up here. Is everything okay?"

Below, the laughter increased. I could hear Daddy saying something, but his words were muffled. Mama pounded harder on the floor. This time, no one below seemed to notice.

Mama sat on the floor, deep in thought. At last, she spoke. "Danny, take the other kids into the living room, over by the French doors—and try not to let them know what's going on. Get their coats and all the blankets from the hall closet. If you hear me tell Mrs. Moen that the temperature is rising, get them outside, quick. It's a short run in a straight line to the barn. You kids'll be safe and warm there. Don't try to light the lantern. Just cuddle them down in the hay. Do you understand?" She turned to me, her soft eyes clouded with concern. "Help your brother, Leah, and remember—straight to the barn!"

Her voice was filled with confidence, but I could sense her fear. As we headed for the playroom, however, her shoulders relaxed—Mama had a plan.

While Danny and I did as she had asked, Mama returned to the kitchen. From my vantage point near the French doors, I saw her put on her coat and open the kitchen door leading out to the porch. I stretched my ears to listen.

"Hal!" Her words were almost lost in the rising wind. She called louder. "Honey, the house is on fire!"

This time Daddy replied. His answer rose from beneath my feet.

"Did you hear that, Frank?" He laughed. "The women think the house is on fire. Ha, ha, ha! Probably see steam rising from these pipes."

"Yeah," grunted Frankie in assent.

My brother looked at me with nothing short of horror on his face. I shrugged. Mama returned to the kitchen where Moan-a still huddled close to the trash burner, cigarette dangling inelegantly from her lips.

"What's all the fuss ovah, sweetie?"

"Moan-a, Danny was right. He did see smoke—the house is on fire, and those big apes downstairs don't believe me!"

"Well, honey, if Hal says ev'rathang's all right, I believe him. You shouldn't let yourself get all worked up ovah nothin'." She rose from her chair and tossed the cigarette into a pail of clean water Mama had saved for dinner. "Heah, let me try peelin' those potatoes." Her petulant little voice droned on; "We nevah did our own kitchen work at home. I was forced to learn these things quite recently."

Mama went to the back porch again.

"Hal, I don't care what you think. This damned house is on fire; and if you don't do something right now, it's going to burn down around our ears!" Lordy! Mama WAS angry.

Daddy muttered something unprintable and started singing about a rooster from Wooster. Mama hated that song. One year, Daddy taught it to me and I sang it for the minister's wife at Sunday school. Mama said she was mortified, whatever that meant, and could never show her face in public again.

The smoke was noticeably thicker now, filling the house with a peculiar, nose-crinkling odor of wet ashes. Danny and I tried to keep the younger boys occupied while we listened intently for Mama's signal. "Don't you think it's get'n warmah in heah?" remarked Moan-a. "My feet are surely cozy for the first time in a week!"

"Yes," replied Mama, "I think the temperature is rising."

"Well, Mayleen Vanac, you do not have to shout! I'm right next to you."

Danny gave me the nod and out we went! Much later, Mama filled in the details.

"Good," she murmured as she heard the French doors slam shut.

"What did you say? Oh, yes. I do so hope the weatha's warmin', 'though I will surely be sorry to leave you all. Your dear Hal is so good to you. I do so hope my Frankie learns a thing or two from him."

I guess my mama had had it, right up to the top of her head.

"Oh, you are SO right," she replied. "He's so good and handsome and strong—and so smart that his house is going up in smoke and he doesn't even believe me—wait a minute."

She ran for the door. Once more, she called down to the cellar.

"Hal, honey, honest, could the house be just a teeny bit on fyah? Will you humor little old me and puh-lease take a look? You are so sweet and brave to go out in the cold and thaw those pipes, but don't you think that little old blow torch could 'a lit some of the timbahs?"

"That you, Moan-a? Sure thing, I'll check for you—**HOLY CHRIST!** Get some buckets! **THE HOUSE IS ON FIRE!"**

"What on earth is all that noise down stayahs, Mayleen, honey?" Moan-a sounded a little puzzled.

"Oh nothing, Moan-a, honey," grinned Mama. "Only those big, brave, handsome men discovered that the house IS on fire."

"What did you say?"

"I said, the house really is on fire. But everything's okay now—Moan-a?" Moan-a's face turned the color of a crushed gardenia—her eyes wide with shock.

"My babies. My little Keith and Sarah. They will surely

burn to death," she wailed. "Whatever can I do? Keith, Sarah! Mayleen, this is all your fault!"

"Oh, for pity's sake, Moan-a! The kids are out of the house. They're safe in the barn. Snap out of it." She momentarily considered giving Moan-a a well-deserved slap but restrained herself. Most likely, that would fall beyond the bounds of graciousness to a guest.

Outside, the wind dropped to a whisper. Mama could hear the men in the cellar, laughing. Suddenly they burst into the kitchen, blackened and soot-stained, demanding hot supper, strong coffee, and copious applause for saving the house. We kids followed close behind.

Mama quickly finished supper preparations as I set the table and Danny settled the boys back into the playroom. Moan-a lit yet another cigarette as she rehashed the events of the last hour. At dinner, Daddy and Mr. Moen told and retold the harrowing story of how they saved the house and both families from certain destruction and death.

"Gee, Moan-a, you sure are sharp," Daddy exclaimed as he helped himself to a third slice of bread. "Noticing the smoke and all. Smart thinking, too, sending the kids to the barn. You Southern gals have beauty AND brains."

Moan-a brightened. "Why Hal, honey! How gracious of you!"

Mama made a muffled sound deep in her throat—a choking sort of sound—and her face twitched. When no one was looking, she stuck her tongue out at Moan-a, and then winked at me.

After supper, the lights came back on. Moan-a and Frankie and their brood gathered their possessions, "and half of our kids' toys," reflected Mama later, and left for home. As we settled in for the night, our beds warmed by rubber bottles of hot water from the tap, my parents' muted conversation filled me with ease. If I listened carefully, I could just make out what they were saying.

"Now we can go back to our own dull routine," mused Mama as she cuddled in bed. "No fat little Keiths or brow-beaten Frankies or wilted Southern gardenias. Just you and me and the kids. Too bad that little phony's got you so fooled..." Mama's voice trailed off.

"What'd you say, honey?" That was Daddy from the kitchen.

Suddenly, a thick, honeyed Southern drawl oozed from Mama's bedroom.

"Hal, honey, would you get a glass of watah for little ol' me? I am surely parched!" In my mind's eye, I could see her grinning as she snuggled deep into the covers.

"Hmmm? Huh? Oh, sure, Moan-a, anything you say—" Daddy's voice sounded puzzled. "Mayleen? Is that you talking, Mayleen?"

Mama started to laugh, a gentle sound filled with her own warmth. "Of course, you-all. Who else but little ol' Southern Mayleen. Remember, Sugar Pie, I come from southern Washington!"

Daddy laughed. "I should have known. I really should have. It was you every time telling me about the fire! But after all, this has been a day. And they're gone. Here we are, just you and me, snowbound."

I felt him kiss her. When things were good like this between my parents, I could almost see the love they had for each other. He kissed her again. "Like being alone without all those people around?"

"Mmm," murmured Mama, snuggling closer. "Turn on the light for a sec, will you?"

"Yeah."

"Well?"

"Damn! The bulb must be burnt out. It won't come on. I'll try this one. Damn, it doesn't work either." A palpable silence emerged from my parents' bedroom.

In unison, I heard them say: "Do you suppose the electricity...?"

"Shhh, Hal. Listen—do you hear someone on the porch?"

We all lay very still, hoping "someone" would go away!

CHAPTER 30

In Which a Marriage Vacillates and I Learn to Listen with my Heart

Tensions continued to grow between my parents during the first weeks of the new year. Mama and Daddy withdrew from each other, imperceptibly at first, then with widening certainty as weeks rolled into months and spring filled the air. Mama continued to confide in me, and Daddy began looking at me as if I were a traitor, although I never breathed a word about the phone call. My brothers grilled me at length in a vain attempt to figure out what was going on. When I began having nightmares, Mama moved me permanently to the guest room so that I wouldn't disturb anyone's sleep. In one regard, the move fulfilled my dream of having a room to myself, away from the noises and annoyances of sharing with two brothers. Unfortunately, it left me alone to think about family dynamics no child should have to ponder.

While it was bad enough that my once stable family was locked in some kind of death struggle for which my father held me partly responsible, now school, once my refuge, became a nightmare. For some unfathomable reason, my teacher, Mrs. Eldon, had taken a dislike to me. She started keeping me in a few moments at lunch or after school to "deal with my attitude." Her comments left me bewildered and intimidated. I hadn't the slightest idea what I had done.

"You are arrogant, Leah. You're too full of yourself," she would tell me. "You must learn your place. Don't come crying to me when the other kids won't play with you." Her face was hard, her eyes squinched into menacing slits that matched the pursed lips, blanched of blood. She truly frightened me.

I didn't know what she was talking about. I liked everybody, had lots of friends, and tried to help my classmates whenever I could. When I asked my mother what arrogant meant, she'd answered me absently, her mind on larger problems, so I kept this one to myself. I gathered it meant something like snooty or being better than other people. Surely Mrs. Eldon was mistaken—I wasn't better than anyone else—I was one of the feed sack kids!

Rural girls who grew up during the forties and fifties know about feed sack kids. Back then, 50- and 100-pound portions of poultry, calf, and other prepared feeds came in gaily printed calico cotton bags. Simply by removing the bottom, side and top stitching, one obtained a straight length of fabric. A little careful selection at the feed store provided enough fabric for sunsuits, dresses, blouses, and skirts. The prints were cute enough and the cotton sacking of decent quality, but every farm kid knew them. After Purina or General Mills issued a new pattern, little girls started showing up in home-sewed outfits sporting the latest prints.

Mother was particularly handy with a sewing machine and made most of my clothing. Using the feed sacks was economical as well as logical. Unfortunately, I could count on several other little girls at school to show up simultaneously wearing the same fabric. We learned quickly who played in the feed sack league and avoided each other on the playground. Feed sack kids might someday develop a sense of pride in their enterprising mothers, but arrogance is not one of their hallmark qualities.

Eventually, I deduced from Mrs. Eldon's comments that she was most unhappy when I made no mistakes on my papers. This puzzled me even more than her comments on my behavior. My first-grade teacher, Miss Benson, had lavished my error-free papers with praise.

I can't remember when I learned the alphabet, or to count and recognize my numbers. By the time I entered school, I could pick up a book or newspaper and read with ease. It didn't occur to me that other kids had to be taught how, that it didn't come as naturally for others as it had for me. Miss Benson recognized my naiveté and nurtured my burgeoning intellectual curiosity, finding special projects to keep me occupied and fulfilled while the other kids learned their ABCs and sounded out their first readers. I didn't even notice, unless she set me to help some less fortunate classmate. I enjoyed helping others, developing patience rare for a first-grader.

My problems with Mrs. Eldon came to a head one soggy March afternoon when my failure to recheck my subtraction left an error on my arithmetic paper. She had stood at the front of the room dictating the lesson, watching while we all tried to print our numbers as neatly as possible on the sheets of paper she handed out from the classroom supply. After a suitable time passed, we handed the finished papers to the front of each row where she collected them, then we put our heads down for a few moments of quiet while she sat at her desk to correct them.

I do not know why I discern she was correcting my paper, but as I surreptitiously peeked from beneath my arm, Mrs. Eldon's eyes meet mine. Her face freezes in a malicious grin aimed right at me! I flatten my head back down onto my forearms and bury my eyes. Something in her look frightens me.

"Class, you may all sit up, now." Mrs. Eldon rose from her desk and began distributing the corrected arithmetic papers to their owners. She passed me by several times on her trips up and down the rows of waiting second graders. Finally, only one paper remained in her hand. She ended at the front of the classroom, facing us, her eyes fixed on mine like a fox hypnotizing a rabbit.

There is a brick in the pit of my stomach. I hear my teacher in a too-loud voice say "Leah, please step to the front of the class." I move in slow motion, Mrs. Eldon and the classroom clock telescoping away from me like a speeding train. Mrs. Eldon's voice sounds very pleased. "I have a special treat for us, class." She grasps me hard by the shoulders and turns me around to face my classmates. I can feel her flourish the remaining paper over my head. My knees go weak and I can feel my legs begin to buckle. I will not fall down, I think fiercely to myself. I will not fall down in front of all my friends and I will not wet my panties, even though my poor, damaged bladder wants to let go.

"Class, here is Leah's arithmetic paper. I want you all to see that it has a red checkmark on it. Leah has made a mistake."

I cringe, sucking myself into as small a space as possible, eyes squinched shut and lips clamped between my teeth. A few of my classmates gasp. Mrs. Eldon sounds very far away. Perhaps she is not talking about me. Perhaps this is just a bad dream and I will wake up in my bed with Danny laughing at me and Mama and Daddy asking what is wrong, Leah!

"Let's laugh at Leah. Come on, children, let's all laugh at Leah! She has made a mistake and needs to be laughed at."

It is not a dream. Mrs. Eldon laughs, loud and victoriously, while she parades me in front of my friends. Hesitantly at first, and then with more volume, my classmates follow suit. Soon everyone is laughing at stupid Leah, who made an arithmetic error. I yank away violently, escaping her clutches, her long, red-painted nails raking lines down the side of my arm. I make a beeline for the cloakroom, where I hide amidst the damp and smelly winter coats and overshoes, the laughter of my friends and classmates ringing back and forth inside my head, trapped behind my eyes, like some demented bell.

Something curled into a neat little ball and buried itself deep inside me that day. Call it self-esteem, confidence, pride of accomplishment, self-worth, whatever—for years afterward, the least mistake rendered me mute. I became a perfectionist, not permitting myself the slightest error in word or deed. As a consequence, I held back, often giving the impression of aloofness or unwillingness to be friendly. After all, if a kid can't trust a teacher, who can she trust? First, my father—now, my teacher!

The smell of old cloakrooms still fills me with disgust.

I don't know how long I sat huddled in the cloakroom before Mrs. Eldon came to check on me. I heard kids going by in the hall next to where I leaned with my back to the adjacent wall and deduced, after a while, that it must be close to lunchtime, when the door opened and a sliver of light illuminated the dark little room. She slipped in and stood staring down at me, backlit against the opened classroom doorway.

"Always making a spectacle of yourself, aren't you, Leah—why can't you be like the other kids? All the other teachers always sticking up for you—she's bright, she's talented—we need to keep her stimulated!" Her voice went all high-pitched and squeaky. "I'm sick of it. Just make yourself fit in, young lady, or you're going to have a miserable life. People don't like someone who doesn't fit in. Someday, you will realize that I did you a favor today."

I do not move, do not make a sound. Her words burrow into my soul unimpeded, slipping into the cracks and hiding themselves in the crevasses, ready to spring forth and trip me up every time that someone compliments me. I really do not understand what she is talking about—the other teachers! Could she mean my picture that won a blue ribbon at the state fair? I did not enter it—the picture with the sky and the green grass meeting and the trees filled with apples like in our meadow.

Miss Benson sent the picture to the fair in my first-grade year, and when the blue ribbon arrived, she called me up at assembly and presented it in front of the whole school. Mama and Daddy came for the presentation and Daddy had framed the picture. It hung in the activity room at home, complete with its little blue ribbon. Daddy pointed it out to company while Mama beamed and Danny shuffled his feet, hissing at me that I liked to be the center of attention.

This must be what Mrs. Eldon means—I like the attention.

She reached down and snatched me up by the arm, lifting me high enough that my feet left the floor and I dangled for a few seconds before she let her hand slip off. "Now, you will come with me to the office, young lady. You can tell Mr. Anders why you are hiding in the closet."

She marches me down the hall in front of all the kids waiting in lunch line, through the open double swinging doors into the cafeteria where Danny sits eating his tuna sandwich and drinking his milk from the little metal cup that serves as a lid on his Thermos bottle. I can feel Danny's eyes boring a hole through me, his dark eyebrows coming together in the middle of his forehead to form a deep vee over his nose. I don't care that all my friends are watching. I only care that Danny will never let me forget being dragged through the cafeteria like a puppy who has messed on the floor.

We pulled up short in front of Mr. Anders who, knife in hand, was leaning down to cut up an apple for Sydney Judd, one of my first-grade classmates. She stared at me for a moment, then turned red and fumbled for her apple. Mr. Anders wiped his knife on a napkin and motioned towards me, a questioning look on his face. Mrs. Eldon leaned forward and whispered close to his ear. I stared straight ahead, not caring what she said. All I could think of was Mama and Daddy. Mr. Anders shifted the knife to his left hand and motioned with his right towards the doors. With me firmly in tow, Mrs. Eldon followed him down the aisle and into the hallway, then to the office.

I sit on the hardwood chair in the corner of Mr. Anders's

office while he asks me what has happened. Cat got your tongue, he asks me. I cannot answer him as my mouth and my brain are no longer connected. If my brain formulates an answer to his questions, my mouth will not open to transmit the words. I look at him with terror in my eyes, my heart beating like a little bird inside my chest, fluttering in its ribcage. Maybe if I can open my mouth, the little heart-bird can escape and take my soul to heaven. Then Mama and Daddy and Danny and Robbie will be saved the humiliation of having a daughter/sister who sits in the principal's office like a criminal.

After several futile attempts at making me speak, Mr. Anders lifted the receiver of the big black telephone on his desk and spoke to the operator. After a short wait, she connected him to someone. I heard him say that the someone should come to his office. I knew in my heart that the someone was Mama.

An eternity passed before my mama burst into the school office, her eyes sweeping from Mr. Anders at his desk to me, where I squirmed on the hard wooden chair. After a brief conference with Mr. Anders and Mrs. Eldon, she came and kneeled at my side.

"Can you speak to me, Cookie?" she asked softly. I nodded and put my arms around her neck, then whispered into her ear.

"I'm so sorry, Mama. I'll try to never make a mistake again. Please don't tell Daddy that I got sent to the principal's office."

Mother was furious! She called Mrs. Eldon's actions monstrous and threatened to go to the school board, and Mrs. Eldon apologized for making fun of my mistake. Daddy dismissed the whole episode as a tempest in a teapot and said

I was too sensitive. Danny laughed at me. I retreated, covering myself with a protective shell that earned me in later years the nickname of Ice Princess. Eventually, I confided in Annie, hoping she wouldn't think me foolish, too.

"Thee must have compassion for thy teacher, Leah." Annie had spent the afternoon rocking and stitching but stopped and sat quite still and attentive as I told my story.

"This lady must have a sore black hole where her heart should be to so mistreat a child, especially one entrusted to her care. Do not believe her poisoned tongue, little one. Pray that God blesses her life and lifts the heavy burden she must carry."

"But Annie, how can I forgive her? She hurt me really bad. All the kids laughed at me—some of 'em still do."

"God does not ask us to do anything we cannot handle, little one. He never gives us a burden too heavy for us to carry. Forgiving thy teacher is a small thing compared to her burden. After all, she must someday forgive herself—a task much, much harder to accomplish."

"I'll try, Annie—really, I will." I put my eyes and fingers back to the task before me, piecing sections of cloth together into the log cabin pattern. "Do you think I'm an arrogant child, Annie?" I asked solemnly, keeping my eyes pinned on my stitching.

"Oh, my goodness! Where did thee hear such a word about thyself? Oh, no need to speak! Thy teacher has spoken of arrogance to thee!"

I nodded.

"Do not worry thyself. Thee are the least arrogant child I have ever met. The woman has an even heavier burden than I thought. She needs thy prayers, Leah. Promise me thee will try to pray for her each night."

I promised with a nod and tried to keep that promise to Annie and God, if not always with a good heart.

Sometimes, especially after Mama and I had one of her heart-to-heart talks about her problems with Daddy, I found it hard to breathe at home and spent more and more time up the hill with Annie. As the days grew longer, it became possible to get away during the week, as long as I finished my chores and homework, and I was home before supper.

"I can see thy heart is sorely troubled, little one. Can thee share thy burden?" Annie had waited several weeks before speaking. "You are too quiet for such a spirited child, and a sadness is growing behind your eyes. Is this problem something to do with your teacher again? Mayhap I should speak with your mother, then?"

I had been nodding my head at Annie's inquiries, not paying full attention, as I pieced my quilt by the fire. Her words startled me.

"No!" I jerked myself upright and touched her arm. "No, Annie. Please don't tell Mama. This isn't about school. I'm praying as hard as I can for Mrs. Eldon, even though it doesn't seem to be doing any good. This is something else."

"Why should we not share this problem with her, little one? If thy problem is not for my ears, then surely your mama should know thy soul is troubled."

"I have been listening to someone with my heart, Annie. It's mighty hard to do, sometimes, but I have learned real well. My heart tells me this thing should not be shared. It is a personal thing and a private thing. Do you understand?"

"Aye-huh, little one. I surely understand that kind of

listening. And I shall not inquire further." She hesitated. "But if you ever need, my heart can listen, too."

Annie's words comforted me. Without my saying a word or betraying my mother's confidence, Annie had eased my burden. A look passed between us. No matter where time and space might take me, I would have a friend as long as this dear woman drew breath.

During that springtime, the last we would spend on this farm, my nightmares started. Several times a week, I woke the entire family with my screams of terror. The dreams involved Jerome, a half-witted boy who lived with his father in a little house we passed every day on our walk to and from school. Shortly after Easter break, there had been an incident with Jerome that resulted in a call to the police. A few weeks later, the dreaming began.

I am walking alone through the cool, fragrant woods above Park View. I am carrying a stick—a peeled willow wand, limber and useful for poking at the puffballs that grow at the base of the tall old trees. I jab with my wand and poof! The fungus pops open, brown powdery spores spurting everywhere. Suddenly, I hear behind me the crack of someone stepping on a dry stick. The hair on the back of my neck stands on end and I feel a sudden chill. Slowly I turn. I am confronted by something that paralyzes me with fear. I wake up screaming, never able to see what has caused my terror.

Mama and Daddy were at a loss to console me. Danny called me crybaby and laughed at my obvious distress. Robbie viewed me wide-eyed from his bed, sucking his thumb hard as if to comfort both of us. Several times, I heard my parents talking about the dreams when they thought they were alone.

Mama thought someone should talk to me about "the incident" as she called it, but Daddy felt the least said the better. "She'll forget about it soon enough if we don't remind her," he observed caustically, remarking a little unkindly that they had enough on their plates without blowing a few bad dreams all out of proportion. I knew, however, that my nightmares disturbed them deeply and feared it was causing a further rift in their relationship.

Postlude

I finished second grade on the farm. Shortly after school let out in June, we sold our livestock, packed up our belongings, and moved away. In the end, we left so quickly that I had no time to scamper up the hill and bid my dearest friend good-bye. My quilt lay unfinished (in my memory it would always wait for me) in the little basket Annie had found and placed on her hearth, next to her own quilting basket. For years, I thought of them side by side on the hearth, gossiping like two old friends—loving each other as I loved Annie and she loved me, waiting for my return.

Mama promised me we'd visit Annie on her hill, but we never did. I think she couldn't bear to go back to a place that she remembered with so much pain. I could neither heal that pain, nor fix her broken heart, but I could lend her mine when the need arose, and console her at night when she cried. In time, I learned to embrace the sound of silence and enfold my mother within the arms of a listening heart.

I didn't know what tomorrow would bring—perhaps my parents believed that the place and not the behavior determines the future. For now, tomorrow held a new chapter and I would try my best to be ready for wherever the road ahead took me.

ABOUT ATMOSPHERE PRESS

Atmosphere Press is an independent, full-service publisher for excellent books in all genres and for all audiences. Learn more about what we do at atmospherepress.com.

We encourage you to check out some of Atmosphere's latest releases, which are available at Amazon.com and via order from your local bookstore:

Out and Back: Essays on a Family in Motion, by Elizabeth Templeman

Just Be Honest, an inspirational collection by Cindy Yates

Detour: Lose Your Way, Find Your Path, by S. Mariah Rose

To BnB or Not to BnB: Deromanticizing the Dream, by Sue Marko

Sacred Fool, by Nathan Dean Talamantez

My Place in the Spiral, a memoir by Rebecca Beardsall

My Eight Dads, a memoir by Mark Kirby

Without Her: Memoir of a Family, by Patsy Creedy

Dinner's Ready! Recipes for Working Moms, by Rebecca Cailor

ABOUT THE AUTHOR

 Lessie Auletti is a writer, poet and advocate for women through P.E.O. and OES. An accomplished artist and Graphics Designer, she grew up in the Pacific NW and is a University of Washington alumna. Lessie's career in journalism began with the *Bremerton Sun* newspaper. She retired as a technical writer/illustrator for General Dynamics, Pomona, CA. Since returning to Washington State, her many readings on the Olympic Peninsula and the greater Seattle area became her memoir, *Holding Up the Sky*. She lives in Sequim, WA with her husband Ron. They have six children. Watch for her continuing journey—Book Two coming soon.